T0340236

America's Trade Follies

America is the powerhouse of the world economy, but will it continue to be in the era of globalization? Today, foreign policy, trade and jobs are closely connected. Thirty-five million American jobs depend just on exports – more than in Europe and Asia. The US has been a leader in opening up the world of trade, but now, Bernard K. Gordon argues, it has taken a wrong turn that threatens to close down the world trading system itself. He warns that the danger is America's love affair with "regionalism": if it isn't stopped, Asia will respond with it's own "regional bloc", and the world will be on the road to disaster . . .

America's Trade Follies controversially challenges the myth of America's trade deficits and shows its consequences for current trade policy. The book argues that the global political economy is hardening into regional blocs, in North America, Latin America, Europe and the Asia Pacific, each organized around a powerful economic base and mutually suspicious of one another. Bernard K. Gordon's masterful analysis shows that this division into regional blocs fundamentally threatens American prosperity by limiting US access to the world's richest and largest markets, and endangers US security by dividing the globe along economic and political lines. It is vital, he argues, that US trade policy recognizes that support for regional trade blocs is an act of political folly in our globalized economy.

Combining foreign trade and world politics, this book looks at issues of US trade and strategy in Europe, East Asia and the West – particularly US–South America relations. Provocative, original and stimulating, this book is essential reading for all those interested in American politics, trade and international political economy.

In articles in *Foreign Policy, Foreign Affairs* and *The National Interest,* **Bernard K. Gordon** first showed that America is the world's only truly global exporter; no single region is America's "Natural Market". Now, uniquely combining economics and politics, this 30-year member of the International Institute of Strategic Studies warns that America's flirtation with regional blocs is both foolish for America and dangerous for the world.

To Pam and Josh, and Eve and Daniel

This reflects some of our travels

America's Trade Follies

Turning economic leadership into strategic weakness

Bernard K. Gordon

Routledge
Taylor & Francis Group

LONDON AND NEW YORK

First published 2001 by Routledge
4 Park Square, Milton Park, Abingdon, Oxon OX14 4RN
605 Third Avenue, New York, NY 10017

*Routledge is an imprint of the Taylor & Francis Group,
an informa business*

British Library Cataloguing in Publication Data
A catalogue record for this book is available from the British Library

Library of Congress Cataloging in Publication Data
Gordon, Bernard K., 1932–
     America's trade follies : turning economic leadership into
  strategic weakness / Bernard K. Gordon.
        p. cm.
  Includes bibliographical references and index.
     1. Trade blocs. 2. Regionalism. 3. Balance of trade–United
  States. 4. United States–Commercial policy. I. Title.

  HF1418.7 .G67 2001
  382'.0973–dc21

                                                          00–054743

ISBN 13: 978-0-415-25320-8 (pbk)
ISBN 13: 978-0-415-23272-2 (hbk)

Contents

Figures

Acknowledgments

Because this book somewhat uniquely combines issues of politics and economics, it has been a special task requiring several years, and my debts are many. At the University of New Hampshire, they include librarians Debbie Watson, Linda B. Johnson, Kathy Foss, and Meredith Ricker, and their truly outstanding Library Collections. Without their help this book simply could not have been written, and that applies also to GEN. Richard Chilcoat and Jeannemarie Faison, for their help in arranging my access to the Library of the National Defense University in Washington, D.C. A word of personal thanks is due to my good friend Tom Fitzgerald, for his encouragement, and no words can ever approach my gratitude, not least for her confidence, to my wife, Anita.

Abbreviations and acronyms

AFTA	ASEAN Free Trade Area, agreed to in 1992
AMF	Asian Monetary Fund, proposed in 1997
APEC	"Asia–Pacific Economic Cooperation," the group of nations (now 21) that convened in 1989 to improve their economic cooperation
ASEAN	Association of Southeast Asian Nations
BDI	Federation of German Industries
CAP	The Common Agricultural Policy of the European Union
DOTS	Direction of Trade Statistics
EAC	"East Asia Cooperation," a collaborative format agreed to in 1999 by ASEAN, China, Korea, and Japan
EAEG/EAEC	Proposals, beginning in 1989, for a "group" or "caucus" of East Asian nations to facilitate economic and related cooperation
"fast track"	a law providing Congress the authority only to approve or disapprove a trade agreement, the specifics having been already negotiated by the President
FDP	Free German Party
FTA	any proposed or existing "free trade area" among nations
FTAA	proposed Free Trade Area of the Americas, called for by the 1994 "Miami Summit"
GATT	General Agreement on Tariffs and Trade
GDP	Gross Domestic Product
IMF	International Monetary Fund
JETRO	Japan External Trade Organization
LDP	Liberal-Democratic Party in Japan
MERCOSUR	Common market in South America's southern cone
MFN	"most favored nation" a clause widely used in international trade agreements that acts to readily extend agreements
MITI	Japan's Ministry of International Trade and Industry
NAFTA	North American Free Trade Agreement, established in 1993 by Canada, Mexico, and the US

NATO	North Atlantic Treaty Organization, established by 12 nations in 1949 to provide for their collective defense, and which now numbers 19 nations
NGO	non-governmental organizations active in public policy issues
NIC	Newly-Industrializing Country
NIE	newly-Industrializing economies
OECD	Organization for Economic Cooperation and Development
OEEC	Organization for European Economic Cooperation, established in 1947 to administer US aid and promote cooperation in the region
OPEC	Organization of Petroleum Exporting Countries
TAFTA	proposed "Transatlantic Free Trade Area"
WHFTA	a proposed Western Hemisphere Free Trade Area
WTO	World Trade Organization, the effective successor of GATT

1 America's folly

The rise of regional blocs

Although they have attracted much recent attention, regional blocs have a long history. As early as 1942–3, as part of the planning for the post-war world, Britain's Prime Minister Winston Churchill outlined a specifically regional framework for dealing with global problems. At meetings with President Franklin Roosevelt and his advisors, Churchill proposed a world based on three "regional councils": one each for Europe, the Pacific, and the Western hemisphere. The councils were expected to be formally subordinate to a supreme World Council, comprised of the wartime "Big Four," but the regions were the keystone. As Churchill put it, "The central idea of the structure was that of a three-legged stool – the World Council resting on three regional Councils ... I attached great importance to the regional principle."[1]

Ultimately, Churchill's plan did not prevail, and the United Nations concept was adopted instead. This was based not on several global regions, but on the idea of a single, all-inclusive global structure. Even so, Churchill's idea did not completely disappear; something like its shadow can be found in the UN's four "Economic Commissions": one each for Europe, Asia and the Pacific, Latin America, and Africa. But no more than that can be said for those early attempts at regionalism. Over the next 50 years, altogether different structures shaped world affairs, and neither Churchill's rejected regionalism, nor the single UN structure had much influence.

Instead, the bipolar Soviet–American conflict dominated most of the period, and as the Cold War was ending, many believed that global interdependence, or "globalization," would shape the next stage in world affairs. The concept of globalization reflected the largely unfettered movement of goods and money across borders, as well as the relative inability of states to do much about it. But the concept had hardly taken root when the ghost of Churchill's wartime idea re-emerged, and took on new life. As Churchill expected, regionalism's revival was based in Europe. Its success in building an economic and political community inspired a reawakening of regionalist thinking everywhere. By the mid-1990s the attractions of regionalism had moved beyond the talking stage, and had become the basis of support and action among many nations in East Asia and South America.

The United States' role in all this has been odd. America emerged from the bipolar conflict as the world's sole political and military superpower (there was even talk of a "unipolar" structure), and the US seemed poised to continue as the prime beneficiary in a world of global economic inter-dependence. Yet despite those gains, the United States has been a key actor and advocate in the return and rise of regionalism. In the Western hemisphere, President Bush took the first steps, in the late 1980s, to promote close trade ties from "Argentina to Alaska," and in 1994 Bill Clinton enthusiastically took up the same cause with his call for a "Free Trade Area for the Americas."[2] Likewise in the Pacific region: in 1993 Mr Clinton breathed new life into the Asia–Pacific Economic Forum (APEC), and called for free trade among its members within 20 years. Nor was Europe – where it had all begun – left out: by 1998 senior American and EU officials were again discussing a 1995 German proposal for trans-atlantic free trade, and already were calling it "TAFTA."[3]

These US policies on behalf of regionalism have been important in two ways: first as a key factor in their own right (for example by establishing NAFTA), and second by helping to legitimize the environment for similar actions by others. Thus in 1991, in South America, Brazil took the lead to create a customs union, known informally as MERCOSUR, and in South-east Asia, the ASEAN states established a free trade area they call "AFTA." In Asia, moreover, these regional proposals have moved beyond just the single issue of expanding trade.

For example, in 1997–8, in the wake of financial and currency collapses in Thailand, Korea, and Indonesia, Japan proposed a specifically Asian answer to Asian problems. Tokyo called for an "Asian Monetary Fund" to supplement the long-established and globally-active International Mone-tary Fund. Malaysia, which strongly supported Japan's initiative, went further. Prime Minister Mahathir suggested that trade among ASEAN members be conducted only in local Asian currencies, and repeatedy urged bigger steps to achieve closer political cooperation in East Asia.

All these efforts have several separate justifications, but they also repre-sent a double challenge. First, they are a challenge to the world's single, or global international political and economic structure. Despite its short-comings, that structure has nevertheless helped at least to bring much material improvement to many of the world's peoples. Second, those efforts challenge the role of the United States, which has acted as the prin-cipal creator and supporter of that single structure. It is in that sense, and for that reason, that I will argue here that American policies that aim to legitimize and promote regionalism look increasingly like the mistakes Barbara Tuchman identified in her famous book, *The March of Folly*.

In that book, Tuchman described how governments have often brought about their own calamities, when their leaders not only pursued "policies contrary to their own interests," but did so in the face of warn-ings at the time. As Tuchman put it, those governments and their leaders were "wooden headed," and to illustrate the high price of their folly, she chronicled three famous errors: how the Renaissance Popes provoked the Protestant Secession; how Britain under George III lost the American colonies; and how America's leaders, in pursuit of unattainable goals, betrayed America in Vietnam. Today, as this book will show, the United States is approaching a folly of similar proportions. It is helping to bring about what it cannot want: the hardening of world politics into three regional blocs – in Europe, East Asia, and the Americas – each organized around a powerful industrial and economic base, and each liable to be suspicious of the others.

Such a global structure would deny the whole point of American foreign policy, especially as it has developed since the beginning of the twentieth century. Throughout that period, the United States had two par-allel aims: first, to prevent the rise of any single politico-industrial force either in Europe or in Pacific–Asia, and second, to assure that no other nation could become dominant in the Western hemisphere. Yet today, just such concentrations are taking shape in Europe and Asia. But Ameri-can leaders, like the man who whistled while walking past the graveyard, contentedly assure themselves that America's dominant role in the Western hemisphere will somehow neutralize, and compensate for, those concentrations in Europe and Asia. Even Henry Kissinger has fallen for this trap. He has written that if the United States develops a "Western hemisphere-wide free trade system" it would retain a *"commanding role no matter what happens."*[4]

The reverse is true: a world of three economic blocs would be critically constraining to the American economy, and would turn the basic strategic concept of America's foreign policy on its head. Consider first the eco-nomic implications. A global structure with economic blocs as its center-piece would relegate the United States largely to the Western hemisphere, in economic terms the least attractive of the three world regions. That point warrants an explanation, and will be fully explored in a later chapter. Suffice to say for now that aside from Canada and to a lesser extent Mexico, the markets of the Western hemisphere – when compared to Europe and East Asia – represent the relative crumbs at the global eco-nomic dinner table.

That does not deny America's obviously strong trade and investment role in the Western hemisphere, but the United States is demonstrably *not* more deeply involved there than with Europe or Asia. On the contrary, America's exports and investments make the US a uniquely *trilateral* eco-nomic actor. It has profoundly important economic interests in both East Asia and Europe, as well as in Latin America and Canada. Any policy or process that diminished that essentially global position would represent a grave threat to America's material well-being, and any steps that appeared *even to move in that direction* would almost certainly provoke a sharp American response.

The political danger of a world based on blocs is that it will transform national economic disputes into international political conflicts. Three closely-related reasons explain why:

- the unprecedently high role that *economic performance* now plays in the affairs of all major governments;
- the role that *exports* play in that performance;
- the fact that the main political measure of a government's economic performance has become its capacity to achieve *high employment.*

A key reflection of this linkage between jobs, exports, and economic performance is that full employment policies are prominently trumpeted throughout the industrialized world, as the speeches at each year's "G–7" summit meeting repeatedly demonstrate.[5]

In the US this commitment to high employment is reflected in the "Full Employment Act" of 1946, and recent American politics reaffirm its top place on the agenda. A good example was the 1992 Clinton–Bush election campaign, which centered precisely on who could best assure more and better jobs. After his victory, Mr Clinton repeatedly cited America's record performance in "job creation" as proof of his administration's success, and he then made it the centerpiece of his foreign economic policy as well.[6]

The same commitment also characterizes the other major industrialized nations: Western Europe has had full employment policies since before World War II, and Japan does today. While Japan's so-called "lifetime employment" policy has never applied to most of its economy, Japan's post-war years are nevertheless filled with tales of firms that have gone to extreme steps rather than dismiss workers. Tokyo's long-ruling Liberal Democratic Party takes special pride in the nation's low unemployment rate, and the usually vibrant economy it reflects. Japan has been in an economic slowdown for the better part of a decade, and most individual Japanese do not believe they are "rich". Nevertheless, the nation's overall and enduring prosperity is the chief reason why the LDP – in the face of much evident corruption, and even incompetence in most other policy respects – has been able to stay in power for more than 40 years, with only a recent brief interruption.

The linkage of jobs, exports, and economic performance has also transformed the relationship between foreign trade and domestic politics. The consequence is that new attention has been brought to the issue of protectionism, whose roots are in the mercantilist era of the sixteenth–eighteenth centuries. Leaders in that period embraced the policy not only for commercial and economic reasons, but as the essential underpinning of national security. The economic rationale was straightforward: protectionist policies were intended to promote particular industries or business sectors, but the political rationale for protectionism was more complex.

A key element was the need for self-sufficiency, often referred to as "autarky," which in turn was grounded in national security requirements. A classic example of the economic argument was Alexander Hamilton's famous 1791 defense of "infant industries." A modern illustration of the national security argument is Japan's policy against significant rice imports. Its ostensible aim is to maintain "food security" – an argument that stretches credulity in the thermonuclear era. The deeper reality is that the interests of a powerful political class are involved, as in Prussia a century ago. In that era, the elite Prussian *Junkers*, who were farmers as well as soldiers, argued on national security grounds for limits on grain imports,[7] just as Japan's rice farmers, who dominate their nation's over-represented rural constituencies, do today.

Today, however, protectionism has a far wider and more powerful domestic base. The reason is that protectionism can now mean jobs, and in an age of mass politics, jobs and employment are the life blood of all major contemporary governments. Those mass-politics roots mean that all modern governments (regardless of whether they meet Western standards of democracy) legitimize their hold on power in terms of the popular will, as reflected by a government's ability to promote its people's material welfare.[8] That, in turn, means that what were once considered merely "economic," or trade issues, are now altogether inseparable from a leadership's possession of political power. Those mass-politics roots also mean that any development seen as likely to threaten a nation's economic well-being, especially the fullest possible employment of its people, will be transformed, as soon as it becomes public, into a powerful issue of domestic politics.

This link is the principal reason for this book's argument that the likely consequences of global "economic" regionalism must be understood not only in economic, but in political and strategic terms as well. We need to go beyond that, however. We need to show why regionalism has not only gained acceptance, but is evidently gaining support. To understand why, two recent developments should be recalled; one grounded in international economics, the other in world politics.

The *economic* change is the post-war explosion of world trade, which can be seen in several ways. In 1960, for example, world *exports alone* were valued at $130 billion, but by 1998, as Figure 1.1 shows, they had risen to almost *$5,500* billion. That represents an increase of more than 40 times – a rise that is far greater than the growth in world production. As the prominent economist Jeffrey Sachs has put it, "In almost every year since World War II, international trade has grown more rapidly than global production."[9]

From 1967–93, for example, among the industrialized nations that comprise the OECD, exports grew at twice the rate of GDP.[10] The contrast

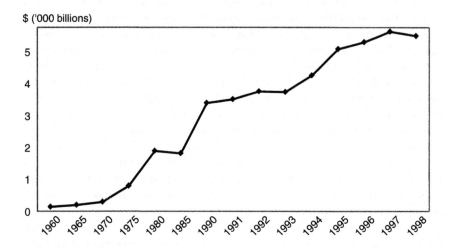

Source: Data in IMF DOTS, annual issues.

Figure 1.1 Value of world exports, 1960–98.

is even more stark at the global level: world GDP more than doubled from 1970–96, but the value of world exports grew by a multiple of more than *17 times*.[11] In other words, however the issue is expressed, the explosion in world trade has been one of the most significant developments of the post-war era.

This explosion in trade has had both economic and political consequences. In economics, it has produced unprecedented benefits for many nations and peoples, and led to what economists call a rise in global welfare. And in terms of politics, the trade explosion has put trade issues – particularly export issues – much higher on the agenda for more nations than ever before. But just as the number of nations deeply affected by world trade has grown, so has their frustration with the global regime that has set world trade rules since the 1950s. That regime was the General Agreement on Tariffs and Trade, or GATT, which in 1995 became the World Trade Organization. The shift to the WTO was the final step in GATT's so-called "Uruguay Round," and it is fair to say that when the change came, dissatisfaction with GATT was so widespread that its future effectiveness, and even its existence, were much in doubt. As the economist Lester Thurow reportedly said at the time, "GATT is dead."

Part of the reason for the general upset with GATT was that so much trade was not covered by its rules. Farm products are the best-known exclusion, and several nations, led by France and Japan, have long aimed to keep it that way. Their leaders would deny it when put this way, but it often appears that Paris and Tokyo (and some others) would prefer agriculture to be altogether excluded from most international rules. Also excluded from GATT was trade in almost all services – for example banking, advertising and insurance. And even in the sectors that GATT did include, its methods for resolving differences and disputes were often slow and unclear.

The result of this combination of weaknesses in the GATT "system" was that, by the early 1990s, in an environment where protectionism was far from dead, a number of nations and their leaders increasingly were tempted to go outside the GATT framework. Some even saw, in the rise of protectionist sentiment, a possible return to the "beggar thy neighbor" sentiments of an earlier era. Under those circumstances, it was not altogether surprising that some national leaders were inclined to write off GATT, and seek instead to make the best bilateral or regional deals they could. This temptation, moreover, was heightened by the actions of the United States. In the 1990s, America's trade partners increasingly were warned of unilateral US trade sanctions, of which the most dramatic were threats of "Super 301."

This was shorthand for an American law that called for trade penalties against a nation whose practices could be found, by the US, to be in violation of principles of "fair trade." A perfect illustration is America's steel industry, which regularly charges foreign producers with "dumping" steel on the US market, at prices alleged to be below cost. Although steel accounts for only 5 percent of US imports, the steel industry is responsible for almost *half* the complaints brought before the US International Trade Commission. Even in those cases where no fault was found, the sheer costs of responding are often enough to choke off imports. In the words of a steel industry spokesman, "That's the great thing about filing [complaints]; even if you lose, you win."[12]

It was in that sort of environment that the attention of so many nations returned to the possibilities of economic regionalism. They reasoned that if the flaws of GATT – the world's one major format for setting the rules for trade were too severe – it might be better to try smaller bodies, closer to home. In fact, the creation of the World Trade Organization resolved a number of the most serious institutional problems associated with GATT, which was, after all, never intended to be permanent. It was created in 1947 only as a stop-gap measure: to replace a proposed formal trade organization that never came into existence. That body, slated to be called the "International Trade Organization," faced powerful opposition in the US Senate, and President Truman scuttled it. GATT arose in its place, and while, like Topsy, it just grew over the years, in fact it had little formal grounding in international agreements.

In contrast, when the WTO was created, it had widespread international support and consensus, including that of the United States. In formal and legal terms, moreover, it has a seemingly much more solid and formal foundation. The WTO also has far better dispute settlement procedures than did GATT, and while agriculture is still not covered, trade in services and intellectual property *are* included. Nevertheless, the essential nature and format of the WTO, as compared with GATT, are unchanged. Like GATT, the WTO's mission is to foster open trade on a global or multilateral basis. Its largest single incentive is the central principle of reciprocity, and the many benefits that come from it. But in 1998 and 1999, the still-new WTO suffered devastating internal and external blows that have weakened it considerably, and called into question its effectiveness, and possibly its legitimacy.

One wound was largely self-inflicted; the WTO, in the full light of public attention, spent more than a year in an ultimately failed effort to find a successor to its Director-General. The result was a compromise that left the organization with a new chief officer, but whose term of office was set at half the normal span. The second blow was the Organization's failure to establish an agreed agenda several months before its next meeting, planned for Seattle. That failure was directly related to its inability to first put a new Director-General into place. The third, and best-known wound, in December, 1999, was the disastrous spectacle of the meeting itself. With all the world's press in attendance, the Seattle meeting came under unprecedented pressures, largely from non-governmental groups (so-called "NGOs"), to abort or fundamentally to change the plans for a new trade "round." In many cases, the NGOs had little or no prior experience in world trade issues, and in the view of many, no prior commitment to open and global trade as well.

The causes for these failures remain in debate, but the result was that the WTO meeting altogether failed to agree on any principles or format for a new trade round. As of this writing, in late 2000, none had yet been developed. One consequence is that the WTO will likely have a much-reduced ability to fend off pressures to create several bilateral or regional approaches to trade. Those pressures were already building under GATT, and the WTO's new troubles make it quite clear that those earlier pressures, rather than weakening, have in some important cases been encouraged.

The clearest evidence is in the regional developments already mentioned: in the Western hemisphere, MERCOSUR and the Clinton FTAA proposal; in the Pacific, the APEC blueprint, the ASEAN Free Trade Area, and a just-emerging East Asian proposal; and in Europe, revived attention to a possible transatlantic free trade agreement between the US and the EU.[13] Consequently, although hopes for a continuation and enlargement of the multilateral system that shaped the world economy since the 1950s now rest with the WTO, the reasons that led many leaders to incline toward regionalism have not disappeared. If states and leaders come to believe that their nations' interests will be better served by smaller clusters, the nascent WTO may never get much of a chance to prove itself.

The broader strategic environment, in particular the end of the Cold War, represents the major *political* change in world affairs that favors regionalism. A decline of confidence in the world trading system was evident even before the USSR collapsed, and that softening of support accelerated as the global fear of communism subsided. The principal reason is that the erosion of the communist threat also eroded many nations' political and security dependence on the US, which until then had been the main force behind every successful effort at post-war trade liberalization. But with America's central rule-making or hegemonic authority weakened, and with the global economic regime it sponsored increasingly uncertain, two clear results have emerged.

One is a revival of earlier international economic patterns, reflected for example by Germany's leading economic role in central Europe, and by Japan's heavy presence in northeast Asia in particular. The other is a resurgence of earlier, and specifically *national*, political interests. These two broad changes, the one in world politics, and the other in the international economy, have given new and unprecedented support to global regionalism, and two concrete developments have reinforced that support. One is the intensification of economic integration in Europe – marked, of course, by the EU decision to adopt a single currency in 1999 – and the other is in a set of recent American actions. In ways that were not intended by the United States, and that are also not in its long-term national interest, America's decision to establish a free trade area with Canada, and then to extend it to Mexico under NAFTA, has acted like an accelerant on a smoldering fire.

Those European and North American developments, "even though fortuitous and prompted by different motivations and historical circumstances," have created a sense elsewhere that "regionalism is the order of the day and that others must follow suit."[14] That belief in the inevitability of regionalism is a wake-up call that has so far been ignored. While the EU has continued its successful program to build a largely single economy in Western Europe, the US has persisted in its efforts to build a Western Hemisphere Free Trade Area. Those two developments have encouraged others to move in similar directions, and if the process continues, the result will be to promote a world structure based on economic blocs.

To assume otherwise – to believe that because regional proposals failed in the 1960s they will fail again today – is to confuse the two periods. The first, in Bhagwati's apt term, was the "First Regionalism." It was marked by many calls for "NAFTA, PAFTA, LAFTA," and it failed for many reasons, including the unconcern of the United States. Today, however, the American role is reversed: "the main driving force for regionalism today is the conversion of the United States [and] ... the resurrection of regionalism suggests [it] is likely to endure this time."[15] For both economic and political reasons, that is an extremely troubling prospect, and as the following chapters will show, it is hardly in the economic and trading interests of the United States.

To see why, we will first explore the role of foreign trade in the American economy, as well as America's place in the world economy. Later chapters will then deal with the forces shaping the rise of regional economic efforts in Europe, the Western hemisphere, and in the Asia–Pacific region. On that basis, we will then aim to lay out the political and strategic implications of these developments, both for American foreign policy, and for global international politics.

Notes

1 W. S. Churchill, *The Hinge of Fate*, New York, Houghton Mifflin, 1950, p. 804. Much of the story, especially from the American side, has recently been retold in Townsend Hoopes and Douglas Brinkley, *FDR and the Creation of the U.N.*, New Haven, Yale University Press, 1997, pp. 64–78.
2 President Clinton unveiled his plan in December, 1994, at the "Miami Summit of the Americas," and President Bush's proposals for the hemisphere began in 1990 with his proposed "Enterprise for the Americas" program.
3 In January 1998, Leon Brittan, the EU Trade Commissioner, resumed talks with senior US trade officials designed to explore a "broad Free Trade Agreement," *Financial Times*, 2 February, 1998.
4 In Kissinger's view, if the GATT–WTO system continues, the Western hemisphere will be a major participant in global growth, but "if discriminatory regional groupings dominate, the Western Hemisphere, with its vast market, will be able to compete effectively with other regional trading blocs . . . ", H. A. Kissinger, *Diplomacy*, New York, Simon and Shuster, p. 832. My emphasis.
5 At the G–7 summit in 1992, for example, leaders agreed that "too many people are out of work . . . We are particularly concerned about the hardship unemployment creates" (from the text of the Munich Declaration, 10 July, 1992). All recent meeting have included a similar emphasis on employment as a main goal of the G–7 leaders.
6 For a full-scale defense of this position, including then Commerce Secretary Kantor's assertion that Clinton is "the first President" to connect economics (which Kantor equated with jobs) with foreign policy, see *The New York Times*, 29 July, 1996.
7 The same point is made by Gisela Hendricks, in "Germany and the CAP: National Interests and the European Community," *International Affairs*, 1989, p. 75. She adds that support for agricultural incomes "has been the central element of Germany's national agricultural policies for over 100 years."
8 Michael Sturmer, writing from a German perspective, has put it well: "National governments are rejected or reelected according to their performance in providing comfort and confidence," in "Resist the Melting Pot", *Financial Times*, 16 August, 1996.
9 "International Economics: Unlocking the Mysteries of Globalization," *Foreign Policy*, Spring, 1998.
10 Export growth averaged 5.4 percent, while GDP growth was 2.7 percent (based on data for world exports in IMF, *Direction of Trade Statistics Annual*, various years, and OECD data calculated from OECD *Economic Outlook*, June 1994, Annex Tables 1 and 9 (pp. A4, A12).
11 CIA, *Handbook of International Economic Statistics*, 1997, Table 1, p. 15 (based on 1993 dollars).
12 *Wall Street Journal*, 27 March, 1998.

13 The TAFTA concept, about which more will be said in Chapter 3, was given its first significant endorsement by German Foreign Minister Klaus Kinkel in 1995, and received a further boost in late 1997, when Germany's governing Christian Democratic Party added its support.

14 Jagdish Bhagwati, "The Threats to the World Trading System," *World Economy*, July, 1992, Vol. 15, No. 4, p. 454. Bhagwati, a Columbia University economist, has also served as Economic Policy Advisor to the Director-General of GATT.

15 In "Regionalism versus Multilateralism," *The World Economy*, September, 1992, Vol. 15, No. 5, p. 540, my emphasis. On the difference between today and the 1960s, Bhagwati remarks that "Those who do not know the history of the First Regionalism are doomed to extrapolate from the current political ferment . . . and assume uncritically that regionalism is here to stay. Those who know the history may make the reverse mistake of thinking that regionalism will fail again."

2 America's trade in its global context

When cautions are raised against the revival of regionalism today, the reasons are rooted in memories of the trade and currency blocs of the 1930s. In that era, Britain and Germany, and unofficially the United States, were associated with a regional trade arrangement based on each nation's currency. For example, Britain's Sterling was the common denominator for its system of "Imperial Preference." London's goal – through tariff, banking, and other advantages – was to foster British industry; to tighten the linkages among the nations of the Empire (today's British Commonwealth); and generally to militate against outsiders. Similarly, Germany utilized trade, and its currency, the *Reichsmark*, to promote German exports; enhance Germany's self-sufficiency ("autarky"); and link several Central European nations to Berlin. Finally, several Latin American nations and Canada were loosely but not formally connected to Washington by means of the US dollar.

What makes this all relevant today is that, simultaneous with the rise of those regional groupings in the 1930s, the Great Depression overtook the world economy, and brought with it the collapse of global trade. In what economists still call an "astonishing implosion,"[1] world trade fell by 50 percent from 1929–32. Moreover, while global production recovered when the Depression eased later in the 1930s, trade did not recuperate. By 1938, for example, global production of goods surpassed 1929 levels by 11 percent, and commodities by 7 percent, but *global trade remained 10 percent lower than in 1929.*

To this day, economists still debate the causes of the Depression and its associated trade collapse. The three economic blocs of the day were not the sole cause, but there is little doubt that they played an important part, especially in the contraction of trade. The result is that today's prospect of a world of separate and potentially competing economic blocs recalls a host of bad memories, and sparks new concerns about a revival of regionalism in Asia and Latin America.[2] The worry is that new regional blocs will not only slow the post-war trade explosion, but threaten the global trade regime that has made it possible.

The revival of regionalism

The essential element of that global regime is the GATT system of world-wide, or "multilateral" agreements that stand in sharp rebuke to the 1930's experiment with regional blocs. GATT, as we saw in Chapter 1, is the acronym for the General Agreement on Tariffs and Trade, and its principles can be summarized in three words: reduction, reciprocity, and extension. GATT members agree to reduce trade barriers by reciprocal agreement and then to extend that negotiated best deal to every other member-nation. This is GATT's famous MFN or "most favored nation" keystone, and it has contributed mightily to the worldwide expansion of trade.

But from its beginnings in 1947, GATT has also had a provision – Article 24 – that effectively exempts from its rules any new regional arrangements (such as customs unions and free trade areas) that aim to reduce trade barriers. A main purpose of the exemption was to legitimize the hoped-for European Economic Community: its original members probably would not have joined GATT unless excused from its principles of universality and MFN.[3] Most observers today, looking back on the success of the EEC over the years, would probably agree that the exemption was justified.

Since then, however, more than 130 regional economic groups have been established, in all parts of the world, and almost all point to Article 24 as the source of their international legitimacy.[4] In practice, little of this now matters, because most of those groups date from the 1960s and 1970s, and have limited contemporary relevance. But today's regionalism is different, because it is being pressed by powerful voices in some of the world's major nations, including the major trading nations.

In that environment, the new regionalism has reawakened earlier concerns that it will not merely slow trade growth, but will lead to new trade complexities, and eventually to new trade barriers. Anne O. Krueger, the 1996 President of the American Economic Association, addressed that issue in a booklet called "The Dangerous Drift to Preferential Trade Agreements." She warned that new regional Free Trade Areas could lead to "greater protection between trading regions," and Martin Wolf, the principal economics writer for the *Financial Times*, recently expressed similar doubts. In a celebratory essay on the 50th anniversary of GATT, he wrote that "the case for liberal trade is now grounded in economic theory and ... experience. Only extreme stupidity would allow the world to forget what it has so painfully learned."[5]

Proponents of regionalism argue that such warnings miss the point. Indeed, every participant in every regional group regularly affirms a commitment to free and open trade, to what increasingly is called "open regionalism." Likewise, economists normally stress that regional trade groupings and preferences do not automatically reduce trade. They argue that regionalism, by virtue of the economic liberalization it represents, can enhance trade and economic activity generally. In a classic expression, regionalism is seen not as a stumbling block but as a "building block" on the path toward globally open trade.[6]

Perhaps so, but by providing preferences to members, any trade group must discriminate against non-members, otherwise there would be no point in joining.[7] That logic has prompted a growing number of observers to caution that whatever the good aims of regionalism's advocates, trade blocs – in practice – will discriminate against non-members. The Carnegie Endowment recently warned against that when it found that several groups – the EU, MERCOSUR, and the Gulf Cooperation Council – all showed signs of distorting trade at the expense of non-members.[8] To that extent, in a phrase famous to economists, regional blocs would be "trade diverting": that is, they will create less trade than they divert.[9]

This was precisely the concern of Asian leaders and others in the early 1990s, when the United States began discussions aimed at expanding the 1989 US–Canada Free Trade Agreement. A major part of the American goal was to broaden and deepen ties with Mexico, and ultimately those discussions led to the establishment, in 1994, of the North American Free Trade Agreement. Then, with the ink hardly dry on NAFTA, those Asian fears were heightened when President Bush, and then President Clinton, began immediately to talk of extending NAFTA to South America. That worried the Asians on three counts: first, that the South Americans would get preferential treatment in the enormous United States market; second, that those preferences would come at Asia's expense; and third, that the whole process would encourage those in Asia already looking for reasons to form their own regional trade bloc.

This was exactly the point made by Ryutaro Hashimoto in 1991, then Japan's Finance Minister. In 1996–8 he was Prime Minister, and has since been leader of Japan's two most powerful political factions in its Diet. In his book *Vision of Japan*, Hashimoto recalled telling former American Secretary of State Henry Kissinger of a Malaysian proposal for a "caucus" of Asian nations that would exclude the United States. Hashimoto reported that Japan was being pressed to support the idea, and when Kissinger asked whether Tokyo would be influenced by American plans to extend NAFTA to South and Central America, Hashimoto answered "Yes, that is what will happen":

> As a member of the cabinet I do not highly regard the Mahathir Plan. But if the United States strengthens its posture towards forming a pro-tectionist bloc by extending NAFTA and closing off South America and North America, then Japan will have to emphasize its position as an Asia–Pacific country. This will inevitably alter the Japan–US rela-tionship . . . so please do not force us into such a corner.[10]

Hashimoto's warning strikes very close to the central theme of this book: that America's emphasis on economic regionalism is likely to bring profoundly unsettling consequences to both the global economy and world politics.

Asia and Japan illustrate the point well. After all, Japan is the world's second largest economy; it is a fully industrialized nation; and it has a *per capita* product and income essentially identical to that of the United States.[11] Moreover, Japan ranks behind only adjacent Canada and Mexico as the largest overseas market for America's exports. But even aside from market issues, it has long been understood that a *sine qua non* of American security and foreign policy is that Japan and the United States must maintain their intimate political and security relationship. Accordingly, a Japan that decided to increasingly focus on its identity "as an Asia–Pacific" nation would imply a policy of distance from the United States, and such a shift would have the most profound economic and political consequences for Japan, the US, and world politics.

In economic terms, a Japan that turned more toward Asia, while the US focused more on the Western hemisphere, would, at a minimum, alter present trade patterns, and probably lead to a contraction at least in US–Japan trade. In addition, because post-war trade expansion has been so great, the severity and consequences of the contraction would be even worse than in the 1930s. Likewise, the domestic political consequences of such a trade reduction, not only in Japan and the United States, but also elsewhere in the Asia–Pacific region, would also be even more severe than before. The chief reason, as I mentioned in Chapter 1, is the centrality of foreign trade today. International trade is far more closely tied to every nation's economic growth, and therefore to every nation's domestic political stability, than in the pre-war period.

The role of foreign trade in America

This is true even in today's United States, where historically, foreign trade has played only a small role. Indeed for the past century, and until very recently – in other words, from the 1870s to the mid-1970s – America's economy was characterized by very low levels of trade. Even in 1939, on the eve of World War II, US imports and exports *combined* represented only slightly more than 6 percent of the Gross Domestic Product, a small fraction of what was common in Europe. Five years after the war's end, in 1950, the US ratio remained only marginally higher, and even 20 years later, in 1970, foreign trade still represented only 8.4 percent of America's GDP.

But in the quarter-century since then, as Figure 2.1 shows, trade's role in America's economy has more than doubled. It now represents nearly 20 percent of America's GDP, and even that is lower than in most other major economies. In Britain and France the ratio is more than 40 percent and in Germany more than 60 percent.

"Trade," of course, includes both imports and exports, and in domestic

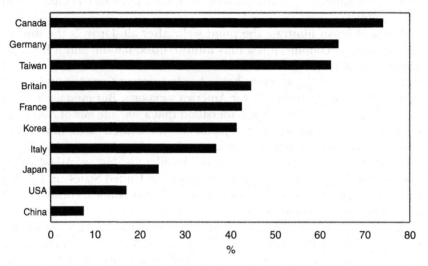

Source: Author's calculations from data in *CIA World Factbook*, 1999.

Figure 2.1 Foreign trade as a percentage of GDP, 1999.

political terms what mainly counts is the place of exports. The reason is that exports relate so directly to jobs, and in the advanced and industrializing economies especially, those exports contribute significantly to high-paying jobs. Just how many such jobs is difficult to say with precision, because the methodology varies by industry, region, and other criteria. But however it is calculated, the number of jobs dependent on exports is always very large, and that reality underlines the political significance of exports in today's economies.

The United States Trade Representative, for example, testified in April, 2000 that 12 million American jobs depended directly on exports.[12] An even higher number, perhaps as many as 15 million, are the result of the ratio used by the Commerce Department and the International Trade Administration: 20,000–23,000 jobs for each $1 billion in exports.[13] *Manufactured exports alone* were reported to be responsible for 4 million jobs, even in the mid-1990s,[14] and another report in that period said 13 percent of all jobs were dependent on manufactured exports.[15] Even higher figures come from particular industries and states. One concluded that "at least 25,000 aerospace jobs are related to each billion dollars of exports,"[16] and Washington state – home to Boeing, Weyerhauser, and Microsoft – reports that more than a quarter of all employment is export-based. These are all very high levels, and as Figure 2.2 shows, in most other nations exports play a far greater role than in the US.

As that illustration shows, exports count for less in America's economy

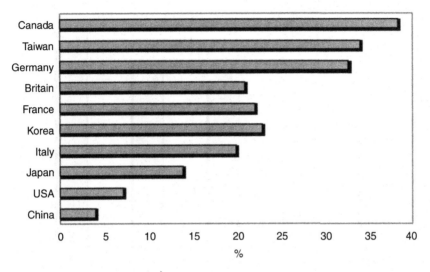

Source: Calculated from data in *CIA World Factbook*, 1999.

Figure 2.2 Exports as percentage of GDP, 1999, world's top ten exporters.

than in most other nations, but nowhere else has the size and recent growth of exports been more impressive than in the US. The result is that America clearly has once again become the world's leading exporting nation. Its sales abroad in 1997 were $678 billion, more than double the $320 billion just ten years earlier. As the *Wall Street Journal* remarked at the time,[17] it was a decade of "amazing export growth": both the value of exports and the number of jobs based on exports doubled, and the export-related share of the American economy rose by more than two percentage points, to 8 percent. Moreover, the *rate* of export growth during that decade, as Figure 2.3 shows, was far steeper in the US than it was in Europe, Japan, or in the world as a whole.

Yet despite that record of strong growth, and its positive impact on US employment, American attention has nevertheless continued to focus more on imports than exports – or, more precisely, on the *difference* between the two. That difference, the nation's "trade deficit," is the best known and most widely discussed issue in American trade, and to understand why, we need to recall US economic history.

The myth of America's trade weakness

From shortly after the Civil War until very recently, the US was largely self-sufficient, and there was little need for Americans to be concerned with the size of either imports or exports. That pattern continued during the

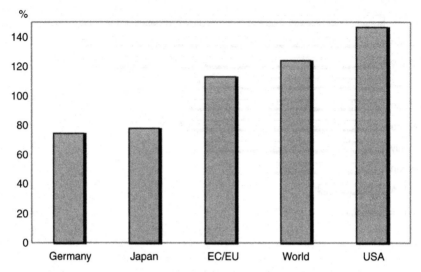

%

Source: Author's calculations derived from data in IMF, *Direction of Trade Statistics,* annual
issues.

Figure 2.3 Comparative rates of export growth, 1987–96.

first two decades after World War II. In those years, wartime destruction in
Europe and Japan meant that in those economies, the first two post-war
decades were devoted mainly to meeting the needs of recovery and
domestic demand.

In that environment of reconstruction and worldwide shortage, there
was a sharp increase in both the dollar-value, and the portion, or share, of
the global market reached by US exports. Both were at levels far higher
than they had ever been before, and America's global share has never
again exceeded or even approached those heights. I have shown this
history in Figure 2.4, which traces a full century of the American export
experience, from 1896–1996. My aim has been to put those exports into
their global context, by showing them as a percentage of all the world's
exports during those years. Since the period covered is a full century,
Figure 2.4 is based on trade data collected not only by the United States,
but by the League of Nations and the United Nations as well.

The illustration shows starkly what happened in the period just before
and just after World War II. In its immediate aftermath, the US accounted
for an unprecedented 22 percent share of the global export market. That
compares with 13 percent in the pre-war year of 1937, and with roughly
the same level – not quite 12 percent – from 1980 to 1996.[18]

That seemingly-significant post-war decline – from 22 percent to 12
percent – is at the heart of a very powerful, but fundamentally misleading

view of America's role in the world economy. It is misleading because it has led to a view of "decline" based on a single and wholly artificial time-span: the 25 years after World War II. The reality is quite different. When the past century of American exports is examined, it reveals not only that America's share of world exports has *not* experienced a secular decline since 1896–1900, but that those exports have instead moved mainly *within the same narrow 11–13 percent range*. Only during short periods, associated mainly with the immediate consequences of the two World Wars, has the global share of US exports been higher, and *since at least 1980 those exports have been rock-steady, at just under 12 percent.*

Because the lessons of this hundred-year record are so different from what is commonly thought, two further points contained in Figure 2.4 should be highlighted. The first is that, in the initial few years after World War II, America's global export share expanded quite suddenly and dramatically, but also quite temporarily. By 1960, and clearly by the mid-1970s, the unprecedented 22 percent level reached in 1949 had already begun to return to its historic 11–13 percent range, where it remains today. The same pattern characterized the years just before and after World War I. In 1913, on the eve of that war, the US share of world exports was just over 12 percent, as it had been since the turn of the century. By 1928, however, a decade after the war's end, it had grown to almost 16 percent. But in 1937, America's share was once again precisely 13 percent.[19]

The explanation in both cases is similar, though the effect was much more pronounced after World War II. That war brought devastation everywhere in the industrialized world, except for the United States, Canada, and a few small economies. In terms of exports and trade generally, there

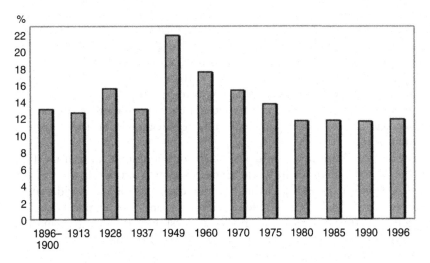

Figure 2.4 100 years of US exports, as percentage share of world market.

were two consequences of that wartime destruction. First, in the early post-war years, no other nation was capable of producing many of the goods that came from the United States. Second, no other nation could yet compete with the US as a supplier to most foreign markets. Japan and Western Europe, in other words, were effectively absent from the global export scene during much of the first two post-war decades; they re-entered world markets only as they completed their domestic recoveries. By the mid-1960s that task was behind them, and by the early 1970s European and Japanese suppliers had returned massively to the opportunities presented by foreign economies.

By that time, moreover, some of those economies, as in Southeast Asia, were beginning to experience their own rapid growth, and in those markets, firms from Britain, Holland, France, Germany, Italy and Japan often had an extensive pre-war presence. The reappearance of those pre-war suppliers, meaning that American suppliers were no longer the only ones available, in fact often represented no more than a *return to pre-war trade patterns*. But that was not how this revival of pre-war patterns was understood by many Americans. Instead it was seen as the beginning of America's export "decline" – a perception that was soon to fuel America's contemporary obsession with trade deficits.

The second main lesson of Figure 2.4 is in the years since 1980. That period witnessed two major events: first, the remarkable growth in world trade discussed in Chapter 1, and second, the arrival of altogether new economic actors. Those newcomers, especially in Asia, *either did not exist as independent players when the century began, or, as in the case of Japan, had just entered export markets*. In 1913, for example, Japan accounted for less than 2 percent of world exports, but Japan alone now represents *nearly 8 percent*.[20] The others – Singapore, Korea, Taiwan and Hong Kong (the so-called "Asian NICs," or Newly Industrializing Countries) – played no separate role at all as export economies before World War II, but today they account for more than 10 percent of world exports. When China, the newest Asian NIC, is added to this group, the world export share of these Asian newcomers becomes more than 13 percent. Thus, when Japan's remarkable rise as a world exporter is included, more than 20 percent of the global export market is now represented by economic actors that had little or no international significance when the twentieth century began.

Yet despite those profoundly important developments, and in the face of the overall explosion in world trade, exports from the United States have consistently maintained their 12 percent share of the world's total. That is a genuinely remarkable accomplishment, and it points to the capacity of the American economy to respond to changed market opportunities in ways that have remained altogether competitive. A good illustration is the changed composition of US exports. As recently as 1975, for example, farm products represented 20 percent of American exports, but today they count for less than 10 percent. The resulting relative "loss" in agricultural exports has been compensated by America's rising sales of manufactured goods – which now account for almost *85 percent of total US exports.*[21]

The most striking finding of this hundred-year review is that the United States, which began the twentieth century with 12 percent of the global export market, ended the century with an identical 12 percent share. The significance of that conclusion is particularly underlined by America's recent export performance. Especially in the context of strong new actors, a constant or rising US share of world exports means that the roles of some other actors have necessarily declined. The accompanying two pie charts (Figures 2.5 and 2.6) demonstrate that point by comparing the 1990 and 1996 world market shares of the United States, the EU, Japan, and the Asian NICs (including China). In those six years the size of the world market grew by almost $2 trillion, but the illustrations show that America's portion remained constant at 12 percent, while the share of the Asian NICs rose from 10 percent to 13 percent, and that of the EU nations *fell,* from 44 percent to 39 percent.[22]

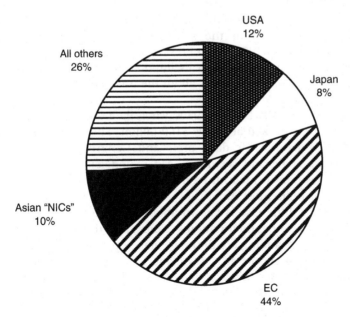

Figure 2.5 World export shares, 1990 (total = $3,386 billion).

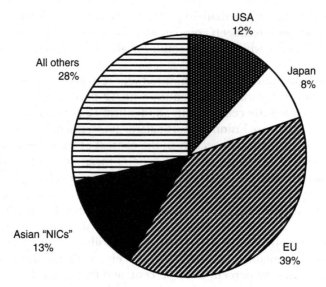

Source: Author's calculations from data in IMF DOTS Annual 1997.

Figure 2.6 World export shares, 1996 (total = $5,266 billion).

The trade deficit

This chapter has so far described a highly positive picture of America's export performance, both in the short-term and over much longer periods. But at least since 1971, when President Nixon devalued the dollar and imposed a surcharge on America's imports, America's trade debate has been shaped primarily by worries about the trade *deficit*. Those worries now drive America's trade policy.

The issue came to a head in the 1980s, when the trade deficit suddenly swelled, and in 1987 peaked at nearly $160 billion. The sheer size of that figure made it a natural for daily press and Congressional attention. Because it was a single and seemingly easy-to-understand number, the "trade deficit" was transformed into a media topic everyone could follow. The result is that while most Americans are now aware that the US runs large trade deficits, little else is known about trade, and most would be very surprised to learn that their nation's exports lead the world.

That gap in understanding continues to shape opinion today, although the issue was never as simple as it was made to seem. The reason is that since the mid-1980s, America's *total* trade has grown very sharply, and the total includes a sharp rise in US exports. To repeat the point made a moment ago, in the decade after 1986, US exports alone nearly tripled: they rose from $223 billion to $612 billion.[23] For that reason, in order to

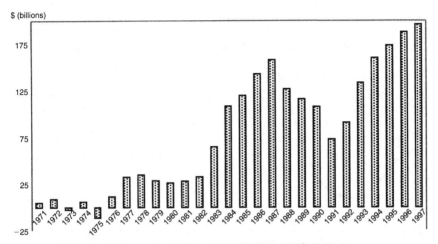

$ (billions)

Source: US Commerce Department, *Foreign Trade Highlights*, 1997, Table 1.

Figure 2.7 The dollar value of America's trade deficits, 1971–97.

judge the significance of any trade deficit number – whether $50 billion or $200 billion – some context is needed. One such context is the size of America's overall trade; another is the size of the American economy.[24] To ignore either or both would be like comparing – without taking into account their size – the weight-lifting ability of a young boy and his 200-pound father. Both might be able to lift a 10-pound barbell, but the boy's achievement is far more impressive.

The same reasoning applies to the trade deficit. In 1987, when America's total trade was $660 billion, the trade deficit caused much alarm when it approached $160 billion. Ten years later, however, US total trade had grown to *$1,560 billion*. For the deficit in 1997 to have the same alarming proportions as in 1987, it would have had to grow to almost $380 billion. In fact, it was just over *half* that amount in 1997. That was larger, of course, than in 1987, but far from proportionately so.

The following three charts will illustrate these points. The first (Figure 2.7), deals with 1971–97, and shows the trade deficit as it is usually seen: measured in dollars. This is the sort of chart that regularly makes the news, because it presents a picture of billion-dollar trade deficits that are almost always rising to new heights.

The next two illustrations deal with a similar period (1977–97), but reveal a very different pattern. Figure 2.8 shows the deficit not in dollars, but instead *as a percentage of America's total merchandise trade*. This chart shows that in the late 1990s, the trade deficit – at 12 percent – was only

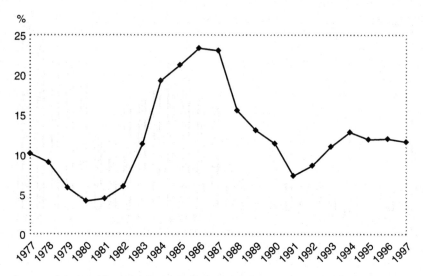

Source: Calculated from data in *US Foreign Trade Highlights*, 1996 and FT900.

Figure 2.8 The rise and fall of America's merchandise trade deficit as a percentage of US total trade, 1977–97.

half the level reached in the peak years of the mid-1980s, and in 1997 it was only slightly higher *than in 1977.*

Figure 2.9 is different in two respects. First, it tracks the trade deficit as a *percentage of America's overall economy,* i.e. in relation to America's Gross Domestic Product, and second, it shows the trade deficit measured in two ways: one for merchandise-only, and the other for merchandise plus services.

As the illustration shows, both rose sharply in the late 1980s, and both have come down significantly since then.[25] As in Figure 2.8, which traced the trade deficit as a percentage of overall trade, the merchandise-only deficit was actually *smaller* in 1997 than in the mid-1980s, and when services are included, the ratio of the trade deficit to GDP was *the same in 1997 as it had been in 1977.*

The lesson of both illustrations is that America's trade deficit, relative either to the size of overall US trade, or to the size of the US economy, is not the shocking figure it has been made to seem. The true picture, despite innumerable press and Congressional references to America's "ballooning deficits," is much different than the hype, and much less of a cause for alarm.

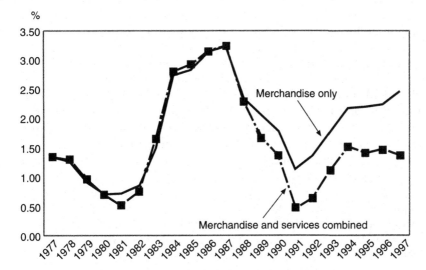

Figure 2.9 The trade deficit, as percentage of GDP, 1977–97.

Lessons from America's trade with Japan

The reason why America's trade deficits have fallen back to levels not seen since the early 1980s is that exports have risen faster than imports. The best and most important example of that reality is US exports to Japan, an example worth close examination for two reasons. The first is that deficits first entered America's consciousness as an important public policy issue largely as a result of trade with Japan, and that subject now needs to be re-examined. The second reason is that the record of US exports to Japan contains important lessons on a wider issue: the ability of American products and firms to compete successfully abroad. We will close this chapter with a discussion of both issues.

The importance of trade deficits has long been downplayed by economists: their discipline teaches that *bilateral deficits in particular* have little economic meaning, and should be ignored. But perversely, what has been ignored instead is the economists' advice. The result is that to most Americans, the nation's trade deficits have been seen as powerful *political* symbols suggesting national weakness and economic decline. Much of the responsibility for that profoundly mistaken view, and for the confusion generally about trade deficits, belongs to America's political leaders, whose statements regularly reinforce the false deficit-decline linkage.

The Clinton administration is an excellent example. From its first days in office, its behavior showed that America's trade deficits, rather than the nation's already-healthy exports, shaped the administration's thinking.

The President himself made this clear during his first formal press conference, on 24 March, 1993. As *The New York Times* reported, "he went broadly after the Japanese." When he spoke about trade, Japan was his entire focus – but *not* the Japan that continues as America's largest overseas market. US sales to Japan were almost $50 billion the year Mr Clinton spoke, and became much higher in the immediately-following years. But the President spoke with irritation only about America's trade deficit with Japan. Other deficits, he remarked, go down and even go away, but "the one that never seems to change very much is the one with Japan." Then, "with an icy laugh," he added that "The persistence of the surplus can only lead one to the conclusion that the possibility of obtaining real, even access to the Japanese market is somewhat remote."[26]

Mr Clinton was wrong on both counts: first, about the "persistence" of the Japan deficit, and second, about its purported uniqueness. The year the President spoke, in 1993, the US also had relatively large deficits with China, Canada, and Germany, and as the list below shows, they all rose very substantially over the next six years.

	1993	*1999*
China	$23 billion	$69 billion
Canada	$11 billion	$32 billion
Germany	$10 billion	$28 billion

Moreover, while the US had trade *surpluses* with both the EU and Mexico at the beginning of the 1990s, both markets soon turned into large trade *deficits*. By 1999, the deficit with the EU was $43 billion, and with Mexico it was $23 billion.

The deficit experience with Japan was quite different. Over the next six years it went both up *and* down; indeed in 1997 it was actually lower than in 1993. Like the others, it was higher in 1999 than in 1993 ($73 billion versus $59 billion), but as Figure 2.10 shows, its *rate of growth* was the smallest of all.

In retrospect, America's trade deficit with Japan was "unique" in only one respect: it was one of a very few which not only did *not* continue to rise, but instead came down sharply in the late 1980s. The next illustration (Figure 2.11) makes this point clearly. It is a particularly accurate and useful way to look at any bilateral trade deficit, because it shows the *deficit in relation to the overall size* of their bilateral trade, and expresses that size as a percentage. As Figure 2.11 shows quite dramatically, America's trade deficit with Japan has gone up *and* down, but it has never returned to the high point reached in 1986, when the deficit represented more than 50 percent of US–Japan total trade.

But however striking these specific illustrations may be, they are not the main point. More important is that an American President, even with the

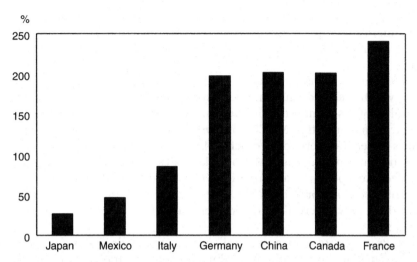

Source: Author's calculations from data in US Commerce Dept., *Foreign Trade Highlights* (FT900), Table 8, Total Trade Balances, August, 2000.

Figure 2.10 Percentage increases in America's trade deficits with major partners, 1993–9.

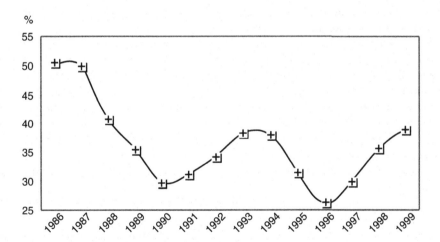

Source: Author's calculations from data in *US Foreign Trade Highlights*, annual issues.

Figure 2.11 America's trade deficit with Japan, as a percentage of their bilateral trade, 1986–99.

full range of US government data available to him, was so wide of the mark on trade issues, especially in connection with Japan. For Japan is not only America's largest overseas trade partner, and the world's second largest economy, but is also America's key political and military ally in Asia.

Yet the misinformation that shaped the President's perspectives on Japan, which included issues in addition to trade, applied not only at the beginning of his administration, but throughout his years in office. The likely explanation is that Mr Clinton's views, both on Japan and on trade deficits in general, were formed before he came to office, and no amount of factual information was likely to shake his convictions.[27] That suggests how deep and pervasive are America's misplaced trade deficit worries, a point of special importance in this case, because the resulting distortions affected not only America's trade policies, but its foreign and strategic policies as well.

The President, of course, was not alone in this trade deficit mind-set, with its familiar, but deeply misleading, view that a trade *deficit* signals something negative about a nation's economy. Nor was it novel to associate a nation's positive trade balance, that is to say a *trade surplus*, with national well-being, and even national "power." Quite the opposite is the case. As I mentioned in Chapter 1, the idea of equating a trade surplus with national strength, and a trade deficit with national weakness, stems mainly from the mercantilist era, i.e. the economic and political history of the sixteenth–eighteenth centuries.

In practical terms, mercantilism has few followers today, especially among the governments of the major economies. But it does have a powerful hold on much popular thinking, which evidently includes the thinking of some political leaders as well. In 1987, when Ronald Reagan was in office, his Council of Economic Advisors wrote that "Unfortunately, interest in bilateral trade balances – *essentially a mercantilist trait* – remains great."[28] They used the word "unfortunately" because mercantilism's principles have little or nothing to do with today's circumstances – although in the seventeenth century, trade balances *were* a legitimate economic and political issue.

The reason was straightforward: in that era, the principal trading actor was the state, or its chartered agents. A trade *deficit* in that period meant literally that in exchange for its exports, a nation had earned too little gold or silver ("specie"), and specie was vital to national security. Why? Because in the age before military conscription, the king had to pay hard cash for his soldiers and sailors. His troops, native born or not, were what we would today call mercenaries. Without them, the state's existence could not be assured. For that reason, trade, and especially the need to assure more exports than imports, was indeed both a central political and economic issue.

Today, however, there is no such direct linkage between trade deficits and state survival, certainly not in the United States. That point must be stressed again: *America's trade figures – whether deficits or surpluses – do not reflect state actions.* They reflect instead a multitude of private transactions, each one intended to be profitable to buyer and seller alike. Nevertheless, the powerful symbolism of a trade "deficit" lives on, with all its connotations of state weakness and profligacy. That is the reason why, for many Americans in the 1980s and 1990s, the Japan deficit came to mean that Japan was strong and America weak. Its dubious corollary – that America's main trade "problem" is its trade with Asian nations – arose from the fact that America also had deficits with most of the other Asian economies. It was then no great leap to conclude that America's best course was somehow to expect less from Asia, and to promote instead closer trade ties with regions thought of as geographically closer and culturally similar.

The reality, though seldom mentioned in the trade debate, is that America's trade deficits are *not* concentrated regionally. This chapter has already pointed to the very substantial deficits the US also has with Canada, Mexico, Germany, Italy, and France. The United States has a trade deficit even with Sweden, as of course it does with the OPEC nations (more than $22 billion in 1996). But those deficits, especially in the light of other prominent US economic indicators that are simultaneously present – and which co-exist with high and geographically widespread deficits – tell us no more than that *trade deficits are essentially irrelevant to economic well-being.* After all, the US economy in this era has been marked by the following features:

- an unemployment rate of roughly 5 percent, lower than anywhere in Europe and almost all other industrialized nations;
- an export *level* that continues to lead the world;
- an export growth rate, as Figure 2.3 showed, that exceeds all other industrialized economies, and that assures America's continued high export status;
- a pattern of historically-low interest rates, combined with low inflation levels;
- very high *per capita* GDP, and a GDP growth rate of more than 4 percent annually, which is higher than in all the other mature industrialized economies.

These summary points should cast much doubt on the American habit of concentrating on trade deficits. They also point to a second reality in US trade that has been largely ignored: the *high value* of America's exports to Japan. Their relevance goes beyond US–Japan relations, because they shed important light on the ability of US firms and products to compete successfully in world markets generally. This chapter closes on that point, because much of America's new-found interest in regionalism stems from two false convictions: first, the belief that American products have *not* done well against competitors in Asia, and second, that America and its products have not been able to "crack" markets in Asia that were effectively closed to outsiders.

Yet consider the following: in the five years from 1985–90, the Commerce Department reported that US exports to Japan more than doubled, from $23 billion to $49 billion. By 1996, despite a relative slowdown in Japan's overall imports after 1991 (when the Japanese economic "bubble" burst), US sales there grew by another $20 billion, to almost $68 billion.[29] That very substantial rise should be compared with Japan's imports from the *other* major manufacturing nations – the economies that are America's principal competitors. Data reported by the International Monetary Fund, which collects both import and export statistics for all nations, allows us to do precisely that.

The IMF reports that from 1990–6, Japan's imports from the US rose by 52 percent, whereas Japan's imports from "Industrial Countries" (an IMF category that includes the US), rose by only 36 percent.[30] Even more dramatically, Japan's imports from the EU rose more slowly than that, by 30 percent, and within Europe, the figures for specific countries are especially instructive. Japanese imports from Germany rose by just 22 percent – less than half the rate of its import growth from the US. Likewise regarding Japan's imports from France, the source of many of its luxury goods: they actually *fell* by more than $1 billion. The American trade experience with Japan in those same years was very different. Its rate of import growth from Japan slowed, and in some years during the 1990s, even declined. Exports, however, as we just pointed out, generally grew: the increase from 1993–6 was more than 40 percent.[31]

These figures are valuable for two reasons. First because they tell us that in Japan, America's allegedly "toughest" market, US exports have been more successful than all other competitors. Second, they underline once again the point made throughout this chapter: that the overall foreign trade position of the United States is far stronger than it is reputed to be. That *global* achievement by America's firms and products makes its official policy of economic regionalism particularly difficult to rationalize, or even to fathom. Yet some of the explanation for America's continuing attachment to regionalism lies in the success of Europe's experience with the concept, and for that reason the next chapter explores the evolution of the European Union – from its beginnings as a simple coal and steel community, to its emergence as a commercial superpower with a single currency.

Notes

1 B. Eichengreen and D. A. Irwin, "Trade Blocs, Currency Blocs and the Reorientation of World Trade in the 1930s," *Journal of International Economics*, 1995, Vol. 38, No. 5, pp. 1–24.

2 For early descriptions of regionalism's revival, see A. Bollard and D. Mayes, "Regionalism and the Pacific Rim," and J. Whalley, "CUSTA and NAFTA: Can WHAFTA Be Far Behind?" in the *Journal of Common Market Studies*, June, 1992, pp. 125–41 and pp. 195–209.

3 The EEC's original six threatened to withdraw from GATT if full compliance with Article 24 was insisted on. See B. Hoeckman and M. Kostecki, *The Political Economy of the World Trading System*, Oxford, Oxford University Press, 1995, p. 219. Good recent discussions of Article 24 are in Carnegie Endowment for International Peace, *Reflections on Regionalism*, Washington, Carnegie Endowment, 1997 and J. Bhagwati, "Regionalism versus Multilateralism," *The World Economy*, September 1992, Vol. 15, No. 5, p. 540.

4 Table A1-1 in J. Bhagwati and A. Panagariya, *The Economics of Preferential Trade Agreements*, Washington, American Enterprise Institute Press, 1996, pp. 55–73.

5 See Krueger's essay, "NAFTA: Strengthening or Weakening the International Trading System," in J. Bhagwati and A. Krueger, *The Dangerous Drift to Preferential Trade Agreements*, Washington, AEI Press, 1995, and M. Wolf, "Why Liberalisation Won," *Financial Times*, 18 May, 1998.

6 The "building block" phrase was popularized by Robert Lawrence (who credits Bhagwati with its first use), in a prizewinning essay in R. Lawrence, *Finance and the International Economy*, Oxford, Oxford University Press, 1991.

7 NAFTA's "local content" provisions already illustrate the point, and as John Whalley reports, the Latin Americans who want to join NAFTA also want "to secure their access to the larger US market . . . before other smaller countries enter into similar access negotiations," Whalley, *op. cit.*, p. 126.

8 *Reflections on Regionalism*, *op. cit.*, p. 23.

9 The dichotomy between trade creation and trade diversion originated with Jacob Viner in *The Customs Union Issue*, Washington, DC: Carnegie Endowment for International Peace, 1950.

10 Ryutaro Hashimoto, *Vision of Japan*, Tokyo, Bestsellers, 1994, p. 71.

11 Japan–US income comparisons are often confused by yen–dollar variations, but the main point is the essential equivalency in Japanese and American living standards and disposable income.

12 Statement of Ambassador Charlene Barshefsky, Subcommittee on Commerce, Justice, State and Judiciary of the Committee on Appropriations, US House of Representatives, 106th Cong., 2nd Sess., 5 April, 2000, cited in Heritage Foundation, *Backgrounder*, No. 1391, 25 August, 2000, p. 4.

13 Commerce Department estimate reported in Heritage Foundation, "Trade Figures Highlight Importance of Exports to Asia for U.S. Jobs," October, 1994. The same figure was confirmed by telephone in 1998. The ITA figure is in "Contribution of Exports on U.S. Employment, 1980–1987," March, 1989, p. 1, as reported by the Heritage Foundation, "How the North American Free Trade Agreement Creates Jobs," in *Backgrounder*, No. 872, 15 January, 1992. Similar estimates are reported by C. Carvounis and B. Carvounis, *United States Trade and Investment in Latin America*, Westport and London, Quorum Books, 1992, p. 78.

14 P. Morici, "Export Our Way to Prosperity," *Foreign Policy*, Winter 1995–6, p. 8.

15 Heritage Foundation, *Backgrounder*, No. 872, *ibid.*

16 V. Lopez and L. Yager, "An Aerospace Profile: The Industry's Role in the Economy, the Importance of R&D," *Facts and Perspectives*, quoted in V. Golich, "From Competition to Collaboration: the Challenge of Commercial-class Aircraft Manufacturing," *International Organization*, Autumn, 1992, p. 912.

17 *Wall Street Journal*, 28 April, 1998.

18 Sources for Figure 2.4 are as follows: world export data for 1896–1937 from P. Yates, *Forty Years of Foreign Trade*, London, George Allen & Unwin, 1959, Table

A18, p. 226, and US data for those years from US Department of Commerce, *Historical Statistics of the United States*, Series U187–200, pp. 884–5. 1970–96 data, for both US and world exports, are from International Monetary Fund, *Direction of Trade Statistics Yearbook*, various years. (This fundamental source is sometimes referred to as "IMF DOTS," and several of this book's charts will indicate "IMF DOTS" as the source of their trade data.) US percentage-shares in 1949 and 1960 are from IMF, *International Financial Statistics Yearbook*, 1979, as reported by T. D. Lairson and D. Skidmore, *International Political Economy*, 2nd. Edn, New York, Harcourt, Brace, 1997, Table 4.2 p. 65.

19 1937 figures from League of Nations, *Review of World Trade*, as reported by Yates, p. 226, and US Commerce Department, *Historical Statistics of the United States*, Washington, 1960, p. 537.

20 Japan's share in 1913 from Yates, *ibid.*, p. 234; 1996 data calculated from IMF, *Direction of Trade Statistics Yearbook, 1997.* Japan's share was again down for a number of years after World War II (in 1953, for example it was 1.7 percent) as compared with its pre-war high of 6 percent in 1937.

21 Commodity-composition data from US Department of Commerce, *U.S. Foreign Trade Highlights 1996*, Table 3.

22 Both illustrations calculated from data in IMF, *Direction of Trade Statistics, Yearbook*, 1997.

23 They were higher still in 1997, at $678 billion (data from US Department of Commerce, *Foreign Trade Highlights*, 1998).

24 A former Chairman of the White House Council of Economic Advisors (Laura d'Andrea Tyson) has made a similar point: "the absolute size of the trade deficit measured in dollars is irrelevant. A preferable measure is the size of the deficit compared with the overall size of the economy," *The New York Times*, 24 November, 1997.

25 Figure 2.9 trade data, for merchandise only and with services included, are from *Foreign Trade Highlights, 1996, op. cit.*; 1997 figure from US Department of Commerce, *Foreign Trade Highlights*, "FT900" Series, 2 June, 1998. GDP figures for 1977–89 from *Foreign Trade Highlights*, 1997, Table 5, p. 15; GDP data for 1990–7 from US President, Council of Economic Advisors, *Economic Report of the President*, Washington, GPO, 1998.

26 *The New York Times*, 25 March, 1993. After fielding a question about the trade policies of his predecessor, the President, "without a further question ... harshly criticized Japan's big trade surplus." He said he was "astonished" that the Bush Administration "gave [Japan] a $300 million-a-year freebie for no apparent reason ... and we got *nothing*, and I emphasize *nothing*, in return." Emphasis added.

27 Mr Clinton's appointment of Mickey Kantor as US Trade Representative did not bring balance or better factual analysis to trade issues. Kantor was a California lawyer prominent in Democratic Party circles, but he had no prior experience or concern with trade policy. His qualifications were high personal loyalty to Mr Clinton, his record as a fund-raiser, and his reputation as a political "fixer" when the President needed help.

28 US, *Economic Report of the President*, Washington, GPO, January, 1987, p. 130. My emphasis. The brief section called "The Case for Free Trade," pp. 127–30, is an excellent brief statement of this classic issue.

29 These are official US figures of US exports, from census data. They are conservative figures, and raise a methodological point that should be identified. In this book, when figures for US *exports* are given, the source is normally the US Commerce Department. However, because those data do not include costs of freight and insurance, they are lower than the figures the IMF

reports as the corresponding imports. For example, in 1996 the IMF, *Direction of Trade Statistics* (DOTS) figure for Japanese imports *from the US* was $79.9 billion, while the comparable "f.a.s." (freight-alongside basis) US Commerce Dept. figure for US *exports to Japan* was $67.6 billion.

30 International Monetary Fund, *Direction of Trade Statistics Yearbook, 1997*, p. 270.
31 US, *Foreign Trade Highlights, 1998*.

3   Regionalism in Europe

A model for the past or the future?

January 1999 marked a truly historic event, when the European Union introduced its single currency, the Euro. For the eleven participating nations, the decision to phase out their national currencies signaled both unprecedented European economic integration, and the possibility of political unity – something not seen since the Roman Empire collapsed 1500 years earlier.[1] And for the world beyond Europe, the new currency meant that the global supremacy of the US dollar, a feature of the world economy since 1945, might also have come to an end.

In its place would be a new duality, in which the Euro would function alongside the dollar as one of the world's two key currencies. A prominent American economist predicted that "the Euro pretty quickly will start to rival the dollar as an international asset,"[2] and European sentiment was similar: "all of the sudden the dwarves . . . are asking whether Snow White always has to be the U.S."[3] The President of Germany's *Bundesbank*, Hans Tietmeyer, went further. He had already termed a single currency essential for Europe ("political union begins here"), and the Euro's introduction led him now to call for a single European constitution.[4]

Not to be outdone, Japan's Prime Minister Obuchi flew immediately to Europe to declare that two main global currencies would not be enough. As leader of the nation with the world's second largest economy, Obuchi insisted that Japan's yen would have to take its place along with the dollar and the Euro. Even Brazil, always aware of its role as South America's largest economy, joined in. Just days before the *Real* lost nearly half its value, Brazil's leaders were reported to believe that "in the future, maybe there ought to be four currency blocs: the dollar, the yen, the euro and the Brazilian currency."[5]

These events are worth recalling for two reasons: first because they are a reminder that economic regionalism comes in several shapes – in this case as a currency issue – and second because they show how topics that seem to be about "only economics" quickly become intensely political. After all, the Euro's advent was intended to promote *economic* integration, but it was nevertheless seen immediately in strongly competitive *political* terms. A good illustration came at a meeting of French and British leaders, who were discussing the meaning of the Euro just weeks after it was introduced. France's participants said it meant "a more integrated, activist, and world-leading Europe," and stressed that was their goal as well. Likewise, a French company director interrupted a British speaker to insist that "the European project was *about the building of a state, not the mere extension of commercial freedoms.*"[6] A reporter described that as the meeting's "defining moment," but that view was quickly denied by France's Finance Minister. Sounding like the inspector in *Casablanca*, who was "shocked, shocked" to find gambling at Rick's place, the Minister insisted there was nothing political about the new currency: "the euro is not being built up as a currency in opposition to the dollar or against US [hegemony]."[7]

Politics and Europe's regionalism

The reality, of course, is that politics, both domestic and international, has always been at the core of every aspect of Europe's post-war integration. In the late 1940s and early 1950s, Europe's leaders made their unprecedented efforts to build a European Community *not* for reasons of trade or economics – and certainly not for such theoretical niceties as "integration" or "functional cooperation" – but instead for the fundamentally *political* imperatives of national security and foreign policy. That is why the notion of European integration as an alleged "model" has been so ill-suited to regional cooperation efforts elsewhere. The European model does not fit, because its roots are in the political conflicts that have afflicted Europe for centuries – conflicts which led to the two nearly global wars that characterized the twentieth century.

Those roots become immediately clear when we recall that the very concept of regional cooperation is itself firmly grounded in European writings of the inter-war years: when economic integration was seen as a way to avoid new European conflicts.[8] The concept was kick-started after World War II, by Europe's bleak conditions in those early post-war years: when food, fuel, and all other goods were in short supply, and when parties of the left preached that they had the answer. The final impetus for regional cooperation and integration – the force that moved it from the drawing table to the negotiating table – was the equally bleak state of post-war global politics: when Western relations with the Soviet Union hardened into the tensions of the early Cold War. That heavily political environment was the soil in which Europe's post-war integration took root; as a recent and authoritative book on the *economics* of European integration put it, "politics led to the EEC's integration."[9]

Two main features of post-war history will help recall that political background. First, precisely because of World War II and its horrific consequences, many Europeans were encouraged to return, not only to the concept of European cooperation that had been outlined before the war, but to take the collaborative steps they believed would prevent another such conflict. The second is that the material incentives that made their collaboration possible came from America's Marshall Plan. That effort was firmly grounded in the American conviction that a more united Europe would be economically healthier, and would therefore be less vulnerable to the siren song of communism. Accordingly, the seeds of what in ten years would become the European Economic Community were sown in 1947, when the Organization for European Economic Cooperation (OEEC) was created. Its immediate purpose was to administer Marshall Plan aid, but the broader OEEC aim was "to promote Europe's economic cooperation and trade liberalization."[10]

Events moved quickly, and as early as the mid-1950s, the steps were in place that led to the European Union of today, with its single market and single currency. The key initiative came in March, 1957, when six European nations (Belgium, France, Germany, Italy, Luxembourg, and Holland) signed the Treaty of Rome. That Treaty was the foundation stone for all that has followed; it called for the establishment the following year of the European Economic Community (EEC), as well as its rule-making body, the European Commission. Ten years later (in 1968), all tariffs on intra-EEC merchandise trade were removed, and in 1985 the Commission called for the establishment of a single European market. That came into effect in 1993, and provided for free movement of both people and services. In addition to these steps, the Community expanded over the years, as nine new members were added: Denmark, Ireland, and Britain in 1973; Greece in 1981; Portugal and Spain in 1986; and in 1995, Austria, Finland and Sweden. The result is that today's European Union is an impressive institution of deep economic cooperation among 15 nations, representing more than 360 million people.

Along every step of the way, often difficult political decisions were involved. Some reflected genuinely different conceptions of what a federal or united Europe would look like, and in those conceptions, the views of France, Germany, and later Britain, were especially prominent. Other distinctions were shaped by different decision-making styles and practices, as well as a host of other separately-important topics. But all those differences paled by comparison with this fundamental point of convergence: at the heart of Europe's integration was a *political decision by France and Germany to achieve an historic reconciliation and rapprochement*. German Chancellor Konrad Adenauer and French President Charles de Gaulle – two giants of post-war history – both personified and were central to this decision.[11] Their agreement was that Germany and France would link their two economies, and would forego any potentially disruptive national political interests. Their path had been pointed to as early as 1946, by Winston Churchill, Britain's wartime Prime Minister. In a rightly famous speech, Churchill had said that "the first step in the re-creation of the European family must be a partnership between France and Germany."[12]

Since then, there have been many reflections of that partnership, but two are worth special mention. The first, which preceded de Gaulle, and indeed preceded the Treaty of Rome, was the European Coal and Steel Community, established in 1951. It had undoubted major economic significance, but the Coal and Steel Community was an essentially *political* act – and was so understood at the time – that "marked a step toward Franco-German reconciliation." No less than Adenauer himself put the point unmistakably in a speech to his Bundestag in 1952:

> It is my opinion and belief that the parliaments of the six European countries which will have to deal with this European Coal and Steel Community realize exactly what it is all about and that in particular they realize that the *political goal, the political meaning of the European Coal and Steel Community, is infinitely larger than its economic purpose.*[13]

The second critical step was the EC's Common Agricultural Policy, or CAP. It was adopted in 1962, and came into force in 1964. By the 1980s and 1990s, the Common Agricultural Policy had become one of Europe's most divisive political issues, because its cost – at more than $40 billion in 1998 – represented almost half the EU budget.[14] But in 1962 the CAP reflected a grand Franco-German bargain that made the EC possible – in somewhat the same way the "Great Compromise" allowed for the adoption of the American Constitution in 1787–8. The issue there was the fear among the small American states that they would always be dominated by their larger and more populous peers – a concern removed when "The Great Compromise" assured all states equal representation in the US Senate.

Likewise in Europe, where despite their relatively small numbers, French and German farmers have long held a veto not only on issues of agricultural policy, but on the success of the EC as well. The Treaty of Rome perfectly reflected their political power, when it stipulated formally that farmers deserved "a fair standard of living." The Common Agricultural Policy was the method chosen to achieve that goal, and it became part of a larger EEC bargain that would ensure markets both for German industry and French farms. The essence of the deal was a *quid pro quo*: France, in return for European protectionism in agriculture, was prepared to accept a free market in manufactured goods, from which Germany would principally benefit.[15]

A key problem from the beginning, however, was that French and German farmers are not equally efficient. German farmers have histori-cally been relatively less productive than those in France; indeed since the nineteenth century Germany has protected its farmers with price supports and barriers against imports. Post-war German leaders were committed to continue those benefits, just as France's leaders were concerned to ensure large export markets for their wheat and other farm products. The Common Agricultural Policy, a complex and increasingly costly system of

guaranteed prices and incomes, met both needs: German farmers continued to receive their high incomes, while French farmers were encouraged
to produce ever-increasing yields.

With the perspective of hindsight, the CAP could be called a great
success, since it achieved what it was designed for. By the early 1990s, for
example, France alone accounted for half the EC's grain exports.[16] But at
the same time, the CAP also became a world-class illustration of how
global markets can be distorted by domestic politics. Those particulars are
less important, however, than this central point: the CAP, which was vital
to the successful first years of the EC, was a political win–win for both
Germany and France.

Even so, their different bargaining positions illustrate yet another
aspect of the EC's essentially political nature. Germany, for at least three
reasons, had a greater "need" for the EC than did France. First, as
Europe's largest industrial producer, with workers in manufacturing and
related fields making up a very high proportion of its labor force, the
German economy sorely wanted the EC's single market. France's situation
was the reverse: almost double its labor force, compared to Germany, were
farm workers.[17] Second, as the CAP process itself reflected, if Germany
were to get the industrial prize the single market represented, it had to
protect its farmers – and therefore Germany needed to contend with the
disproportionately strong domestic political pressures *they* represented.
But above all, Germany's post-war leaders had a deep historical–political
need to demonstrate that their nation could be a good citizen in a peace-
ful Europe, as Adenauer himself personified, and as German participation
in NATO also underlined. Combined, all those factors meant that in the
bilateral French–German negotiations surrounding the EC, France always
had the upper hand – as de Gaulle dramatically illustrated with his first
veto threat in 1961, and again in late 1964, when CAP differences led
France once more to threaten to withdraw.[18]

Europe as model or a fortress?

Although politics and foreign policy have always been the genuine key to
understanding EC goals and processes, its accomplishments in trade and
economics largely explain the EC's role as a model for others. Since the
1950s there have been scores of efforts, in all parts of the world, to
promote regional economic cooperation,[19] and explicitly or implicitly,
almost all identify the effort in Europe as their inspiration. The result is
that the European Community serves as a model in two ways: first, as a
standard against which existing regional efforts can be measured, and
second, as the inspiration for regional proposals not yet established.

An example of the first type, Europe as the standard against which
to be measured, is a study of the MERCOSUR effort in South America,
prepared in 1997 by several World Bank economists.[20] It carefully and

explicitly identified several MERCOSUR features and goals, and then, one-by-one, it measured those features against particular EC steps and accomplishments. A clear example of the second type – the EC as an inspiration for something *not* yet created – is a recent and potentially very important speech by Japan's former Prime Minister, Keizo Obuchi. This event, in March, 1999, marked the first time a Japanese leader publicly called on Asian nations to emulate Europe and create their own "free trade zone in Asia." Because the statement represented such a departure, Mr. Obuchi's words are worth quoting. Speaking to students at Korea University, he asked them to

> realize the dream of the 21st century in which Japan and the Republic of Korea would play a central role in realizing a *free trade zone in Asia that stood on a par with the European Union.*[21]

That speech, along with many like it, underlines an important point: the EC has a widely-known, and well-deserved, *reputation* for promoting intra-European trade and economic cooperation. The EC's *record*, however, raises the question of whether it has succeeded too much. To say that is not to deny that a main EC goal from the outset was to promote more intra-European trade, largely by reducing internal trade barriers. Nor is it to deny that a principal measure of EC accomplishments is precisely that expansion of trade. Instead, it is to ask whether the building of Europe's internal market has now succeeded to the point where the EC/EU has become "Fortress Europe" – the increasingly closed and self-contained system that many critics feared and predicted.[22]

The Fortress Europe label, with its charge of growing insularity, dates mainly from the late 1980s – the years leading up to the Maastricht Treaty. It was at Maastricht, in 1991 (a town known more for its art sales than diplomacy), where the EU formally agreed to establish, by 1999, a European central bank and single currency. As the planning for those momentous developments proceeded – planning that envisaged a genuinely single market of roughly 350 million consumers – officials and business people in the US, Japan, and other major exporting nations openly worried that their products would be frozen out. EC spokesmen just as often denied any such intent, and pointed to Europe's commitment to the WTO, as well as the Uruguay Round that created it, as evidence that "Fortress Europe" was a groundless worry.

The record, however, does not support their denial. It shows, for example, that in 1995, 68 percent of EC imports of *manufactured goods* were from other EC members, an increase from an already high level of 61 percent in 1985.[23] Moreover, the EC's broader and long-term record in *overall* imports (not just manufactured goods), is equally clear. Figure 3.1 illustrates the point: it begins a decade after the EC was formed; traces 30 years of its imports (1968–97); and shows that, from 1968–92, those

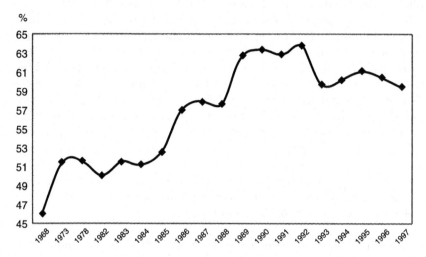

Source: IMF, *Direction of Trade Statistics,* annual issues.

Figure 3.1 Intra-EC imports, as percentage of total EC imports, 1968–97.

imports *rose from 46 percent to 64 percent.* That level has declined some in recent years, but is likely to stay in the same, roughly 60 percent, range in the future. Not surprising, therefore, that in 1994 a very qualified British observer wrote that Europe remains "appallingly protectionist,"[24] and that in early 2000, a former Chairman of the President's Council of Economic Advisors wrote that the Euro and other EU policies will intensify Europe's protectionism.[25]

The illustration, because it shows that two-thirds of the world's largest single market is effectively dominated by internal EU suppliers, demonstrates very clearly the concerns of the "Fortress Europe" critics. It underlines their point that world-class industrial exporters outside of Europe – which means not only the US and Japan, but significant newcomers Korea and Taiwan as well – must all compete for the remaining one-third of Europe's market. And, of course, the same daunting prospect is faced by the world's major *agricultural* exporters, including Australia, Brazil, Canada, and again the USA, as they seek to enter Europe's CAP-dominated farm market.

Another striking feature of the 30-year EC record can be seen by taking a second and separate look at Figure 3.1: the sharpest rise in intra-EC trade began in the mid-80s – when the world's newest exporters were also coming on line. For example, at the beginning of the period, Japan was still in its early post-war growth stages as a major exporting nation. In 1969 its products represented less than 6 percent of global imports, but grew to

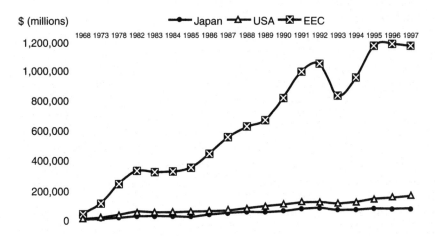

Source: IMF, *Direction of Trade Statistics,* annual issues.

Figure 3.2 Who supplies the EC, 1968–97.

8 percent by 1997. Today it ranks behind only Germany (9 percent) and the US (12–13 percent) as a leading world exporter, but despite that new global prominence, EC imports from Japan did not come close to reflecting the change. Instead, Japan's share of the EU market in 1997 was just 3.7 percent. That was an increase from the 1969 level – when the EC imported just over 1 percent of its products from Japan – but the rise was very far from proportionate to Japan's global export role. And rather amazingly, the US record in the EC market was even worse. *EC imports from the US actually fell over the past 30 years*: from 10 percent in 1969 to just over 8 percent in 1997.

Figure 3.2 illustrates this history in absolute-value terms: it shows the dollar-value of EC imports from three sources: the EC itself; the United States; and Japan.

Why the EC is no model

These high levels of intra-EC imports, and correspondingly low levels of non-European imports, should surprise nobody, given the frequent predictions that the EC would, in fact, become "Fortress Europe." After all, reducing Europe's internal trade barriers, precisely for the purpose of achieving more intra-European trade, was among the earliest announced goals of the EC. That goal has now been reached, and while non-Europeans may not be happy with the results, they are as expected.

Quite another matter is the EC's role as a model and inspiration.

Europe's experience with integration is constantly held up as a model for others to emulate, but there is little or nothing, either in the EC's historical background, or its recent record, that fits it to other regions. In terms of history, we have already seen that Europe's long and violent familiarity with war is inseparable from its modern efforts in regional economic cooperation and integration. One without the other is hardly imaginable. But even aside from history – and that is a very big aside – important aspects of the European economies, and their intra-regional trade, also make the EC/EU experience largely inapplicable as a model for cooperation and integration elsewhere. Nevertheless, *every other regional effort*, whether in Latin America, South Asia, or Southeast Asia, routinely proclaims as its goal the same ideal that has long been an EC/EU mantra: "more intra-regional trade."

That ostensibly common feature masks a fundamental difference that separates the EC from integration efforts almost everywhere else. The difference is that outside of Europe, and with only one exception,[26] the concept of greater intra-regional trade among geographically-close economies has little applicability, and even less likelihood to be achieved. That difference, between the EU experience and all other efforts, means that however much cooperative steps elsewhere might accomplish *other* worthwhile goals, significantly greater intra-regional trade is not likely to be among them.

The reason is that the nations in any given region – especially in the early stages of their economic development – heavily overlap one another, in what economists call their "factor endowments." The economic factors they have in common particularly for nations in the pre-industrial stage, are their natural and related agricultural resources: their rubber, rice, timber, tin, copper, coffee, oil and gas are examples that come quickly to mind. Largely for that reason, those economies have little need or opportunity to trade with their neighbors, and they have not done so, either in their earlier histories or in modern times. Among the developing nations of Asia, for example, it has long been a commonplace to note that historically, their economic and all other ties were far more intense with their *metropole* – their colonial rulers in Europe or America – than among themselves, and that those patterns continued in the post-independence period.

Essentially the same factors also apply to the newly-industrializing countries, the "NICs." That is an important point, because the newest and most active proposals for regional cooperation – as in ASEAN and MERCOSUR – have come from the NICs. Like economies in the pre-industrial stage, the NICs too have important economic features in common, though not necessarily their natural resources. For example, as part of their growing competition for foreign investment, the developing and newly-industrializing nations have emphasized, since the 1970s, their supplies of relatively inexpensive labor as an investment incentive. In that respect, their "factor endowments" are as similar as those among the pre-industrial economies, and the NICs likewise have little or no reason to engage in much intra-regional trade. As in the case of the pre-industrial economies, the NICs' efforts at regional cooperation – whatever other benefits they may produce – are not at all likely to include significant gains in "greater intra-regional trade."

But in a first hint of the national economic *differences* that do explain most trade, the NICs have also learned that their relatively cheap labor – the one factor they tend to have in common – does indeed have national variations of economic significance. They have found, in other words, that relatively cheap labor in one nation is not the same as equally cheap labor in another, even closely-neighboring nation. To put it another way, the labor supply among developing or newly-industrializing economies is not as interchangeable, or "fungible," as their supply of rubber, timber, or copper. If it were, those nations with the greatest supply of cheap labor would excel at attracting foreign investment, and a nation like Bangladesh would today be a global manufacturing center. Instead, developing nations searching for foreign investment have emphasized their nationally-specific labor-force *differences*. Those differences, which include their national literacy and educational levels; the familiarity of their people with widely-used languages; and those infrastructure features that affect labor productivity (such as harbors and roads) have become today's arenas for foreign investment competition.

A good illustration was the mid-1990s competition between Thailand and the Philippines for a proposed General Motors plant. It was valued at $750 million, and would be capable of producing 100,000 cars annually for the then-growing Southeast Asian market. As inducements, both Thailand and the Philippines offered relatively cheap labor, but in practice the competition focussed on more specific differences. Thailand had two main advantages: an existing network of Japanese auto-parts suppliers, which meant a labor force already attuned to the production of cars and trucks; and a higher rate of economic growth, which implied a larger domestic market. Thailand's demerits, however, included Bangkok's notoriously crowded streets and arteries, and a population generally not educated beyond middle-school level. For its part, the Philippines had a generally better-educated population, which often included English-language skills, as well as the availability of a recently empty former US naval base.[27] Both nations offered various tax-holidays and related subsidies.

In 1996, GM's closely-watched decision went in favor of Thailand, mainly because of its already-existing automotive industry, principally its network of suppliers and relatively experienced workers. The decision was another reminder that comparably cheap labor – based on the fact that both nations are at comparable levels of economic development, and are in the same geographic region – was not decisive. It underlined two points: first, that *national* economic distinctions had greater influence on GM's investment decision; and second, that factors associated with geography, or geographic proximity alone, are not likely to be decisive on issues of trade or economics.

Those national economic differences are the other side of a single coin, whose message is that the similarities among developing and newly-industrializing nations will continue to limit the likelihood for much intra-regional trade. Their *similarities* will instead continue to lead developing nations to trade principally with distant others, as the cases of several Asian and Latin American economies show very clearly. In the 1980s and 1990s, for example, the annual exports of the Philippines were much larger to distant *Holland* than to geographically very close neighbors Thailand and Malaysia. Likewise, Thailand's exports were almost always higher to Switzerland and France, than to ASEAN-partner Indonesia – despite the fact that Indonesia has sometimes imported large quantities of Thai rice.[28] In sum, the Philippines, Thailand, and Malaysia traded far more with the advanced economies of Europe – and with the United States – than they did with their closer but similar neighbors.

Much the same pattern exists in South America. Chile, for example, trades more with *Japan* than with Brazil, and more with the US than with any other nation.[29] Chile also trades more with any *one* of the following in Europe – Germany, Italy, or Britain – than with the *combined* South American economies of Venezuela, Colombia, and Bolivia! Peru's much smaller economy shows a similar pattern: its total trade with *all* of Latin America, even including Mexico, is less than with the United States. Similarly, its trade with the European Union is only slightly less than its total trade with Latin America (Mexico again included). Even Argentina, whose trade *is* dominated by neighboring Brazil (the region's largest economy), shares this feature: it trades more with Italy than with Chile; more with Belgium–Luxembourg than with Bolivia; and much more with either Britain or Holland than with Colombia, Peru, and Venezuela *combined.*

These low levels of intra-regional trade should also not be surprising, however much they contrast with Europe's trade patterns, and however much they tend to be deplored by well-meaning observers, both local and foreign. The trade patterns of the developing regions tell us that until their economies, along with those of the newly-industrializing nations, reach levels of economic differentiation of the sort that prevail in Europe, their levels of intra-regional trade will continue to be very low. This is simply another way of saying that trade among Europe's nations is high, *not* because of their geographic proximity, but because of two factors: the complementary nature of the European economies, and the workings of the principle of comparative advantage.

By complementary I mean that their economies do not substantially overlap, and that each produces some goods that another needs. In practice, that most often means that advanced industrialized nations trade mainly and most heavily with other advanced industrialized nations. The reason is the second factor: each economy concentrates on, produces, and exports those products where it has an important degree of *comparative advantage*. This keystone concept of modern approaches to foreign trade – largely missing from the intra-regional trade prospects of the NICs and developing nations – was introduced by David Ricardo in 1818, and expressed with somewhat greater clarity three years later by James Mill. It holds that an economy and its people are best off when its production and its exports concentrate on goods where its efforts are most efficient, i.e. where it has "*comparative*" advantage over other producers.[30]

Ricardo's famous example was the trade in wine and cloth between Portugal and England. Portugal could produce both at lower absolute cost, but held a comparative cost advantage only in wine. The reason was that England's efficient ability to produce and export cloth was such that its earnings from cloth – where its comparative advantage lay – made it beneficial to import just wine. A good contemporary example is America's textile industry – another instance of an economy that imports large quantities of a product where it has absolute, but not *comparative* advantage. As a knowledgeable economist has pointed out, in textiles the US is "undoubtedly more efficient than Asian countries such as Sri Lanka and Bangladesh ... (e.g. output per worker hour is higher), but the US is a net textile importer because we have comparative advantage in other goods."

Europe, because it has long reflected the workings both of complementarity and comparative advantage, has been characterized for a similarly long period by uniquely-high levels of intra-regional trade. Even in 1913, for example, the single greatest concentration of all the world's trade was intra-European. With Britain aside for the moment, the region's exports and imports represented 37 percent of the total, and for Europe as a whole the ratio was 40 percent.[31] In 1928, ten years after World War I, the level appears to have been even higher: an early GATT study showed that *more than 50 percent of Europe's exports* were intra-regional.[32] A decade later, under the impact of the global depression, the level of intra-European trade may have declined by about 10 percent, but by the mid-1950s the roughly 40 percent ratio was resumed.[33] In 1953, for example, among the nations that five years later established the EC, 45 percent of their imports were intra-regional, and as Figure 3.1 showed, that same level continued for roughly the first ten years of the EC's existence.

None of this, of course, applied in the developing regions. One study showed that in Southeast Asia between 1984–90, Indonesia's exports to its ASEAN partners were no more than *2 percent* of its global exports, and the ratio in Thailand actually declined. The only increases were the ASEAN-directed exports of the Philippines and Malaysia – but both of those remained below 5 percent and 8 percent.[34] By 1997 – *ASEAN's 30th year* – the group's intra-regional trade had generally dipped further. For example, Thailand's total trade with both the Philippines and Indonesia was 1–2 percent of its world total – the same level reported by both Malaysia and Indonesia for most of their ASEAN trade. The only exceptions to this strikingly low pattern were in some ASEAN partners' trade with Malaysia – but even in those cases the ratios never reached more than 4 percent.[35]

Long aware of these persistently low levels, leaders in both Asia and Latin America have looked with envy at Europe's strikingly high levels. In the mid-1970s, for example, Albert Fishlow, one of America's leading scholars on Latin America, wrote that "the great success of the European Common market, combined with the stagnation of Latin American exports in the latter 1950s, made regional integration appear both feasible and highly attractive."[36] Perhaps so, but in terms of the objective facts on the ground, both in Asia and Latin America, that "highly attractive" European model was never genuinely applicable to the world's other regions

TAFTA and its "marketplace": last stand of the Atlanticists?

Although Europe's economic regionalism is unlikely to be applicable anywhere else, its model continues to figure prominently in one final way – as "TAFTA": a Transatlantic Free Trade Area. The TAFTA proposal came to major public attention only in the early 1990s, but its roots are much deeper than that, and the idea has well-placed supporters on both sides of the Atlantic. The result is that TAFTA-like free trade area proposals are likely to remain high on the trade-policy agenda, and if its supporters – who can generally be called "Atlanticists" – have their way, transatlantic "free trade" in one form or another will move once again to center stage.

At least three main forces have been behind the idea. One stems from a deep-seated belief both in Europe and the US that for too long there has been a "Pacific tilt" to American policy, and that it needs correction.[37] Some who express this view are overtly anti-Asian and especially anti-Japanese, but the main strand is a frankly pro-Atlantic understanding of America's world role. It is rooted in the links of culture, language, and history shared by Europe and America, and it argues that those links also call for tighter European–US economic connections. This view has been largely fueled by the trade irritants that have often nettled European–US relations in recent years, but it has also drawn support from defense and foreign policy specialists, and it includes both liberals and conservatives.

A good example is Clyde Prestowitz, a former senior US trade official who first became prominent with his book *Trading Places*.[38] The book may not have been the anti-Japanese screed derided by some of its critics, but it was very strongly critical of Japanese trade and business practices, and it was very widely read. Prestowitz charged, among other things, that Tokyo, by using unfair and discriminatory methods, had won the contest with the US for global economic and export prominence, and the result was that Japan and America had "traded places."

With his reputation thereby established, Prestowitz then went on to create a public-policy "think tank" called the Economic Strategy Institute. The Institute drew much of its early funding and support from America's labor unions, who were of course already much concerned about job losses attributed to Japan, and the Institute soon produced a publication called *Shrinking the Atlantic*. It was co-authored by Prestowitz, and it provided an early and major public rationale for TAFTA that rested on two main points: the undoubted high value of America's trade with Europe, and the view that US exports to Asia were not as large as they seemed.[39] Moreover, while the report's authors insisted that their purpose "is to illuminate the contribution of Europe, not to denigrate US ties to Asia," its emphasis on America's cultural and political affinities with Europe conveyed a different message. That message was that because Asia – and Japan in particular – are not "fair traders," America's best long-term trade partner is Europe.

The same message came to the fore again in 1997–8, when TAFTA-like issues resurfaced in a new policy debate – this time in the context of what came to be known as "The Transatlantic Marketplace." A central theme in that proposal was that in contrast to most or all of Asia, Europe was "like" America: it had strong labor unions, high wages, and strong environmental laws and regulations. Therefore, Americans were told, a trade partnership with Europe would not pose the problems that Asia or other regions represented, and it would have the added advantage of organized labor's support. Indeed, the Institute, and specifically Prestowitz, were early endorsers of the transatlantic proposal: "the labor unions and Democratic leaders in Congress," he wrote, "might well embrace a trade deal with Europe."[40]

Interestingly, however, support for TAFTA-like arrangements can also be found in some Republican quarters, where it is motivated by much the same Atlanticist impulse. In 1995, for example, Clayton Yeutter, a former US Trade Representative, and Secretary of Agriculture in Republican administrations, proposed what he called "A Nafta for Europe." He wrote that aside from Chile (always a US darling because of its low tariff and free market policies), a "North Atlantic Free Trade Area" would be a better candidate for US free trade ties than anything that might be worked out with Asia *or* Latin America:

> The European Union is already one of the largest overseas customers for US goods and services. ... A North Atlantic Free Trade Area would bring together three of the four largest export customers for US goods and services – Canada, Western Europe, and Mexico.[41]

Finally, similar Atlanticist views have come from prominent Americans concerned mainly with European security issues. In 1999, Robert Hunter, President Clinton's former Ambassador to NATO (and, in party terms, presumably a Democrat), urged leaders in the US and Europe to "supplement the military dimensions of transatlantic relations [with] economic ties across the Atlantic." He pointed out that while NATO and the EU were headquartered in the same city (Brussels), they "behave as though they live on different planets."[42] The result was no formal or institutional way to coordinate or integrate their interests, and Hunter proposed solving the problem by adding an economic dimension to NATO.

In addition to these Atlanticist views, the second major impetus for TAFTA stems from Europe's worries about NAFTA, and its implications for future US trade policy. Europe's concern, shared by some in Asia, is that the US – having already established special trade links with Canada and Mexico – will not only deepen those ties, but will move to extend them to South America.[43] That, after all, was the purpose of President Clinton's "Miami Summit" in 1994. Leaders of all 34 Western hemisphere nations attended (only Castro was not invited), and all endorsed the summit's goal: a "Free Trade Area of the Americas" (FTAA) by 2005 – essentially a duty-free economic zone stretching from Alaska to Argentina.

The FTAA is a bold concept that will be explored more fully in the next chapter. Although it has not yet proceeded much beyond its initial call in 1994, it needs a brief mention now because European and other observers are aware of two important considerations: first that the FTAA remains a very high US priority; second, that its supporters – who believe strongly in its inevitability – are very well-placed. In mid-1999, for example, Mac McLarty, Mr Clinton's former chief-of-staff and later special envoy to the Americas, argued once again that the time was ripe for an all-hemisphere trade agreement.[44] As a first step, he urged the US to begin free trade talks with Chile, "using NAFTA as a model." Only weeks later, Chile's new Foreign Minister announced that just such discussions had indeed begun,[45] and shortly after that – in a step described as "moving out of first gear and into second" – the region's 34 Trade Ministers met once again to restart the FTAA process. They promised a draft treaty for the FTAA within 18 months,[46] a decision the US trade representative welcomed, in a clear sign that Washington remains quite committed to its all-hemisphere "free trade" proposal. And perhaps needless to say, European leaders are well aware that in the US Presidential campaign in 2000, the Republican candidate formally promised to achieve all-hemisphere free trade.

But it is the third factor, stemming from powerful forces within Europe itself, that may be the most important element promoting TAFTA. This component is often referred to as "Eurosclerosis": the widespread evidence that Europe's economic vitality and industry have fallen behind the world's more productive economies, especially the US, Japan, and some in Asia. Prominent European leaders and specialists have been alarmed by their region's continuing high unemployment; by its low investment at home, coupled with high investment abroad; and by Europe's generally declining "competitiveness." As a result, some have begun to conclude that only in direct competition with the Americans will Europe's own industries prosper and expand. Their thinking is similar to those Chinese reformers who were anxious to join the WTO, because they believed the enhanced competition would ultimately benefit China's industries. The European analog is that to improve *Europe's* economic health, a formal trade link with the US may be just what the doctor ordered.

Such views have been expressed most often and openly in Germany, and by some in Britain. Germans in particular point to their high production and labor costs as the cause of declining competitiveness, but the issues go well beyond costs. Other factors frequently mentioned are low research and development budgets, an absence of European entrepreneurial skills and venture capital, and of course high unemployment and too few genuinely new jobs. A leader of Germany's aircraft industry, fed up with the problem in his country, described it this way:

> If you know the strategic importance of the industry, and then consider its public standing and apparent value in public opinion and in wide sections of the political establishment, you can only conclude that there is a grotesque lack of proportion. In complete contrast to Japan, where aerospace has been declared a "strategic industry," in Germany there is far more concern about the dying industries of the 19th century.[47]

Other industrial and business leaders have put the issue into even broader terms: they argue that Europe "looks like a rigidified, self-obsessed society which has lost sight of its reference points and values," and that its mentality is "in many ways the mentality of a dying society. We suffer from hedonism, narcissism, and the unwillingness to take risks."[48] DuPont's chief executive summed it up when he said that no company "with $1 billion to invest" would choose Europe: "it costs more to produce in Europe today than anywhere else in the world. One factor is the high cost of labor and the inflexibility of rules and regulations."[49]

The practical consequence of such views is that a growing number of European firms, in order to escape high costs and other limitations at home, have shifted their investment and production out of Western Europe. The best example is again Germany, because of its industrial prominence and its role as Europe's leading economy. Germany's inward foreign investment stopped growing in 1989, and it has since been either flat or, as in 1996 and 1997, has actually *declined*.[50] In a perfect illustration of the problem, in 1996 almost a third of Germany's industrial firms – more than ever before – reported plans to move production to less costly and less restrictive sites abroad,[51] and there were soon concrete examples. In 1997 the world's fourth-largest tire maker (Continental) moved half of its production from Germany,[52] and two German industrial icons – BMW and Daimler-Benz – both decided to establish large new car factories in the United States.

The explanations are not hard to find. In 1996, German manufacturing costs (wages plus benefits) were more than $30 per hour, higher than anywhere in Europe, or indeed anywhere in the world. Germany's $30 figure compared with $22 in Japan, $19 in France, $17 in the United States and $14 in Britain.[53] And as if to put a final seal on these comparisons, in 1999 the World Economic Forum's "Global Competitiveness Report" showed once again that Germany did not make it into even the top 20 world economies, but fell to 25th place, one step lower than the year before. France was only marginally ahead, in 23rd place, whereas the US was second in the 1999 rankings – one step *higher* than the year before. Singapore, with its transparent business environment and generally free-market approach to trade and economics, ranked first.[54]

It was amid these signs of economic malaise, along with Europe's recurring and often bitter trade disputes with the US, that several leaders began to consider some broad resolution to the issue – even including the admittedly radical form of a formal EU–US "free trade" deal. The idea was first sounded out in 1994 by Canada's Prime Minister,[55] but the movement began in earnest in 1995. In a Chicago speech, Klaus Kinkel, then Germany's Foreign Minister, introduced the concept, and quite deliberately called it "TAFTA." His words are worth recalling, not only because of Kinkel's long tenure as Foreign Minister (1990–8), but because he reflected themes in German thinking that will remain central to its foreign policy.

His speech first placed the trade issue within the context of European–US security and foreign policy, and then stressed two main points. The first was that although European–American security cooperation arose initially from the Soviet threat, its collapse must not end that cooperation: it "must not move the United States further away from us . . . Europe is and will remain America's natural partner . . . we share the same values." Accordingly, Kinkel proposed a formal tightening of political cooperation, probably in some institutional format, and he then moved on to Europe's trade relationship with the US.

Here he pointed out that only Europe had no formal economic connections with the US. Unlike the Western hemisphere, where Washington already had NAFTA in place, and Asia, where it was pushing the APEC framework, there was nothing like that for Europe. This called for "the creation of a Transatlantic Free Trade Area (TAFTA)":

> The three big trade and industrial regions – Europe, America, and the Asian Pacific Basin – are reestablishing themselves. Across the Pacific, America and Asia have envisaged a bridge called APEC, a zone of free trade and investment. . . . There is no transatlantic equivalent to this . . . *our common history and the logic of the new challenges call for the creation of a transatlantic security and economic arena.*[56]

Probably aided by the easily-remembered "TAFTA" label, Kinkel's speech succeeded in placing the issue on the agenda in both Europe and the US.

In June, 1995, Secretary of State Warren Christopher spoke in Madrid on the subject of "Charting a Transatlantic Agenda for the twenty-first century." Borrowing a phrase popularized by Newt Gingrich, then Speaker of the House in the US Congress, Christopher argued that the Atlantic alliance could not be maintained "by nostalgia alone" – it needed an economic dimension. He then gave TAFTA his support, and put it squarely in the context of Bill Clinton's Western hemisphere and Asian goals:

> A hallmark of the Clinton presidency is its focus on global economic growth ... his efforts include leading the way to the Miami agreement ... on a free trade area in the Americas by the year 2005 [and] APEC'S decision to achieve free and open trade and investment in the Asia–Pacific region by 2010. ... Our vision for the economic relationship between Europe and the United States must be no less ambitious. *The long term objective is the integration of the economies of North America and Europe, consistent with the principles of the WTO.*[57]

Mr Christopher qualified his endorsement with the words "consistent with the WTO," but the central point is that from mid-1995, transatlantic free trade was now on the US policy agenda.[58] Christopher remarked that "careful observers" supported the idea, and promised that Washington would now undertake its own study of the issue, following on one already undertaken by Sir Leon Brittan, the EU trade commissioner. Brittan, as we will see later in this chapter, was a central mover in the transatlantic undertaking, but there were important others as well.

Among them were Douglas Hurd, Britain's Foreign Secretary at the time, and his successor, Malcolm Rifkind. In a 1996 speech, Rifkind announced "I am committed to extending transatlantic free trade,"[59] and former Prime Minister Margaret Thatcher, in an essay devoted primarily to strengthening and expanding NATO, made the same point. Like Foreign Minister Kinkel, she too put TAFTA in precisely the same political and security context:

> The most practical way forward ... is to merge the North American Free Trade Area with the European Union, including the countries of Central, and perhaps in time, Eastern Europe. A Trans-Atlantic Free Trade Area would be able to push effectively toward global trade liberalization. It would prevent trans-Atlantic trade wars from jeopardizing wider trans-Atlantic links. *It would bring our Atlantic civilization closer together.*[60]

In Germany, these steps were then followed by a concrete sign of the pragmatic seriousness with which the TAFTA issue was seen. Germany's leading industrial group, known as "BDI" (the Federation of German

Industries), commissioned a study of what a TAFTA might mean in practice. Its findings, however, were at best a lukewarm and reluctant endorsement of the idea, a surprising outcome because Germany has been in the absolute forefront of European regional integration. As our discussion of CAP pointed out, no nation has been more willing to compromise its specifically national interests for the sake of European unity, and a very recent episode shows that the pattern continues to this day. In 1999, Germany (along with Britain and several other EU members) attempted once again to achieve genuine CAP reforms and cost reductions. A German diplomat vowed that this time "we are going for broke ... It's the end of March or nothing." But nothing in fact was what they achieved: confronted by an unyielding Jacques Chirac, the German-led group deferred again to France.[61]

Against that background, of Germany's long and intense familiarity and support for European regionalism, the BDI's lukewarm endorsement of TAFTA is worth recalling:

> Recognizing the high costs which protection inflicts on the economy, German trade policy should strive to promote *global* free trade. *If it is possible* to apply a Transatlantic Free Trade Area (TAFTA) as a lever for this purpose, most German firms will win."[62]

Those cautiously chosen words reveal two important points. The first was the report's careful, but evidently tortured effort to position itself between Germany's needs for "global free trade" on the one hand, and the possibility on the other hand, that TAFTA might be established. Clearly, the BDI study regarded TAFTA and the regionalism it represents as a less than ideal outcome: it awarded that first place to "global free trade," while TAFTA came out no better than second best.

The study's second point was equally important, because it reflected Germany's forty years of very close experience with EC/EU European regionalism. With the phrase, "recognizing the costs that protection inflicts," the BDI report highlighted its view that *European regionalism is inseparable from European protectionism.* To drive that point home, the report concluded that while "the WTO is an open club ... regional liberalization *discriminates* ... the foremost risk of TAFTA is that bilateral agreements can hit third countries."[63] Those words perfectly describe the distinction between true trade liberalization, and the false flag of "free trade areas," that is regularly flown by supporters of preferential trade agreements.

Nevertheless, and however reluctantly, the BDI study did endorse TAFTA, and one final consideration – the role of TAFTA's chief sponsor, Klaus Kinkel – helps explain why. Kinkel was not only Germany's Foreign Minister, but was also the only representative in Germany's Cabinet of the Free Democratic Party (FDP) – the one group that to this day is ideologically closest to the open market and free trade principles of the BDI.[64]

Consequently, when the authors of the BDI study gave their lukewarm endorsement to TAFTA, they probably acted in accordance with Tip O'Neil's famous dictum that "all politics is local politics." As professional economists, no doubt they supported global free trade, but in order not to be out of step with party leader Kinkel, they held their noses and embraced TAFTA's advertised label as a "free trade area" – but which in practice they knew would be a preferential trade arrangement.

But even such tepid endorsements of TAFTA were not universal. Both the WTO and OECD cautioned that any new regional economic group would undermine the just-established global rules, and a Dutch leader had similar worries. He warned that TAFTA would mean "trade relations will be governed by the right of the strongest rather than by multilateral rules of the game." The views of Europe's heavyweights, however – Germany, France, and Britain – were more complicated, because they were shaped not only by what each saw as TAFTA's assets and liabilities, but just as important, by what TAFTA might mean for their *bilateral* relations with the United States. A special new economic relationship with the US – which is what TAFTA would mean – would magnify how each nation's economic ties with the Americans would affect its own political and strategic posture within Europe. That factor alone should cause the US to be extremely wary about the TAFTA proposal, or anything like it.

The reason stems from the fact that, although the United States continues to have an over-riding strategic interest in European unity ("a Europe whole and free" in post-Soviet terminology), almost everything else has changed dramatically. The strategic environment of America's relationships with the major European states today differs profoundly from the circumstances of the 1960s or 1970s – to say nothing of the 1950s, when NATO took shape. In those earlier years, the US role was very close to hegemonic, though there were hints that America's dominance would soon end. One signal came in 1968, when French President de Gaulle challenged America's economic supremacy, and another was in 1971, when President Nixon announced major shifts in America's foreign economic policy.

But until the final collapse of the Bretton Woods system in the mid-1970s, America's writ established the rules of the game in transatlantic affairs. Its hegemony stemmed from the two indispensable ingredients the US provided in that period: the receptive markets and stable currency that were essential to Europe's prosperity, and the military guarantees that assured Europe's security. All that has now changed – as a result of the Soviet Union's collapse and Europe's recovered strength – but what *remains* is America's vital interest in Europe's continued unity. That makes it decidedly not in America's interest to pursue any economic or trade policy that could dilute that hard-won unity, or worse yet, to be the cause of any new intra-European tensions. In an era when much that was sought has now been achieved, the United States could do much worse than adopt, as its policy guide, the Hippocratic oath to "First, do no harm."

Even so, Europe is not a single entity: as Henry Kissinger put it in a rightly famous *bon mot*, he would gladly telephone "Europe" if somebody would please give him the number. The point still applies: despite much economic integration, Europe's nations remain quite separate and distinct. An easy example, of course, are some French policies, but France is merely the best-known case. Within Europe, there are other major differences, on several policy issues, that reflect each nation's separate history and *national* outlook; and one of the most important is the potentially decisive role of the United States itself in each of the major European capitals.

We can illustrate the point by recalling the domestic roots of Europe's differences on TAFTA – which range from strong official interest in Germany, to possible but heavily qualified support in England, and finally to clear opposition in France. In the case of Germany, as Kinkel's initial speech on the subject pointed out, the idea for TAFTA grew directly from the conviction that TAFTA would reinforce German links to the US. In Germany, those links are regarded as absolutely indispensable, both for Germans and for other Europeans. And as we saw earlier, for those in Germany who are concerned mainly with the nation's sluggish economic performance, a close relationship with the United States would be seen as the best medicine to help speed the structural reforms their economy so badly needs.

In Britain, in contrast, there are continuing doubts about the whole European project, and support for TAFTA has been rooted in part in the belief that closer ties with the US – either in TAFTA or something like it – might prove a viable alternative to closer integration with Europe. In that event London might be rescued from all the demons that "Europe" is feared to represent: the new single currency; "harmonization" of taxes; the Brussels bureaucracy with its "over 230,000 pages of mind-numbing regulations"; and much else that continues to separate England from the continent.[65] All those doubts were further inflamed when France decided, in late 1999, to continue its restrictions on British beef.

In that already heavily politicized environment, British interest in TAFTA, which in the mid-1990s was supported by the Conservative Party Prime Minister and two of his Foreign Ministers, has begun to appear increasingly *instrumental*. By that I mean that the TAFTA concept would still have much support, but less as a policy goal in its own right than as a way to bring London even closer to the US, and correspondingly *less* heavily involved with Europe. Indeed Foreign Secretary Rifkind was cautioned precisely on this point:

> Mr Malcolm Rifkind . . . is not the first prominent Conservative politician to declare his government's enthusiasm for . . . transatlantic free trade. . . . Margaret Thatcher called several years ago for a free trade area embracing the US, Canada, and the European Community, as did her cabinet colleague . . . Mr Nicholas Ridley. The idea's popular-

ity with such prominent Eurosceptics ... invites questions about his motives. It is tempting to conclude that they are heavily coloured by his party's deep divisions on Europe, and *the notion that closer Atlantic ties could somehow offer an alternative to further EU integration.*[66]

The French position on TAFTA, like Germany's, is rooted strongly in *national* politics, but is at the same time inseparable from France's view of its role in international affairs. Paris argues that TAFTA will be impossible to implement because of Europe's "special problems" in agriculture, textiles, and services. All are undeniable, but the more compelling reason for French opposition is a combination of traditional protectionism, combined with France's long-standing resistance to what it sees as America's global political aims. It is a view firmly rooted in France's famous and continuing unwillingness to accept America's dominant power in world affairs and world politics, and it is buttressed by the French conviction that the United States also seeks to shape the global economy in its own image.

The French Agriculture Minister, for example, has argued that US farmers seek to "flood the world with their products,"[67] but the note closest to France's truth was struck by Foreign Minister Hubert Vedrine. He does not go so far as the late President Francois Mitterand – who reportedly said "France is at war with America ... *they are voracious, they want undivided power over the world*" [68] – but Vedrine nevertheless repeatedly refers to the US as a "hyperpower," and warns against "the overriding predominance of the United States and [the] lack of any counterweight":

> This phenomenon of hyperpower extends into all sectors ... everywhere in the world you have CNN, Hollywood. ... Virtually all the world's governments include ministers who were educated in the United States ... its predominance leads it to adopt an hegemonic behavior and ... causes it to adopt a unilateralistic approach. That is not acceptable.[69]

While these sentiments undoubtedly stem from a deep resistance to see the world organized along "Anglo-Saxon" lines, they are also rooted in more pressing and practical protectionist concerns. As we saw when we discussed Europe's Common Agricultural Policy, France's farmers count heavily in its everyday politics, and have a well-known ability to mount impressive and disruptive strikes. In 1998, to cite just one example, cauliflower growers seized the main railway line to Paris – a step that interrupted traffic for almost a week, and caused serious damage to the city's electrical network. Yet the behavior of those farmers caused far less urban resentment in Paris than might be supposed. The reason, in the agreed judgment of several close observers, lies in the French self-image: France regards itself as a nation that "regularly visits the rural homestead and is ready to defend the farmer and his way of life."[70] In the words of another long-time and close observer of French society and politics, "Scratch an urban French man or woman and they will speak nostalgically of the village or small town where they grew up or where their parents hailed from."[71]

Europe's American factor and the role of proximity

Ironically, it is the United States, by virtue of the sheer size of its economic involvement in Western Europe, that has the greatest potential to bring to the surface Europe's underlying, but very real fissures and separations. Two dimensions of that US involvement, direct investment and foreign trade, are illustrated in Figure 3.3. It deals with Britain, Germany, and France in 1996, and shows first the US percentage *share* of each of those nations' total foreign investment. Next it shows the percentage share of each nation's foreign trade represented by the United States.

As the chart demonstrates, the US was the source, quite remarkably, of almost 40 percent of total foreign direct investment stock in Britain, and a quarter or fifth of all foreign investment stock in Germany and France.[72] In all three nations, moreover, the share of foreign investment from the United States was *greater than from any other single nation*. The pattern in trade is similar, though necessarily less dramatic, because two-thirds of EU members' trade is with other EU nations. Even so, in every case the US was the *largest single trade partner of each of the three major European nations*.

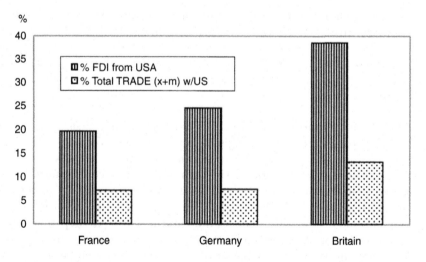

Sources: for FDI, *OECD International Direct Investment Statistics,* 1998 (Table 7), pp. 144–5, and for Trade, WTO, *Annual Report,* 1998, International Trade Statistics.

Figure 3.3 America's share of foreign investment and foreign trade in France, Germany, and Britain, 1996.

The other side of the coin – the location of French, German, and British investment abroad – shows the same close connections to America's economy. In the cases of France and Germany, their investments in the US are at roughly similar levels. To be precise, in 1997, nearly 20 percent of France's investment abroad was in the United States, as was 22 percent of Germany's. And both French and German investments in the US, like those of Britain, were larger in the US than in any other economy. In fact, total German investment in the US (more than DM90 billion by 1997), was actually *double the amount anywhere else*, and will soon exceed that 22 percent figure, because annual flows to the US are now running at about 25 percent of the total.

Those are impressive figures, but even more striking is the extent of Britain's investment and trade ties to the US. Those figures will illustrate perfectly one of this book's main themes: *geography has little or nothing necessarily to do with intensive economic interactions.* Geography still "counts," of course: America's long-standing economic dominance in Mexico and Canada – a century before NAFTA – is rooted in proximity, as is Germany's past and present economic dominance in central Europe. But geographic proximity is *not* destiny, and especially under contemporary circumstances, geography does *not* determine the shape of economic interactions among nations. As Robert Conquest has recently argued (in his campaign to resuscitate the idea of an "English Speaking Union"), "The obstacles of geography are grossly exaggerated."[73]

We can illustrate the point by showing reciprocal economic relations between Britain and the US. As Figure 3.3 showed, in 1996 almost 40 percent of investment in Britain was from the US, and British investment in the US mirrors that: in 1998, the US accounted for 41 percent of Britain's total investment abroad. Moreover, for the first time, British investments in the US were *greater than in the entire European Community.*[74] Add to that what Britain's statistical yearbook reports about the nation's total trade: "the United States was both the UK's top export market in goods and the leading supplier in 1998."[75]

It is worth noting here, though the issue will be more fully explored in a later chapter, that this evidence about Britain's trade with the US is very similar to the Japanese pattern. As Figure 3.4 shows, Japan, "on the other side of the world," also has the United States as its leading market *and* leading supplier, and has very intensive trade with the EU as well.[76]

Both cases show clearly that physical closeness is *not* critical, either to large-scale international trade, or to intensive foreign investment, and both cases underline the point that the *main flaw in today's economic regionalism is its critical dependence on geographic proximity.* Proximity was of course a key factor in foreign trade before World War II – when knowledge of foreign markets for one's products, and the cost of transporting them, made neighbors and near-neighbors each others' most likely best customers. But in an era when containerized shipping has drastically lowered

$ (billions)

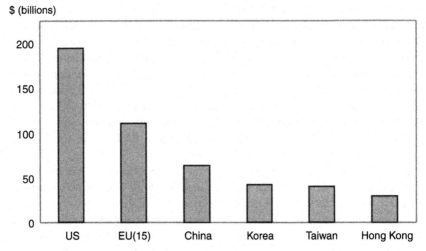

Source: WTO *Annual Report,* 1998, International Trade Statistics, Table A15.

Figure 3.4 Japan's trading partners, 1997.

all the costs associated with bulk freight, and when the most distant markets for great quantities of high-value products have been opened by air-transport firms such as DHL and Fed-Ex, and finally when electronic communication has made price and product data instantly available, proximity has become essentially irrelevant. From the viewpoint of seller and producer, what counts is not whether Kuala Lumpur or Rio de Janeiro is closest; what counts is which market has the customers with the money.

Nevertheless, the sheer size of cross-Atlantic trade and investment helps explain why, even aside from TAFTA, there continue to be proposals for new transatlantic ties, and two final ones should be explored before this chapter closes. One was in Ellen Frost's careful 1997 book, devoted entirely to transatlantic issues.[77] Frost, a former US trade official with a background in US–Japan affairs as well, recommended in effect an economic counterpart to NATO: a "North Atlantic Economic Community." The other main proposal is closely associated with Sir Leon Brittan, the former EU Trade Commissioner. Throughout the 1990s, he called for a "Transatlantic Marketplace": a set of sector-specific arrangements designed to deal with concrete problems faced by business and industry on both sides of the Atlantic.

Both proposals aim to reduce the frequency and intensity of trade-related tensions between Europe and the US, but they differ very strongly in their broader goals and likely outcomes. Frost stressed from the outset the primacy of political and strategic goals: she argued that the need to "repair broader political strains in the . . . alliance" was the main impetus behind transatlantic free trade proposals. She analyzed at length three options to deal with the frequent EU–US economic conflicts, but rejected two that appeared not to meet that foreign policy threshold. The first was a "piecemeal, pragmatic" approach. She quickly cast that aside, partly because it would lack the urgency and institutions that Frost believed the EU–US problem warranted, but also because it "passes up a foreign policy opportunity to reinvigorate the transatlantic partnership." TAFTA was also rejected – though it has a "certain foreign policy appeal" – because it would discriminate against outsiders in general, and lead Asians and Japanese in particular to see it as "ganging up" on them. That, Frost correctly concluded, "could strengthen the hand of those Japanese who favor . . . an 'Asian' way."

She recommended instead a full-scale counterpart to NATO called NATEC: a "North Atlantic Economic Community." Unlike the piecemeal approach, NATEC would not ignore such politically-sensitive fields as agriculture, and because it would be "comprehensive," and would spread liberalized trade to economies beyond the Atlantic sphere, it would not – unlike TAFTA – offend Asians. It would instead combine "APEC-like trade and business initiatives with a strategic political–economic orientation corresponding to NATO."[78]

Nevertheless, a new transatlantic economic institution would represent a major error – both for US foreign policy and the global economy. Like TAFTA, it would formally tie the United States to the EU, in a new institutional format designed specifically to further integrate the American and European economies. That step would strongly reinforce global economic regionalism, and would at the same time represent a major step backwards in international trade and politics. The reason, as this chapter repeatedly has shown, is that in this era, so much of foreign trade and investment is increasingly independent of close regional geographic connections. In that changed environment, new efforts at economic regionalism are a dangerous anomaly, because they move toward a world of regional economic blocs. Frost implicitly recognized that when she wrote that NATEC would accelerate the global movement towards regionalism: "Regional organizations that have dithered on the implementation of free trade would have a powerful new motive to move faster."[79]

In sharp contrast to that ambitious, but flawed goal, is the "Transatlantic Marketplace," an idea that became prominent after 1995, but whose origins are in the "Transatlantic Declaration," agreed to by the US and the European Community in 1990.[80] The "Declaration" was a product of that period when the Soviet threat had begun to decline sharply; under those circumstances both American and EU leaders saw a need to recall their common heritage and shared interests. Accordingly, the Declaration reaffirmed their "close historical . . . and cultural ties," and with the Soviet collapse fully in mind, it pointedly recalled that "transatlantic solidarity" had been essential to "the recent developments which have restored unity in Europe." But beyond agreeing to meet regularly, and to "take further steps towards [trade] liberalization," the Transatlantic Declaration was not a call for action.

That process began in 1995, and owes much to Sir Leon Brittan. He became European Commissioner for External Economic Relations and Trade in 1993, and as early as 1985, he had significant British government responsibilities for trade.[81] With that extensive background, Brittan was very familiar with many of the arcane details of US–European trade, and as EU Trade Commissioner, he was at the center of their sometimes testy disputes over bananas, beef, aircraft noise and much else. Those tensions were very much in the air in April 1995, when – to cite one instance – Sweden's Foreign Trade Minister proposed that the US and EU reach "an extensive economic agreement."[82] As an example, the Minister pointed to the need for common standards for medical and communications equipment, and with an eye to governments that discriminate against foreign products (as in the "Buy British" and "Buy American" programs), he proposed that they adopt more even-handed procurement policies.

Only weeks later, these and similar issues rose to the top of the EU–US agenda. The impetus came when Secretary of State Christopher gave his landmark Madrid speech to which I referred earlier.[83] In addition to endorsing Brittan's transatlantic trade proposals, he proposed "a comprehensive investment regime."[84] Moreover, and probably reflecting his own long experience as an attorney involved in these issues, Mr Christopher listed several familiar topics for EU–US negotiations, including common standards for hi-tech and industrial products.

Those were precisely the sort of practical problems faced regularly by business people on both sides of the Atlantic, and which Commissioner Brittan had identified in his "Marketplace" concept. None was particularly "regional," but within weeks, in June, 1995, all such proposals were scuttled when French President Chirac announced his opposition to the whole concept of a transatlantic "single market." He specifically rejected both Kinkel's TAFTA proposal, and Brittan's suggestion for a "transatlantic agenda." Chirac argued that the concept would undermine the GATT–WTO global trading framework.[85] After that, although reports continued to circulate that the EU and US had essentially accepted a transatlantic free trade agreement, for the next several years the issue moved off the public policy agenda.[86] Private groups kept it somewhat alive with several meetings: a "Transatlantic Consumer Dialogue"; a conference on "Bridging the Atlantic: People-to-People Links"; and at least four meetings of the "Transatlantic Business Dialogue." Nevertheless, high-level attention did not return to transatlantic free trade until the eruption of East Asia's economic crisis in 1997.

By the end of that year, Thailand, Indonesia, Korea, Malaysia, and the Philippines had all suffered sharp economic reverses. In some cases almost a decade of growth was wiped out. In 1998, for example, the imports of Indonesia and Thailand *fell back to 1992 levels*,[87] and the economic distress of these and other Asian economies further weakened the prospects for revival in already-troubled Japan. Its imports in 1996, for example, were almost $350 billion, but by 1998 they had fallen to just $280 billion. All these Asian declines inevitably were accompanied by sharp drops in European and US *exports* to the Asian economies, which in turn led to fears of a downturn in the Western industrialized world. That realization – that Asia's collapse could spread to Europe and the US – turned American attention again to Europe, and to Brittan's "new drive to sweep away barriers to transatlantic trade and investment." As a US official put it, "Sir Leon's proposals [were] boosted by Asia's financial crisis, which had refocused US attention on Europe's attractions as a stable market for exports and investments."[88]

Yet it did not happen. What took place instead in 1998–9, with EU Trade Commissioner Brittan always in the vanguard, was a set of near-approaches to the goal of more open transatlantic trade, followed in every instance by forceful and equally-decisive rejections. It is a tale worth recounting in brief detail. In February, 1998, amidst reports that America's trade unions were already in support of a European trade deal, and that Britain's Prime Minister Blair also was "enthusiastic," US Trade Representative Barshefsky conceded that she had been talking with Sir Leon Brittan about the idea. She insisted, however, that "the dialogue is at a very preliminary level ... we do not envision a free trade agreement."[89] Nevertheless, in March, 1998, the *Financial Times* reported that the European Commission was discussing a "New Transatlantic Marketplace," which would eliminate all industrial tariffs by 2010, provide for free trade in services, and liberalize government procurement practices.[90]

That same package, described as a "US–EU free trade area," was approved by the European Commission just days later (11 March). It did not include aviation, or trade in agriculture and audio-visual materials – the two most sensitive areas for France – but it did cover most financial services and shipping, and it dealt with conflicting product standards. Trade Commissioner Brittan applauded this as a "huge leap forward,"[91] but France remained opposed, and gave as its reason issues of *process and procedure*. For example, while Leon Brittan said the "New Transatlantic Marketplace" was the idea of the entire Commission, French Prime Minister Lionel Jospin, in a French radio interview, disagreed: "This latest move was done without consultation." Amplifying on the point, he cleverly added that "in matters of trade, the priority should go to the World Trade Organization, which operates in a *multilateral* framework."[92]

Jospin's statement was both true and wise, especially for a middle power like France. His words were also especially suitable for a middle power concerned, as France is, about the dominance of a "hyperpower." To a nation in that circumstance, coalition politics, including coalition-building and coalition-maintenance, inevitably represents the main arena for achieving state goals. In that context, it made perfect sense for France to insist that the WTO – the "multilateral framework" – was the best approach, and it was equally rational for France to charge that the steps Paris opposed were also steps taken "without consultation." Both responses emphasize the rules under which a coalition is expected to operate, and they draw particular attention to the non-conforming behavior of an adversary whose policies one opposes. Thus France's explanations of why it was against the "marketplace" concept were the most plausible, and therefore the most effective rationales a middle power could employ.

Yet France's public explanation did not quite capture the true essence of its reasons for opposing the marketplace idea. In a variation on the Japanese distinction between *tataemae* and *honne* (the public face shown to outsiders versus the genuine or "inside" feeling that is seldom shared), Jospin revealed the inner core of France's position:

> We are against becoming involved in the negotiation of a new *bilateral* treaty . . . a purely *bilateral* agreement between the United States and Europe will . . . destabilize the recent [WTO] framework . . . through such a specific free trade area the United States would again *pick as targets the audiovisual media, creativity, communications, and agriculture.*[93]

A year later, at the failed WTO Seattle meeting in November–December, 1999, those same US "targets" – agriculture and the audiovisual media in particular – were once again the issues on which France was most adamant. Precisely because of the deep importance of those issues in French politics, it was not surprising that these issues were also at the heart of France's effective veto of the Transatlantic Marketplace in March, 1998. The method was again *procedural*: France simply prevented the proposals from being placed on the EU Commission's agenda – no easy task for a nation that had been emphasizing processes and procedures. A Foreign Ministry spokesman admitted as much: "Leon Brittan is a very clever man. He said he would discuss the matter and it is *very hard to voice opposition to a mere discussion.*"[94]

The formal execution and death of the marketplace proposal came a month later, in April, 1998, when the European Union's Foreign Ministers were planning their forthcoming summit meeting with President Clinton. Once again, French goals were achieved through coalition politics. In this instance, Paris drew on Europe's already widespread resentment against what had come to be seen as America's heavy-handed "unilateralism" in trade policy.[95] By closely associating itself with that resentment, France added *Europe's* support to its campaign against Brittan's free trade proposal, and the assembled Ministers agreed not to put it on their agenda. That same day, the Multilateral Investment Treaty, proposed by Secretary Christopher in 1995, was also killed; those two events led the Paris newspaper *Figaro* to comment that "27 April was a black day . . . for advocates of free trade and globalization." France's official spokesman had a different view of the transatlantic proposal's burial: "This represents a major, extremely unambiguous acknowledgement of our position."[96]

Two concepts in conflict

From that time to the present – in events that testify to its resilience and continued vitality – the transatlantic free trade idea has experienced sporadic efforts at revival. Only months after its seeming final demise, Leon Brittan announced, in September, 1998, that the European Commission would try to restart his plan. This time he called it a "Transatlantic Economic Partnership." He insisted this was "not the same initiative by another name . . . the Partnership proposes a rolling agenda . . . rather than a single big bang agreement." Then in November, 1998, an EU Foreign Ministers meeting endorsed the partnership's "action plan," and as recently as April, 1999 (with his term as Trade Commissioner soon to end), Brittan gave an impassioned speech at Columbia University on behalf of the idea. Once again he called on Europe and America to set common standards for products that have the same function, and also to establish "regulatory cooperation." He called this "the very heart of EU–US economic relations":

> They are the key . . . the alternative is to continue to burden our industries and consumers with unnecessary costs and to deprive our citizens of the benefits of more open, but safe-guarded, trade.[97]

New life will probably be breathed into the concept early in the first decade of the twenty-first century. The reason, as this chapter has pointed out, is that the idea of a special transatlantic trade arrangement has had very powerful supporters – both in the US and in some European capitals, and there is little evidence that those voices and their influence will weaken.[98] Quite the contrary, and especially in the United States and in Britain. For example, while the 1999 Seattle meeting of the WTO was disastrous in its own right, it also sent a strong signal that in the politics of trade policy, the influence of environmental and labor groups has much strengthened. Indeed the American President reinforced their new-found power when, in Seattle, he specifically aligned himself with their views.

One clear consequence is that the fortunes of the transatlantic free trade concept have also been enhanced, because those same labor and related groups are likely to prefer a trade agreement with Europe over any competing claims – from either the WTO or any other regional grouping. The reason, of course, stems from the widespread American view that only Europe is "like America." In this view, only Europe has the necessary range of laws and administrative capacities – in ways acceptable to Americans and comparable to US practices – to protect both workers' rights and the environment. That argument, when added to the views of those who have long sought an EU–US trade agreement for substantive economic reasons, is likely to represent a powerful combination that may be politically unbeatable. That would be good news for those who regard regional free trade areas – which by definition must be preferential trade areas – as building blocks towards a world of generally open trade. It will be bad news for those who hold, as does this book, not only that such groups must inevitably become a source of tension in international politics, but who also believe that *any* successful association of nations must be grounded in a solid and long-term *community of interest.*

That need, for a community of interest, points to the second-oldest rule in international politics; the first being that all nations act in what they believe to be their national interest. When nations have a common interest in a goal or concern, as did the Atlantic nations when their shared security needs led them to build NATO in the 1950s, or the Southeast Asian nations, when their shared political interests led them to create ASEAN in the 1960s, they also have a sufficient community of interest on which to base a long-term cohesive relationship. However, under today's circumstances of increasingly *global* trade and investment, the situations surrounding the United States and members of the European Union are quite different. They share important economic interests, but they nevertheless have powerful divergences. Those differences are incompatible with a community of interest that is defined principally in terms of its participants' trade and related economic interactions.

The clearest example is the United States, with its *trilateral,* and relatively equal economic interests in the Western hemisphere, East Asia, and Western Europe. Another illustration is Britain, though on a smaller scale. Britain's major foreign economic activities, as this chapter has pointed out, are increasingly intertwined with those of the United States, Canada, and even Australia, rather than with the economies of Western and Central Europe. Moreover, as the EU itself enlarges towards the east, the divergence between Britain and the US on the one hand, and Germany and to a lesser extent France and Italy on the other, will only diverge further. That divergence will be reflected in an already-growing tension between a single, global trading system that is independent of geographic regions, and a competing, regionally-based system called – in the Atlantic region – by any one of the similar-sounding names already identified here (TAFTA, NATEC, "Marketplace," "Partnership," etc.)

There are very powerful indications that the regional concept may prevail, largely because the United States implicitly regards regionalism as an acceptable model for the world's trading system. A former Secretary of the Treasury, Dr Lawrence Summers, added important new light to that subject in January, 2000. In response to my question, Secretary Summers drew a sharp distinction between a regionally-grounded global *financial* system – which he did not accept – and a regionally grounded global *trading* system, which he did. For example, while Secretary Summers regarded the existing regional banks (the ADB and IADB, for example), as no problem, he was adamant that there must *also* remain in place the single, globally-responsible central institution, in particular the International Monetary Fund. In the trade sector, however, Secretary Summers had no such insistence. While "of course" stating that the World Trade Organization is the main framework, he specifically singled out APEC, the "FTAA" (Free Trade Area of the Americas), and the European Union as "constructive" models that laid out America's future directions.[99]

The clear implication is that in Europe, Latin America, and in East Asia, the United States will be in the camp of those who regard regional trading blocs as desirable. Moreover, once a post-Clinton Administration has come to power, it is a near-certainty that US attention will again focus on the stalled FTAA, and may also resume the momentum for a transatlantic trade agreement. In that case the conceptual and policy conflict will have been joined, with heavily ironical consequences for the US. The irony is that France, though motivated by uniquely national reasons, will again be the great champion of the "multilateral WTO framework," and will once again be America's principal trade protagonist. The difference, however, is that in the coming contest, France will be arguing for the genuinely *new* global system, while the United States, still mired in the oldspeak of regionalism, will be carrying the banner of a cause no longer supported by today's realities.

Notes

1 The history of Europe's single currency dates from the Middle Ages, when trading partners tried to unify coins. In the modern era it dates from the nineteenth century, when a "Latin coin union" was attempted by France, Italy, and others, and a more successful "Scandinavian coin union" was also created.

2 C. Fred Bergsten, Former Assistant Secretary of the US Treasury in *The Wall Street Journal*, 4 January, 1999. Also see his "America and Europe: Clash of the Titans?," *Foreign Affairs*, March/April, 1999, pp. 20–34.

3 Norbert Walter, chief economist at Frankfurt's Deutsche Bank, *Financial Times*, 25 January, 1999.

4 Hans Tietmeyer, *Financial Times*, 3 February, 1999 and 4 November, 1995.

5 Sebastian Edwards, *Financial Times*, 16 January, 1999.

6 *Financial Times*, 11 February, 1999 (emphasis added).

7 Dominique Strauss-Kahn, *Financial Times*, 12 February, 1999.

8 For some of the many famous voices advocating a "federal Europe," see the documents in Chapters 1 and 2, in D. Weigall and P. Stirk, *The Origins and Development of the European Community*, Leicester, Leicester University Press, 1992.

9 R. Baldwin, *Towards an Integrated Europe*, London, Centre for Economic Policy Research, 1994, p. 7.

10 *ibid.*, p. 8.

11 The story is well told in E. Kolodziej, *French International Policy under De Gaulle and Pompidou*, Ithaca, Cornell University Press, 1974, pp. 260–4.

12 Document 3.1 (p. 40) in Weigall and Stirk, *ibid.*, also quoted by British Foreign

Secretary Malcolm Rifkind, in a speech in Zurich on 18 September, 1996, New York: British Information Services, 20 September, 1996.

13 Adenauer's Bundestag speech of 12 July, 1952 in Weigall and Stirk (Document 4.12), *ibid.*, p. 67. My emphasis.

14 *Financial Times*, 12 March, 1999. This was a relative decline from 1984, when the CAP represented 70 percent of the total (*ibid.*, 23 March, 1999).

15 Michael Davenport, "The Economic Impact of the EEC," (1982), in R. Griffiths (ed.), *The Economic Development of the EEC*, Cheltenham, UK, Elgar, 1997, p. 276.

16 *Financial Times*, 22 May, 1992.

17 W. Averyt, Jr, *Agropolitics in the European Community*, Boulder, CO, Praeger, 1977, p. 3.

18 This point is well made in Gisela Hendriks, "Germany and the CAP: National Interests and the European Community," *International Affairs*, Winter, 1988–9, p. 79.

19 For a full list of the 134 "Preferential Trade Arrangements" notified to the WTO as of 1995, see J. Bhagwati and A. Panagariya, *The Economics of Preferential Trade Agreements*, Washington, AEI Press, 1996, Appendix A-1, pp. 55–72.

20 See, for example, "Principle Provisions of Mercosur and the European Union" (Table 2) in Leipziger, Frischtak, Kharas, and Normand, "Mercosur: Integration and Industrial Policy," *The World Economy*, May, 1997, Vol. 20, No. 5, p. 588.

21 Text of Obuchi's speech at Korea University, 20 March, 1999, as provided by the Embassy of Japan in Washington. Emphasis added.

22 An early example was the article by C. Michael Aho, "'Fortress Europe': Will the EU Isolate Itself from North America and Asia?" *Columbia Journal of World Business*, 1994, Vol. 29, No. 3, which argued that "the endeavor Europe is now embarking upon ... will only reinforce its traditional self-preoccupation." Later examples include "The Growing Fear of Fortress Europe," *New York Times*, 23 October, 1988; "Protectionism Looms as Europeans Unify," *The Wall Street Journal*, 10 May, 1988; "Europe Offers Assurance of 'Free and Open' Trade," *Financial Times*, 20 October, 1988; and "Fortress Europe," *The Economist*, 16 April, 1994.

23 Data from the European Commission, in the *Financial Times*, 31 October, 1996.

24 Vincent Cable, head of the economics program at the Royal Institute of International Affairs, in *The Wall Street Journal*, 3 March, 1994.

25 Martin Feldstein, "Europe Can't Handle the Euro," *The Wall Street Journal*, 8 February, 2000.

26 The one important exception is the pattern of deep ties between Americans and the economies of both Mexico and Canada, but those ties have existed for well over a century, and long predate not only NAFTA, but all other modern regional efforts.

27 For a summary, see *The Economist*, 17 August, 1996.

28 These examples are calculated from data in International Monetary Fund (IMF), *Direction of Trade Statistics Yearbook*, annual issues.

29 All trade calculations in this paragraph are based on data in IMF, *Direction of Trade Statistics Yearbook*, 1997.

30 This discussion borrows heavily from D. Irwin, *Against the Tide: An Intellectual History of Free Trade*, Princeton, Princeton University Press, 1996, pp. 90–1. I owe the contemporary example in the next paragraph, regarding textiles, to correspondence with Professor Irwin.

31 A. G. Kenwood and A. L. Lougheed, *The Growth of the International Economy, 1820–1990*, London, Routledge, 1992, pp. 210–12.

32 This figure is derived from a matrix of world *exports* that covers the years

1928–57. See GATT, *Trends in International Trade*, Geneva, 1958. Often known as the Haberler Report, it was the work of four of the world's most prominent trade scholars, led by Professor G. Haberler of Harvard, and shows slightly higher intra-regional trade levels in Europe than those reported here. For example, a calculation of the Haberler data for 1953 (Table A, following p. 130), shows that 49 percent of Europe's exports were intra-regional.

33 For the inter-war and early post-war years, see W. Woytinski and E. Woytinski, *World Commerce and Governments: Trends and Outlook*, New York, The 20th Century Fund, 1955, especially p. 80.

34 V. Simone and A. Feraru, *The Asian Pacific: Political and Economic Development in a Global Context*, White Plains, NY, Longman, 1995, p. 335, Table 8.5. A slightly more up-to-date assessment, that intra-ASEAN exports in 1990 might have been as high as 5 percent of total ASEAN trade, is in W. Mattli, *The Logic of Regional Integration*, London and New York, Cambridge University Press, 1999, p. 165.

35 1997 levels calculated from data in IMF, *Direction of Trade Statistics Yearbook*, 1998.

36 A. Fishlow, "The Mature Neighbor Policy," in Joseph Grunwald, (ed.), *Latin America and the World Economy*, London, Sage Publications, 1978, p. 43.

37 One of very many examples, this one from a European perspective, is in J. Donges, A. Freytag and R. Zimmermann, "TAFTA: Assuring its Compatibility with Global Free Trade," *World Economy*, August, 1997, Vol. 20, No. 5, p. 567. Two Americans who have also remarked on foreign complaints about an alleged "Pacific tilt" in US policy are C. Barfield, "The Deceptive Allure of a Transatlantic Free Trade Agreement," *Intereconomics*, Sep/Oct. 1998, and E. Frost, *Transatlantic Trade*, Washington, Institute for International Economics, 1997, p. 25.

38 *Trading Places: How We Allowed Japan To Take The Lead*, New York, Basic Books, 1988.

39 C. Prestowitz and R. Gaster, *Shrinking the Atlantic: Europe and the American Economy*, Washington, Economic Strategy Institute, 1994, p. 6.

40 Quoted in *Financial Times*, 2 February, 1998. Unlike its views on Latin America or Asia, organized labor – focusing on pay and job benefits more than job security – thinks it likes what it sees in Europe and is likely to support a TAFTA proposal.

41 C. Yeutter and W. Maruyama, "A Nafta for Europe," *The Wall Street Journal*, 19 May, 1995.

42 In "Personal View," *Financial Times*, 3 March, 1999.

43 Canadian leaders, most notably its Ambassador in Washington (who is also the nephew of Prime Minister Chetrien), have already begun to discuss such deepening. See "Ottawa Starts to Test the Waters for Further Economic and Trade Agreements with the US," *Financial Times*, 25 May, 1999.

44 "Fast Track Isn't Fast Enough," Op-Ed, *The New York Times*, 20 July, 1999.

45 Juan Gabriel Valdes, as reported in *Financial Times*, 17 August, 1999.

46 "Free Trade Zone for the Western Hemisphere Moves Forward," *The Washington Post*, 5 November, 1999.

47 Wolfgang Piller, president of the industry's federation, *Financial Times*, 25 October, 1993.

48 The director of Europe's Industrial Round Table, and the chief economist at Deutsche Bank, quoted in the *Financial Times*, 29 October, 1996 and 12 June, 1997.

49 "Europe Must Sharpen Competitive Edge," *Financial Times*, 12 June, 1994.

50 Organization for Economic Co-Operation and Development (OECD),

International Direct Investment Statistics Yearbook, 1998, Paris, 1999, p. 138, and *Financial Times*, 21 October, 1999 for related data.

51 "A report of Germany's Chambers of Commerce in "Germans Flee High Labour Costs," *Financial Times*, 11 December, 1996.

52 The Continental decision was reported in *Financial Times*, 2 July, 1997.

53 European data from Price Waterhouse, in *Financial Times*, 6 November, 1997; others from the Institute for the German Economy, Cologne, in *The New York Times*, 21 March, 1998.

54 World Economic Forum, *Report on Global Competitiveness*, 13 July 1999, available http: www.weforum.org (10 August, 1999).

55 The *Wall Street Journal*, 5 June, 1995, reported that in 1994 Prime Minister Chretien and Trade Minister Roy McLaren had spoken with French officials about the concept.

56 From his speech to the Chicago Council on Foreign Relations, 19 April, 1995. Bonn BULLETIN, 24 April, 1995, in Foreign Broadcast Information Service (FBIS), Europe, 4 May, 1995, my emphasis. Kinkel's speeches in the US were little noted in the American press, but were well-reported in Germany.

57 US Department of State, *Dispatch*, 5 June, 1995 (my emphasis).

58 *The New York Times*, for example, reported on 3 June, 1995 that the Secretary "praised the idea of establishing a trans-Atlantic free trade area."

59 Speech before the British–American Business Council, "Transatlantic Free Trade," 12 March, 1996, in FBIS, 14 March, 1996.

60 Margaret Thatcher, "The West After the Cold War," *The Wall Street Journal*, 14 May, 1996. My emphasis.

61 *Financial Times*, 3 January and 28 March, 1999.

62 From the Executive Summary in Andreas Freytag and Ralf Zimmermann, "The Effects of a Transatlantic Free Trade Area on German Industry", Institut fur Wirtschaftspolitik, University of Cologne, October, 1996. Emphasis added.

63 *ibid.*, my emphasis. Freytag and Zimmermann made the same point – that "regional liberalisation is discriminatory by nature" – in their paper, "What Role for TAFTA", 43rd International Atlantic Economic Conference, London, March, 1997.

64 In 1999, for example, the BDI was in the forefront of those attacking the government of Social Democrat Gerhard Schroeder for his anti-free market interventions on behalf of failing industries (see *Financial Times*, 8 December, 1999).

65 For an elaboration of why Britain continues to be ambivalent about tighter integration with Europe, see C. Black, "Britain's Atlantic Option," *The National Interest*, Spring, 1999.

66 Editorial in the *Financial Times*, 11 October, 1995.

67 Agriculture Minister Jean Glavany, quoted in the *Financial Times*, 30 August, 1999.

68 Black, *ibid.*, p. 22. My emphasis.

69 Interview with French Foreign Minister Hubert Vedrine, in *Liberation* (Paris), 24 November, 1998, in FBIS, 24 November, 1998.

70 Robert Graham, "A Symbol of Ancient Values," *Financial Times*, 14 October, 1998.

71 Jonathan Fenby, *France On the Brink*, New York, Arcade, 1999, p. 96, but see all of Chapter 4.

72 These and the next-shown investment figures for France and Germany were calculated from data in OECD, *International Direct Investment Statistics*, 1998.

73 Robert Conquest, "Toward an English Speaking Union," *The National Interest*, Fall, 1999, p. 66.

74 The total in the US was almost £122 billion; in the EU £99 billion, and the world total was £296 billion (United Kingdom, Office for National Statistics

["MA4 Overseas Direct Investment 1998"] and author's correspondence with ONS officer Simon Harrington.

75 UK Office for National Statistics, "Britain 2000: The Official Yearbook of the United Kingdom," HMSO.

76 In 1997, Japan's exports to the US were $118 billion and its imports from the US were $76 billion. That was three times larger than China, Japan's next-ranked trading partner.

77 Ellen L. Frost, *Transatlantic Trade: A Strategic Agenda*, Washington, Institute for International Economics, 1997.

78 This is similar to Prestowitz' recommendation in "Shrinking the Atlantic," where he urged the US and Europe to start "down the path toward an economic parallel to NATO."

79 Frost, *ibid.*, p. 79.

80 Available at http://europa.eu.int/comm/dg01/eu-us.htm

81 He was Britain's Secretary of State for Trade and Industry in 1985; became European Commissioner responsible for competition policy in 1989; and from 1993–9 was EU Trade Commissioner.

82 *Dagens Nyheter* (Stockholm), 29 April, 1995, in FBIS, 29 April, 1995.

83 US Department of State, Dispatch, *ibid.*

84 The investment issue was taken up by the OECD, where negotiations for a "Multilateral Agreement on Investment" collapsed disastrously in 1998. See David Henderson, *The MAI Affair: a Story and its Lessons*, London, The Royal Institute of International Affairs, 1999. In the US, the episode was a precursor of the same fears and occasional hysteria that led to the dismal collapse of the Seattle WTO meeting in 1999; common to both was the widespread and demonstrably false belief that the US is a "loser" in international trade. At public meetings on the investment treaty, I heard it reviled as an effort to remove American sovereignty and substitute instead a UN-sponsored "new world order"; missing only were references to the UN's proverbial "black helicopters."

85 *Les Echos*, Paris, 14 June, 1995, in FBIS, 15 June, 1995. French and Spanish leaders later joined to say all such "free trade" ideas were "premature" (Agence France Presse [AFP], 21 November, 1995, in FBIS, Western Europe, 22 November, 1995).

86 Reportedly they had agreed on everything except the title: the US preference was "Transatlantic Marketplace," while the EU choice was "Transatlantic Partnership", *Financial Times*, 21 November, 1995 and *El Pais* (Madrid), 20 November, in FBIS, 24 November, 1995.

87 Thailand's imports in 1992 were more than $40 billion and grew steadily to $72 billion in 1996 – but then dropped back to just $43 billion in 1998. Likewise for Indonesia: its 1998 import figure was $27 billion, a figure also not seen since 1992 (World Trade Organization, Geneva, *Annual Report 1999*, Table A4, p. 151).

88 *Financial Times*, 2 February, 1998.

89 *The Wall Street Journal*, 3 February, 1998 and *Financial Times*, 4 February, 1998.

90 *Financial Times*, 4 March, 1998.

91 *Financial Times*, 12 March, 1998.

92 From Jospin interview in Toulouse, as reported by Agence France Presse, 11 March, 1998, in FBIS, 11 March, 1998 (my emphasis).

93 *ibid.* (my emphasis).

94 *Les Echos*, 31 March, 1998, in FBIS, 1 April, 1998 (my emphasis).

95 Europeans were angry over both the Helms–Burton Law, designed to punish nations trading with Cuba, and the "d'Amato" Congressional resolution to restrict the US operations of European firms that had not fully satisfied the claims of World War II Holocaust survivors.

96 *Le Figaro-Economie*, in FBIS, 28 April, 1998.
97 From the text of Brittan's speech at the Columbia University Law School "Conference on Transatlantic Regulatory Co-operation," 16 April, 1999. Leon Brittan, who was succeeded as EU Trade Commissioner by Pascal Lamy in September, 1999, is now Lord Brittan.
98 As one example among several, Henry Kissinger has also called for a "North Atlantic Free Trade Zone" (*The Wall Street Journal*, 27 September, 1996). He joined with Brent Scowcroft (National Security Advisor in the Bush administration) in a call to the NATO allies to stop the trends that "were eating away" at the alliance.
99 From remarks following Secretary Summers' speech on the global economic structure, at a Washington, DC meeting sponsored by the Institute for International Economics, 14 January, 2000.

4 The Western hemisphere
America's blurred vision

Tug o'war in the south

In December, 1999, after the spectacular collapse of the WTO meeting in Seattle, Brazil's President Cardoso remarked that "after that substantial blow, I do not see the possibility of an FTAA, as the United States proposes."[1] He was referring to President Clinton's call for a "Free Trade Area for the Americas," announced at the Miami "Summit of the Americas" in 1994. The Summit convened all 34 Western hemisphere leaders (except for Castro), and all agreed to its goal of hemispheric free trade by 2005.

This was hardly the first time Brazil warned that because the FTAA threatens "MERCOSUR" (the acronym for Brazil's own plan for trade cooperation in the region's southern cone), Washington's trade proposal must be slowed down or stopped altogether. In 1997, when the US was last promoting an FTAA speed-up, President Cardoso argued that, because the US has "the potential to destroy Brazil's industrial base," Brazil should first consolidate its trade arrangements with smaller economies, "like Canada."[2] In late 1999, when Foreign Minister Lampreia also commented on the WTO collapse, he found a silver lining in the disaster. In something of a Latin version of *schadenfreude*, Lampreia remarked that "on the other hand, conditions are favorable for ... MERCOSUR."[3] That was followed up days later, when Brazil created a new office and special Ambassador for one task: to "promote ... MERCOSUR."[4]

The US, meanwhile, has sought to paper over any signs of difference with Brazil on the issue. Since the Miami summit, Washington has sponsored or attended a substantial number of meetings of the 34 governments, all aiming to assure that the Summit's goal – a hemispheric free trade area by 2005 – is maintained. In mid-1999, for example, the White House appointed a new special envoy for the FTAA, one of whose tasks was to insist that despite President Clinton's failure to get Congressional "fast track" negotiating authority, the 2005 schedule would not be affected.[5] But even on that point, the Brazilians pointedly disagreed:

> the Bill Clinton administration has never been able to have Congress pass fast track authority, which is an authorization for the

administration to conduct trade negotiations without congressional approval. Without the fast track authority, it is virtually impossible to conclude agreements.[6]

The wonder, however, is why the United States launched its "Free Trade for the Americas" initiative in the first place. There are evident political obstacles, and because Brazil is by far the largest and most populous nation in South America,[7] whose dispute with the US (about MERCOSUR versus the FTAA) will continue so long as American policy remains unchanged, the question is whether there are good reasons to press ahead nevertheless. Are the potential gains – for example, in terms of US exports to South America – large enough to outweigh the *disadvantages* of directly confronting Brazil? To raise that question is not to deny that the United States has already-important export markets in South America, and certainly those markets will grow. But this chapter will show that US markets in South America, in the context of America's overall trade patterns, are *not* large and important enough to overcome two very likely negative consequences; one in South America, the other in East Asia (which will be dealt with in the next chapter).

In South America, if the US continue to press for hemispheric "free trade," the result will be to further alienate Brazil politically, and further aggravate an already-strained relationship. Tensions between the US and Brazil were brought to the surface when MERCOSUR was established in 1991, but their differences are deeply-rooted and will be present for the foreseeable future. President Cardoso has worked successfully to improve ties with the US, but he and those who follow him will always find this to be a very challenging task. Especially from Brazil's perspective, its differences with the US are real, and in this era, the largest obstacle to closer US–Brazil ties is MERCOSUR itself. The reason stems from what MERCOSUR is intended to mean. Ostensibly, it is an economics-only venture, but in Brazil it has existential significance. Its success is seen as vital, not only to affirm Brazil's economic leadership in South America (especially in its southern cone), but also to legitimize the nation's regional *political* pre-eminence. For that reason, the net effect of Washington's FTAA proposal has been to sharply reinforce Brazil's long-standing view that, in terms of regional leadership, the United States is its main rival.[8]

In fact, of course, Argentina has been the only genuine "rival" for that role, but with a population of just 40 million (a quarter of Brazil's), and a GDP only a third as large, Argentina is no serious contender today. Both nations, moreover, have sheathed their military daggers, although shadows of the old rivalry are often still visible. In 1997, for example, Brazil made one of its regular bids for a permanent seat on the UN Security Council (an effort, incidentally, that should not be underestimated), and when Argentine President Menem complained that this would "break the balance of power" in South America," there was an uproar in Brazil.

Brazil's former President Sarney (now a Senator) charged that Argentina's Menem was acting for the United States: "turning himself into an instrument of division in our continent . . . to destabilize Mercosur."[9]

A further uproar came in 1998 when the United States designated Argentina a "close non-NATO ally." Washington had already done that for Chile, entirely for the purpose of allowing sales of surplus NATO equipment. Nevertheless, some reactions in Brazil seemed paranoid, and provided new evidence that Brazil sees the United States as its true problem. Again, it was former President Sarney who harshly criticized both Argentina and the United States:

> It is impossible to comprehend that the Argentine Government asked to be included under the nuclear umbrella of the United States *and to become a member of NATO*, as a military ally of the United Kingdom, which killed hundreds of young Argentine men in the Malvinas [Falklands] War. As a defense against whom? What threat is circling Argentina? That action was serious, because it demonstrated that, according to [Argentina's] Foreign Minister, *Mercosur is nothing more than an economic adventure.*[10]

Finally, problems in Brazil's economy – most recently the collapse of its currency (the *Real*) in 1999 – drew new attention to Argentine–Brazil tension. Both because of and in spite of their close MERCOSUR trade ties, the currency crisis led to several cases of outright protectionism, mainly by Brazil but also by Argentina, and caused much bitter recrimination on both sides.[11]

For its part, the US has regarded Brazil not as a "rival" but as an important regional player, though one that often tries to punch above its weight. Brazil's past uneven economic performance, including its "lost decade" and the 1999 collapse of its currency, have all contributed to that American assessment. The consequence is that Washington regards Brazil's regional aims with "deep skepticism,"[12] and has not given them much weight. Further compounding the problem is the unofficial (but reportedly common) perspective in the US capital that Brazil's foreign policy elite, and its bureaucratically powerful Foreign Ministry (known as "*Itamarati*"), are regarded as the home of "traditional anti-American nationalism."[13]

In that environment, it is hardly surprising that officials in both nations regard the other as a spoiler, committed to frustrating the other's legitimate foreign policy goals, and both can point to actions that confirm their worst suspicions. The Americans, for example, readily recall that in the preparations for the Miami Summit, Brazil's Deputy Foreign Minister gave what the US side regarded as a "preachy, paternalistic presentation . . . the Brazilians sought to stir up latent resentments against the United States."[14] For their part, the Brazilians see American attitudes towards Brazil and its policies as patronizing and presumptuous. A good example was the wording in US Trade Representative Barshefsky's Congressional testimony about the failure of fast track:

> [It] left a vacuum in *our own* hemisphere with respect to leadership. What the absence [of fast track] has done has been to lead ... other countries ... in *our own* hemisphere [to build] their *own little unit* ... *Mercosur is one such example.*[15]

The policy-relevance of these Western hemisphere tensions, as in Europe, is that they can enmesh and entangle the United States, *as a regional actor*, in Latin America's regional and local affairs. In Europe, as Chapter 3 acknowledged, the US has important trade and security relations with the major states of Europe, but it simultaneously has *uniquely global* political and economic interests. The reason is that the US is in fact unique, both in strategic and political terms, as well as in terms of the nations and issues ultimately dependent on America's capacity and behavior. It is like no other nation, either in its capabilities or its responsibilities, and for that reason the United States needs to keep its distance from each region's strictly local concerns.

Yet, in the Western hemisphere, because of Washington's insistence on the FTAA proposal, American policy comes dangerously close to that entanglement. In a sub-region where Brazil – by virtue of its size, population, and present and potential economic capacity – has a reasonable basis to expect a role of regional pre-eminence, the US risks hardening the perception that it is Brazil's regional "rival." Not only would that grossly distort the nature of the Brazil–US relationship, in ways that recall Aesop's fable about the gnat who landed on the bull's horn, but much more importantly, it would be contrary to America's foreign policy and security interests.

Nevertheless, the United States has so far ignored these warning signs. Since at least the 1980s, both Republican and Democratic administrations have adopted the view that South America in general, and Brazil in particular, are among America's "Big Emerging Markets" (what President Clinton and others quickly called the "BEMs").[16] That view was a key element in efforts by both Presidents Bush and Clinton to expand NAFTA to the rest of the hemisphere. It was an appeal, under the rubric of "free trade," to build an all-hemisphere trade and economic bloc, and it recalled Henry Kissinger's remarkable – but unsupportable – statement that if the United States develops a "Western hemisphere-wide free trade system," it would retain a *"commanding role no matter what happens."*[17]

That concept, however wrong-headed, apparently has bipartisan support, which alone promises to keep the FTAA on the agenda. In February 2000, for example, US Commerce Secretary Daley predicted that because support for the FTAA transcended party lines, it would continue as US policy regardless of which person or party next gained the White House, and his confidence appears well-founded.[18] It stems from a widespread American belief that there is a long history of intimate economic connections between the US and Latin America, and that the entire Western hemisphere is America's "natural market."

US trade and "Pan Americanism"

That belief has its origins in a romantic concept that developed in American thinking in the late nineteenth and early twentieth century, which historians refer to as "the Western Hemisphere Idea" or simply "Pan Americanism."[19] It is a concept that both urges and celebrates the goal of close ties between the United States and the nations of Latin America *in general*, although few facts support such a broad US role. The historical reality instead is that America's deepest and longest economic connections in Latin America have been quite limited: to Mexico, to Cuba before Castro, and finally to some of the small Central American economies. Beyond that, the notion of especially close or dominant US economic involvement elsewhere in the region, particularly in South America, has little basis in hard evidence.

United States economic relations with Brazil are a good example: on close analysis, and from a US perspective, the effort to give Brazil the "BEM" label is not persuasive. Though it is a big country, with a big population, Brazil actually buys relatively little from the United States. When compared, for example, to the much smaller populations of Australia, Singapore, and Korea, as Figure 4.1 shows, Brazil is not a heavy-hitter. Of

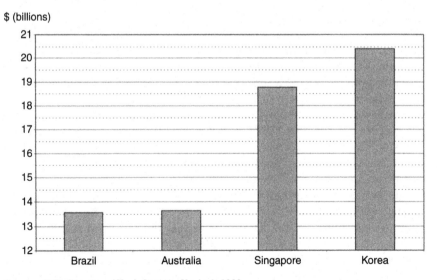

$ (billions)

Source: IMF, *Direction of Trade Statistics Yearbook*, 1999.

Figure 4.1 Imports from the US in 1998 in Australia, Brazil, Singapore and Korea.

course its imports from the US, roughly $13.5 billion in 1998,[20] are obviously no small amount – just a bit less than Australia's. But Brazil's population is more than 172 million, while Australia's is just 19 million. That means Australia's per capita imports from the US were more than $700, *while Brazil's were $80.*

More striking is the case of tiny Singapore, with only 3.5 million people. Even in the midst of the Asian economic crisis, Singapore's per-person US imports were more than *$5,000* in 1998, compared with Brazil's $80. Finally, consider South Korea. Its population of 47 million is not quite a quarter of Brazil's, and Korea's economy was the second-worst hit by the Asian crisis. Yet despite its resulting 30 percent drop in imports, Korea's US purchases remained much larger than even Brazil's best year.

It is a safe bet, however, that most Americans would be quite surprised to learn that Brazil, like South America more generally, has never been a particularly good customer for US products. It would come as news because Americans have been brought up to regard the nations of Latin America as *neighbors*, with whom they share not only the same landmass, but some common historical features as well. They have been taught, for example, that George Washington, and the American Revolutionary War, have parallels in the revolutionary struggle of Simon Bolivar, the hero of Latin America's independence. Some Americans also know that the "Monroe Doctrine" in some way connects the United States to Latin America – in this instance by warning nations outside the hemisphere to stay out. Others have heard of FDR's "Good Neighbor" policy, or JFK's "Alliance for Progress," and some have seen, just blocks from the White House, that symbol of US–Latin American ties, the splendid building of the Organization of American States.

In sum, while Americans may indeed be "parochial and "Eurocentric," they nevertheless are likely to know a bit more about Latin America than about any other region. But that very surface familiarity has a major downside, because it treats as a *single* entity – "Latin America" – what in fact is a very large region, with very large internal differences. A quarter-century ago, when the visionary goal of economic "integration" was much the fad all over the world, Albert Fishlow, an economist and Latin American specialist, cited those differences to explain why the concept never took root in Latin America: "The fact [is] that Latin America is not a cohesive economic region."[21] Nevertheless, Americans treat the region as if it *were* a single and undifferentiated entity, and they are encouraged in the error by their popular culture, which also lumps together the Latin nations, and calls the product "*Latino*." The result is that the food and music, the art and literature, and much else that reflects the *separate* national cultures of, for example, Brazil, Mexico, Cuba, Argentina, and Puerto Rico, are often treated as if they were one entity. And in that perceived single entity, it is Mexico that plays the dominant role. The consequence, in the words of a prominent specialist, is that "most Americans – and many legislators – view

Latin America through the optic of Mexico. To them, Latin America is a continent of *sombreros* and *serapes.*"[22]

The Mexican distortion

As misleading and plain wrong as that Mexico-tinted lens is in connection with popular culture, it is compounded when applied to issues of public policy – especially by members of the US government and America's press. Yet journalists and officials, when they write and speak about Western hemisphere trade, routinely cite the imagined single entity of "Latin America" when what they mean is the Mexico-dominant, Hispanic culture region, south of the United States. Two recent examples will illustrate the point. In 1997, a journalist with seemingly impeccable credentials to write about Latin America (he was the editor of the *Wall Street Journal Americas*) wrote that "Latin America ... which *absorbs some 18 percent of US exports, is our fastest-growing export market.*" Weeks earlier, the same words had been used in Congressional testimony by Ambassador Barshefsky, the US Trade Representative. She announced that "Latin America and the Caribbean *were the fastest growing market for US exports in 1996.*"[23]

Both statements were wildly misleading, because each included *US exports to Mexico* in the single market they referred to as "Latin America." That lumping-together is akin to putting into one bag a tenderloin steak and a sack of potatoes, and calling the bag "groceries": the label misses the important differences. Likewise, combining Mexico's US imports with those of South and Central America erases what most distinguishes them as US markets: the value of their imports. Combining them, as if they were one, exaggerates the receptiveness of South and Central America to US products, and distorts American thinking about their economic importance to the US.

The exaggeration stems from two factors: the enormous value of US exports to Mexico, and the fact that its very great size is altogether *disproportionate* to any and all others in Latin America. Think of "Latin America" as a fishing-sinker, with most of its weight and density at one end. To use the term "Latin American market" implies that the density is distributed relatively evenly, when the reality is that Mexico accounts overwhelmingly for the weight. Moreover, Mexico's importance as a US market is *not* a mainly recent development, tied perhaps to NAFTA. Quite the contrary: Mexico has been a major US market for more than a century, and since 1990, i.e., several years before NAFTA, the US has sold more to Mexico than *to all the rest of South and Central America combined.*[24]

These facts, especially the stark contrast between Mexico's market-size and the size of all other Latin American markets, are – or at least *should be* – well-known to those writers, reporters, and of course US officials who deal with issues of foreign trade and foreign policy. Nevertheless, in their enthusiasm for the idea that South and Central America represent a "natural

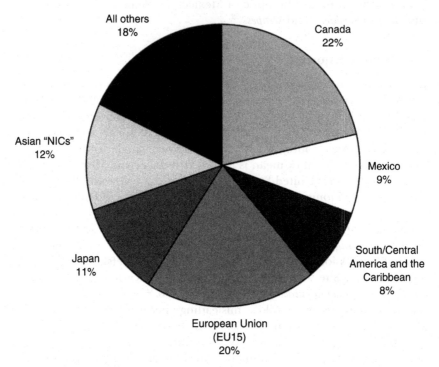

Source: Author's calculations from Table 6 in US Department of Commerce,
        Foreign Trade Highlights, 1996.

Figure 4.2 US export markets, 1996 (total = $625 billion).

market" for the US, they have largely ignored the strong evidence that no such market exists. Figure 4.2 shows South America's market size in relation to US exports to all other areas. It deliberately deals with 1996, the year cited by Ambassador Barshefsky, when she argued that "Latin America accounts for 18 percent of total US exports."

This illustration underlines two points. The first is that in 1996, Mexico *alone* took 9 percent of US exports; almost as much as Japan's share. Second, when exports to Mexico are separated out from those with which it is too often thrown together (South America, Central America, and the Caribbean), Figure 4.2 shows us that those three *combined* represent not 18 percent of US exports, but *just 8 percent.* Yet if we were to follow the practice of most journalists and officials, i.e. simply *add Mexico's export-portion* to the 8 percent sent to South and Central America, and then compound the error by labeling the resulting 17–18 percent package "Latin America," we might also believe – wrongly – that "Latin America" is America's second or third largest market.

Separating Mexico's US imports from the rest also helps put Latin America's true market size in comparative perspective. For example, the more than 450 million people in all of Latin America's 36 remaining economies – from the micro-states of the Caribbean, to the middle players of Central America, and finally to the regional big powers, Argentina and Brazil – account for a *smaller* US export market than the 72 million people in Asia's "NICs": Taiwan, Singapore, and South Korea.

The next two charts (Figure 4.3 and Figure 4.4) show that the second Barshefsky and *Wall Street Journal* assertion is equally false – that "Latin America is the fastest growing market" for the US. Indeed, this notion is even more dramatically affected when Mexico's imports are shown separately. The two charts illustrate *growth rates* for imports from the United States: they show Mexico alone; "Latin America" both with and without Mexico; and for comparison, US exports to three other markets (ASEAN, the Pacific Basin, and the European Union). Again, the first chart deliberately uses data for 1996: the year cited by Barshefsky and the *Wall Street Journal*.

Several conclusions can be drawn from Figure 4.3. It tells us first that Mexico's 1995–6 growth rate as a US market was strikingly high, and that Latin America's growth rate for US imports – *when Mexico is included* – is likewise very high. But the chart also reveals that when Mexico is separated out, Latin America's true growth rate as a US market *is just 7 percent*. In other words, and contrary to what Ambassador Barshefsky and the *Wall Street Journal* asserted, Latin America's growth rate was not high at all. It was *less*

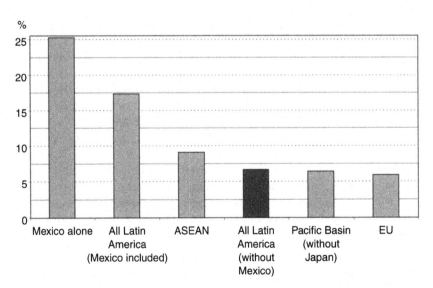

Source: Author's calculations from data in IMF, *Direction of International Trade Statistics*, annual issues.

Figure 4.3 One-year (1995–6) growth rates (%) for imports from the USA.

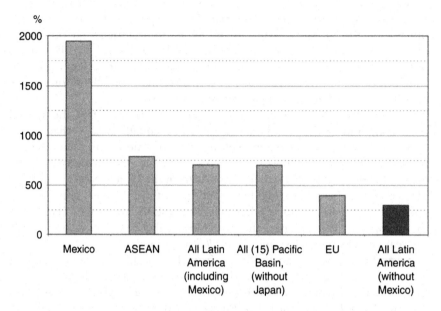

Source: Author's Calculations from data in IMF, *Direction of Trade Statistics,* annual issues.

Figure 4.4 20-year (1978–98) growth rates (%) for imports from the USA.

than ASEAN, and not much different than the Pacific Basin and even the EU, the most mature and presumably the slowest-growing of all US markets.

Since Figure 4.3 dealt with just one year (1995–6), it could be faulted as atypical, or as a one-time aberration. The next illustration (Figure 4.4) avoids that by comparing the same markets over the *20 years* from 1978–98; it provides a very accurate portrayal of the rates at which America's global export markets grew in the 1980s and 1990s.

The lesson of illustration is that without the inflating factor of Mexico's very high US imports (*$93 billion in 1998*), Latin America has had the slowest of all growth rates as a US market. Its rate over the 20-year period has been less than *half* that of the Pacific economies, and lower than even the mature economy EU. In sum, despite the assertions of boosters and officials who should know better, Latin America wins no contest for US import growth.

America's trade with South America

The starkness of that finding forces the question: has the US, in its attempt to build a Western Hemisphere Free Trade Area, lost sight of vital larger objectives? Here we need to remind ourselves of America's unique-

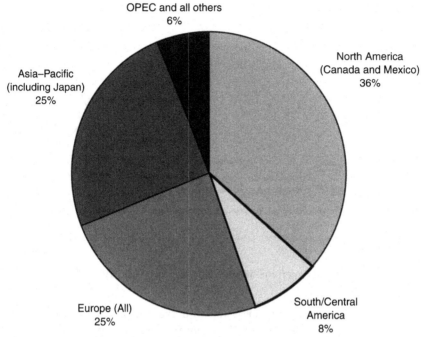

OPEC and all others
6%

North America
(Canada and Mexico)
36%

Asia–Pacific
(including Japan)
25%

South/Central
America
8%

Europe (All)
25%

Source: Author's calculations from data in US Commerce Department, *Foreign Trade Highlights*, 1999, Table 14.

Figure 4.5 Global shares of US exports, 1999 (total = $695 billion).

ness, even aside from its role in military and political terms. The United States is the *only* major exporting nation with a genuinely globally-diversified export record: it has a very large and *nearly-equal share in each of the world's three major markets.* Figure 4.5 illustrates this for 1999, a year that was – because of the striking equality in size of its major markets – both typical and quite remarkable. In 1999, 25 percent of US exports went to *Western Europe;* an equal *25 percent to the Pacific Rim;* and *36 percent to North America,* meaning Canada and Mexico.

As in 1996, this chart also shows that only 8 percent of US exports are directed to *all* of South and Central America. Since those markets are the only new ones that would be covered by an FTAA, an important question is whether they are likely to grow sufficiently to overcome the many political complications that will be encountered – for example, with Brazil and several in Asia – if the US presses its FTAA concept. To put the question baldly, do export prospects in South America, and Brazil in particular, warrant the "Big Emerging Market" label they were given by former Secretary of Commerce Ron Brown?

$ (billions)

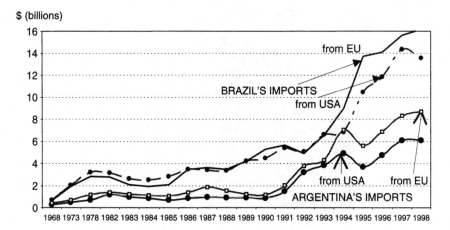

Source: Author's calculations from trade data in IMF, *Direction of Trade Statistics,*
annual issues, 1969–99.

Figure 4.6 Brazil and Argentine imports from EU and USA, 1968–98.

The almost certain answer is no, and the two accompanying illustrations, which deal with Brazil and Argentina over long periods, show why. The first (Figure 4.6) deals with their *imports* during the 30 years from 1968–98, and compares their value from the EU and from the US. It shows that during that 30-year period, both Brazil and Argentina have

$ (billions)

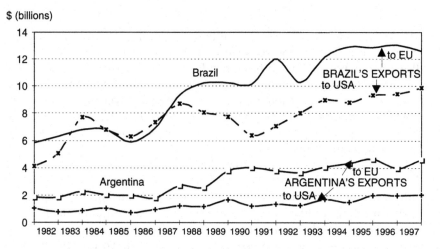

Source: Author's calculations from trade data in IMF, *Direction of Trade Statistics,*
annual issues, 1969–99.

Figure 4.7 Brazil and Argentine exports to the EU and USA, 1982–98.

steadily purchased *more from Europe* than from the United States. There were occasional exceptions, for short periods in the 1980s, when Brazil bought more from the US, but not for long. From the mid-1990s through to the present, both Argentina and Brazil have steadily and increasingly imported more from the EU than from the United States, and by 1998, the gap was $2.5 billion in each.

Figure 4.7 covers the years 1982–98, and concentrates on Brazil's and Argentina's *exports*. As with their imports, it shows that both nations regularly have exported more to Europe than to the US, and here too the gap is widening. In sum, if a developing nation's exports are any indication of its "dependence" on an industrialized metropole, this illustration shows that South America's two largest economies are "dependent" on Europe.

Taken together, these two illustrations underline four main points:

- widely-held assumptions about America's "dominance" of the Latin American market are just that: assumptions with no basis in fact;
- in the trade of both Brazil and Argentina, as an earlier study also found,[25] "the EU (and not the United States) is a more important trading partner";
- the pattern favoring the EU is so long-standing, and in recent years so pronounced, that there is no reason to expect a change any time soon;
- for the US, the concept of South America as an especially favored "natural market" makes little sense.

Nevertheless, as a result of the "Pan American" vision that both assumes and calls for close ties between the United States and the nations of Latin America, the belief in the existence of a Western hemisphere "natural market" persists, and has powerfully affected several generations of American thinking. One consequence is that Western hemisphere advocates – for which there is no real counterpart on behalf of the other regions – both exaggerate those US ties with Latin America that do exist, and minimize the likely problems if closer relations were pursued. Officials guilty of such boosterism have a special responsibility, since they seek to shape policy in the face of readily available and contrary evidence.

To help explain how this special pleading came about we need to recall what has been wisely called "the *myth* of a 'special relationship' between the U.S. and Latin American peoples."[26] To some, the myth implied a primarily helpful or supportive US role, but more typically it portrayed the United States as dominating both the trade and investment of the region. A post-World War II by-product was the *dependencia* thesis, a perspective on economic development that ascribed a principally exploitative (and presumably intended) relationship of overall dependency on the US.

The *dependencia* approach influenced much thought on economic development in all global regions from the 1960s to the 1990s, but even before that, Latin American–US relations were commonly portrayed as "big brother/little brother." The following examples reflect the recurring and common theme:

> Since 1900 it has been the United States that has loomed largest in the *Latin American* trade and investment picture. . . . During World War I, American capital began to surpass European capital in the southern republics. The United States itself was a nation of surplus capital, looking for foreign investments. . . . In the 1930s 43 percent of all investment abroad by American nationals was in *Latin America*. . . . Sixty percent *of Latin America's* imports come from the United States, and only 21 percent from Europe. In return the United States is *Latin America's* biggest market, absorbing 44 percent of their exports.
>
> Bailey and Nasatir, *Latin America: The Development of its Civilization*[27]

> As the United States grew in population, industrial production, and wealth, *Latin America* became the source of the staple goods and natural resources we [sic] needed to meet the demands of our [sic] consumers and our [sic] factories. Once this traditional relationship developed, the *Latin Americans* found themselves dependent on economic decisions and trends in demand within the United States. Since most of these countries had but one or two major export items which provided a substantial portion of their national revenue, the US economy played a critical role in determining the prospects for development and financial solvency in much of *Latin America*. . . . For years the United States has held all or most of the economic cards. The *Latin Americans* now want a better distribution of the cards . . .
>
> Michael J. Kryzanek, *U.S.–Latin American Relations*[28]

> Between 1914 and 1929 the United States definitively replaced Great Britain as the dominant commercial and financial power in *Latin America*.
>
> William Keylor, *The Twentieth Century World*[29]

Although these and similar writings reflect the preponderant view of US–Latin American relations, there were exceptions. After all, as an economic historian put it, "the countries of Latin America were all once colonies of one or another European power," and most of their trade and investment remained with Europe for "almost a century after independence." Yet even that careful writer went too far when he then concluded that "Much of this [European dominance] changed during the first half of the twentieth century. *The United States took the place of Europe as the principal provider of trade and investment.*[30]

Brief interlude: the myth of American dominance

The reality is far different and much less dramatic. The 25 or 30-year period from the worldwide depression of the 1930s, through Europe's post-war recovery in the 1950s and 1960s, was a unique interlude in the history of America's relations with Latin America. It was unique because it was the only time in which US investments were clearly dominant in all of the hemisphere: not only in Mexico, Cuba, and Central America – the areas of America's traditional geographic focus and dominance – but for the first time in *South America* as well. Moreover, those wartime and Depression years were a time of high-profile political events, including Franklin Roosevelt's "Good Neighbor" approach as applied to Latin America; the region's wartime cooperation with Washington (Argentina excepted); and when the war was over, the creation of the Rio Pact and the establishment of the Organization of American States. The combination of those events pervasively shaped American thinking about the region for years to come. A major consequence is the contemporary view that the United States has had an especially close relationship with all of Latin America, and that the US is the dominant foreign actor in the region's economies.

Yet those years represented only an interlude. By the late 1960s, when Europe returned to its earlier role as global investor, America's earlier status also re-emerged: as just one among several major investors. This was especially true in South America, as the investment records for Argentina and Brazil show most clearly. They are, of course, South America's two largest economies, and the two for which the most complete data are available.[31] In both cases, the US share of private direct investment again became smaller than Europe's, and that remains its status in Argentina and Brazil in the twenty-first century. In 1973, for example, while Western Europe accounted for 44 percent of total investment in Argentina, the United States represented less than 40 percent. Similarly in Brazil, as Figure 4.8 shows, Western Europe accounted for 38 percent of investment in 1976, while the US share was 32 percent. (Japan, the relative newcomer, already represented 11 percent by the mid-1970s.)

In other words, in neither of these major South American cases was the US the "dominant" outside investor, even in the 1970s. Its role as "principal provider," was instead quite limited, in terms both of geography and time. Its economic dominance extended first to Mexico, where the US eclipsed Britain in trade and investment in the 1880s; second, to parts of the Caribbean; and lastly to Cuba, where Spain's defeat at the turn of the century left the US the leading foreign presence – until Castro ended the American role 60 years later. Only in Mexico and Central America did America's role remain overwhelmingly large. Long *before* NAFTA – in 1971 and 1976 for example – the US accounted for 81 percent and almost 69 percent, respectively, of Mexico's total investments.

In *South America*, in contrast, especially in the larger economies of

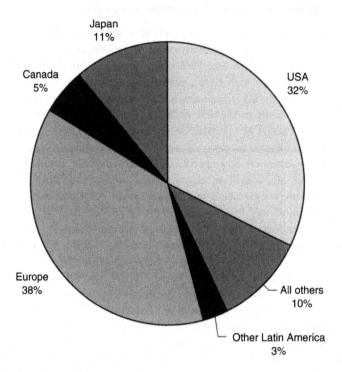

Source: Table 4 in Isaiah Frank, *Foreign Enterprise in Developing Countries,* Johns Hopkins,
          1980, p. 14.

Figure 4.8 Sources of foreign investment (stock) in Brazil, 1976 (total = $9 billion).

Brazil and Argentina, America's investment "dominance" was altogether a
consequence of the worldwide and temporary dislocations associated with
two World Wars, and the depression in-between. Those three cataclysmic
events largely explain the rise and relative decline of America's role in
South America, to the point where the United States is again a large actor,
but not "dominant" in comparison with Europe. The progression can be
seen by looking first at global foreign investment in Latin America in
1914, on the eve of World War I. Figure 4.9 illustrates the pattern.

As this chart shows, of the almost $8 billion that foreigners invested in
all of Latin America in 1914, Britain *alone* was responsible for almost half
the total. The US share – at just over $1 billion – was overwhelmingly con-
centrated in Mexico and Cuba. A UN study in 1965 summarized America's
role in Latin America before World War I:

> before the First World War, United States capital was confined to a
> limited area. ... 77 percent [was invested] in the Caribbean ... in

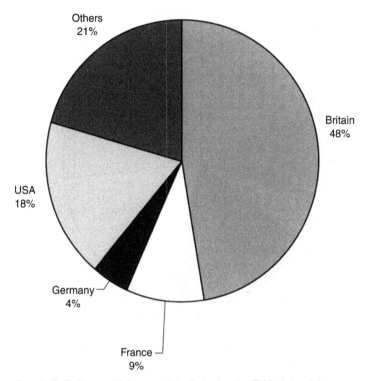

Source: Data in R. E. Grosse, *Multinationals in Latin America,* Table 1.4, p. 12.

Figure 4.9 Foreign investment in Latin America, 1914 (total = $7.6 billion).

Central America, and in Mexico. *Cuba and Mexico alone accounted for 65.8 percent of total US investment . . .* while *little was invested in South America.*[32]

There were two consequences of this Mexico–Caribbean concentration: first, any US capital remaining in Latin America was clearly no match for the Europeans; second, "in the Latin American region as a whole," the US *"ranked far behind Britain."*[33] In Argentina, for example, British investments in 1914 were 40 times larger than America's; French and German investments were 7 and 5 times larger. The same 20:1 ratio existed in Brazil: British and French investments were *$1 billion,* while US investments totaled just $50 million.[34] With the end of the World War I, however, Europe's investments in Latin America fell off dramatically, and as the UN study concluded, "Europe was no longer the main supplier."[35]

The principal explanation lay in the economic consequences of World War I. In order to pay their war debts and rebuild their economies at

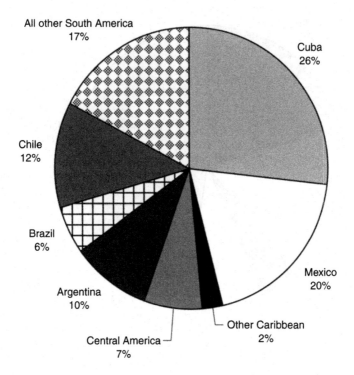

Source: Data in R. E. Grosse, *Multinationals in Latin America,* Table 1.7.

Figure 4.10 Cuba and Mexico dominate US investments in Latin America, 1929
(total = $3.5 billion).

home, France and Britain withdrew from the global investment scene, while German holdings, even aside from Allied demands for war reparations, were confiscated by South American governments. To appreciate the extent to which these new circumstances led to the evaporation of European investment capital, it helps to recall the dialogue in international politics and economics after World War I: it was dominated by the famous issues of "war debts" and "war reparations." Thus while the principal pre-war investors had been Britain, France, and Germany, their post-war financial straits were aggravated either by their enormous debts to the US, or in Germany by the demand for reparations.

While US investment increased modestly in the 1920s (and included some prominent meatpacking and mining enterprises in South America), its role nevertheless remained heavily concentrated in Mexico and Cuba, with smaller amounts in Central America. Figure 4.10 illustrates the distribution in 1929; it shows that 46 percent, or $1.6 billion, was in Mexico and Cuba alone, more than in all of South America.

The lesson of this chart is that ten years after World War I, America's investment choices had not changed. Although new European investment in Latin America was still largely absent, US capital hardly rushed in to fill possibly-vacant opportunities in South America. Instead, half of America's total investment in Latin America went to the *same two economies – Mexico and Cuba – as before the war*, while South America's two largest economies, Argentina and Brazil, attracted just 6 percent and 10 percent.

After 1929, what was left of Europe's presence was then almost entirely withdrawn: first as a result of the global depression in the early 1930s, and then as a consequence of the outbreak of World War II in 1939. British investments, which accounted for two-thirds of Latin America's foreign capital before World War I, "virtually ceased" after 1929–30. London prohibited new investment altogether between 1932–4, because of Latin American defaults and exchange controls, and when the ban was lifted (in the late 1930s), capital did not return because of difficulties in repatriating profits. World War II, of course, put a stop to new investment altogether, and when that war ended, capital needs at home led London once again to ban most overseas investment."[36] The result was that British investment did not recover until well after World War II, and of the holdings that remained, half of those in Brazil and Mexico – and close to 90 percent in Argentina – were disposed of in what amounted to forced sales.

America's investments had also slowed in the 1930s, for some of the same reasons, but the departure of the Europeans was by far the most important factor: "British investments in Latin America had been three times as large as those of the U.S.A. on the eve of World War I [but] by the end of World War II, *U.S. investments were . . . about four times as large as those of Britain.*"[37] In other words, by default rather than by design, and as a result of the three-part drama of war, global depression, and then war again, the US was left in the largest position.

That entirely modern and singular phenomenon has led to the widespread, but fundamentally false, view that US investments have "dominated Latin America" since World War I. It is false for two main reasons. First, because despite the continuing use of the label "Latin America," the reality is that in no meaningful political or economic sense does "Latin America" represent a single entity – certainly not in terms of relations with the US. What Fishlow wrote in the mid-1970s – that "Latin America is not a cohesive economic region" – is as true today as it was then. The second reason pertains to the nature and size of US investments in Latin America as a whole. South America is home to the great bulk of Latin America's population, and is the site of three of its four major economies (Brazil, Argentina, and Chile), but US investments there have been far smaller, even of a different order of magnitude, than in Mexico, the Caribbean (and in the past, Cuba).

Today this disparity is extraordinarily clear. Based on figures from the OECD, which tracks the foreign investment patterns of 28 nations, the US

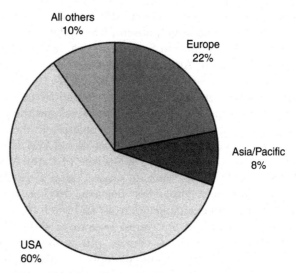

Source: OECD, *International Investment Statistics Yearbook,* 1998, Mexico, Table 7.

Figure 4.11 Sources of foreign investment in Mexico, 1996 (total = $47 billion).

is far and away the single largest source of *all* FDI in Mexico. In 1996, as Figure 4.11 shows, American investment accounted for almost 60 percent of Mexico's total. And needless to say, the US is also Mexico's single largest trading partner.

In South America, in contrast, the US has not held that leadership role, nor has American capital been distributed remotely evenly throughout "Latin America." Instead, and largely as a function of its overwhelming concentration in Mexico and the Caribbean, US investment almost everywhere else in the region has not been the dominant element. In the few cases – one of which we will look at now – where it has been at least prominent, its role has been short-lived and temporary.

Venezuela in the 1950s provides the perfect illustration. In the wake of the Suez Crisis in 1956, America's late 1950s investments in Venezuela's oil sector quickly rose from 3 percent to *almost 10 percent* of the US world total. That level rivaled the traditionally largest US investment destinations anywhere, but after the 1960s they fell very sharply. By 1998, as Figure 4.12 shows, US investment in Venezuela was roughly a *half percent* of America's global foreign investment.[38]

That one-time, and somewhat exceptional episode aside, the point of this recounting is to emphasize that after World War I, any assertions of US investment "dominance" in South America represented, in fact, no more than a brief and temporary interlude. The interlude came to an end

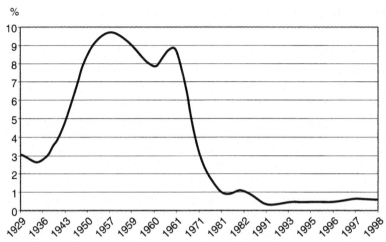

Source: Data in US Commerce Department, *Survey of Current Business*, various issues.

Figure 4.12 US investment in Venezuela, 1929–98, as percentage of US global investment.

within 15 or 20 years of the end of *World War II*, when Europe's major investment role in South America was restored. The result was broadly reminiscent of pre-1914 patterns, when Britain dominated private foreign investment in most parts of the world, and usually led in trade as well.[39] After World War I, however, as we have seen, that pre-war system of global trade and finance entirely and effectively collapsed. US investments were relatively less affected, but overall, in the words of an early UN report, there was a "clear declining trend [and] the 1929 Depression marks the beginning of a period of about 15 years during which hardly any foreign capital flowed into Latin America."[40]

In fact, the investment hiatus was longer than just 15 fifteen years. Not until at least a decade after World War II, and in most places and respects not until the early 1960s, was there true recovery from the Depression and the turmoil of both wars. The revival of global investment was no exception, and the result was that in the *early* post-war years, the United States was often the principal actor in South America. The reason, however, was that no other major investors existed, aside from Canada and a few others, such as Switzerland. By the mid-1970s, that was all over. In 1976, as Figure 4.8 showed, Western Europe's investments in Brazil were once again larger than those from the United States, and the same was true in Argentina. Since then, the pattern has remained unchanged: Europe has held its lead over the US.[41]

The meaning of Europe's investment return to Latin America

A new series of UN "World Investment Reports" has made it clear that these long-term realities were actually *resumed* realities. The 1991 UN Report introduced the concept of the investment "Triad" (the US, Europe, and Japan), and the method cast new light on the issue I have raised here: the question of investment "dominance" in the developing regions.[42] The UN study showed, for example, that just as the United States was the dominant investor in Mexico in 1980 – with a 70 percent share that year – it also showed that the US did *not* play that role in either Brazil or Argentina.

The UN report found instead that, while two of the triad members, the US and the EC, "competed" for investment dominance in Brazil and Argentina in 1980, *the EC already had the larger share in both.* The report then analyzed Brazil's investment data for 1987, by which time the EC had a 38 percent share. That led the UN report to drop the United States altogether as a "competitor" in Brazil, and to list *Brazil as solely EC "dominant."*[43] The EC lead was clearer yet in 1994, the year of the most recent full UN study of the issue. That showed Brazil with a total of $37 billion in foreign investment, of which *50 percent* was from Western Europe, and only 28 percent from the United States.[44]

The clear conclusion is that there has been much mythologizing about the investment role of the United States in South America. Figure 4.13 shows that since 1976, European investment in both Brazil and Argentina has consistently been greater than from the US. Its broader lesson is that the US is not, and for long has not been, the "dominant" investor either in South America's two major economies, or in the region as a whole.

In addition to those already-clear patterns, there are two new and powerful reasons why the Europe–US gap in South America will certainly grow even wider. The first is that, since the mid-1990s, Western European investment has surged in South America, and Latin America in general is once again Europe's principal investment destination. In yet another reminder of the nineteenth and early twentieth century, the source of the largest new investments is Spain, for the first time in generations rivaling those from Britain, the usual leader. These European–Latin American developments are closely monitored by the Inter-American Development Bank (IADB), which concludes that, as a result of the EU's trade agreements with MERCOSUR and Chile in the mid-1990s, "European investment is expected to increase further in the next few years." Its summary is compelling, and bears repeating:

> Since 1994, the largest flows [into Latin America] have come *from Spain* and the United Kingdom. Spanish investment increased sub-

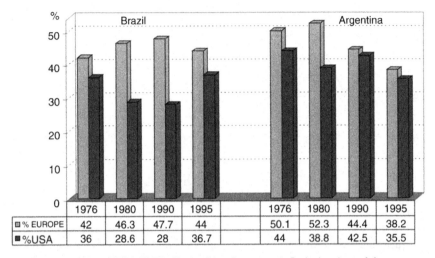

	1976	1980	1990	1995		1976	1980	1990	1995
▣ % EUROPE	42	46.3	47.7	44		50.1	52.3	44.4	38.2
▪ %USA	36	28.6	28	36.7		44	38.8	42.5	35.5

Source: 1980–95 from SELA/IADB, *Foreign Direct Investment in Latin America and the Caribbean*, 1999; 1976 data from I. Frank, *Foreign Enterprise in Developing Countries*, 1979.

Figure 4.13 Percentage share of European and US investment (stock) in Brazil and Argentina, 1976–95.

stantially in 1999 with the purchase of the largest Argentine oil company [for $15 billion] ...

Latin America and the Caribbean is the *main non-OECD investment destination* for ... Germany (60 percent), the Netherlands (55 percent), and the United Kingdom (44 percent). In 1995 and 1996, the manufacturing industry received 82 percent of British investment, 81 percent of Dutch, 72 percent of Italian and 67 percent of German investment.[45]

The second likely cause of a growing EU–US investment gap is the largely unheralded and relative decline, *since the mid-1950s, of US investments in South America*. This surprising pattern is illustrated in Figure 4.14. which covers the 70 years from *1929–98*, and traces the percentage of US investments in South America as a proportion of US global investments. The severity of the decline it illustrates – from a high point of 25 percent in the 1950s to just 7 or 8 percent in 1998 – is both startling and strongly inconsistent with the record of US investments elsewhere.

The explanation for the steep relative decline of US investments in South America is not that American capital has failed to focus on the region. New US investments *have* continued to go to South America, but even greater proportions and amounts have gone to other areas. The next

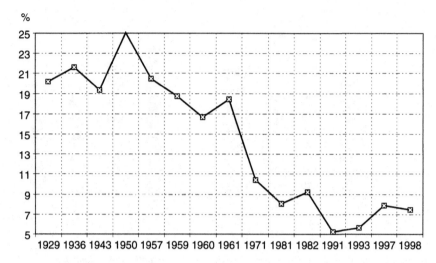

Source: US Department of Commerce, *Survey of Current Business,* various issues.

Figure 4.14 US investment (stock) in South America, 1929–98, as percentage of total US FDI.

two illustrations show how these changes have been reflected in America's worldwide investment patterns. The first (Figure 4.15) shows the global distribution of US investments in 1998, in both percentage shares and dollar-values.

This illustration clearly reflects the changes that have affected US investments. In the 1950s South America was the destination for 25 percent of US investment, but today it represents less than 8 percent. Much of this is the result of the sudden prominence of the Asia–Pacific region, in recent years the fastest-growing locale for US investments. In 1991–2 it replaced Canada, traditionally America's second-favorite investment location, and by 1998 the Asia–Pacific area held $162 billion, or 17 percent of total US investment.[46] Europe, for generations the first choice of US investors, was home to roughly $500 billion in 1998, essentially half of America's total foreign investment.

The final illustration (Figure 4.16) is perhaps the clearest evidence that the United States has not for many years been the dominant investor in South America. It covers the almost 20-year period from 1980–98, and compares the dollar value of American investments in South America with the value of *all* foreign investment in the region.

In each of the years shown, the US portion of foreign investment was substantially smaller than total investment. This chapter has already shown

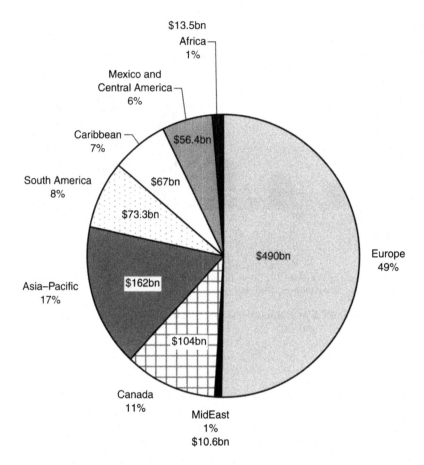

Source: Author's calculation based on *US Commerce Department Survey of Current Business,*
July 1999.

Figure 4.15 Directions of US direct investment, 1998 (total = $980 billion).

that both Brazil and Argentina consistently trade more with Europe than
with the US (Figures 4.6 and 4.7). The combination of these investment
and trade data, all of which demonstrate that the United States is *not* in
the leading position, should dispel all remaining suspicion that the US has
been economically dominant in South America.

American foreign policy and the FTAA

NAFTA has its modern origins in the mid-1980s, a period when the future
of GATT was in doubt, and when Canada and Mexico, to help ensure

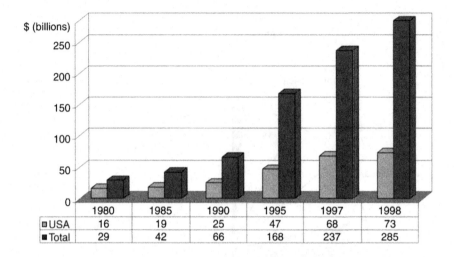

$ (billions)	1980	1985	1990	1995	1997	1998
▣ USA	16	19	25	47	68	73
▪ Total	29	42	66	168	237	285

Source: South America totals in *UN, World Investment Report,* 1999, Table B.3; US data in
        Survey of Current Business, 1981–99.

Figure 4.16 Value of US investment, compared to total foreign investment in South
        America, 1980–98.

their futures, sought a formal trade arrangement with the United States.
In the first case, with Canada, "free trade" proposals have come from both
sides of the border since the nineteenth century (one was in force from
1854–66), and in the modern era, NAFTA was preceded by several concrete bilateral accomplishments. An early step was the Canada–US pact on
cars and car parts in 1965, and 1989 brought their landmark "Canada–US
Free Trade Agreement." After that, in the lead-up to NAFTA, the driving
force for Ottawa was mainly "to cement trading practices ... already
defined by the FTA."[47]

The same idea – to "cement practices" – also fits the circumstances that
brought Mexico to the NAFTA table, and which encouraged the United
States to give it a place there. The aim, both in Mexico and the United
States, was to solidify and give added legitimacy to the economic reforms
Mexico had haltingly begun in 1983, when Miguel de la Madrid became
President. His successor, the later-discredited Carlos Salinas de Gortari,
went further, and sought a way to "lock in" the reforms.[48] NAFTA provided the way: after 150 years of Mexico's mistrustful and often bitter dealings with the US, Salinas proposed to President Bush in 1990 that Mexico
join with the US in a formal free trade agreement.[49] His widely-
acknowledged goal was the stability and predictability that hopefully
would come from improved economic conditions in Mexico:

to provide ... investors with guarantees of continuity of economic policy and access to the US market through an ironclad agreement with Washington. NAFTA, it was hoped, would satisfy both requirements.[50]

For the United States, however, trade and economics was never the main issue; the US goal in NAFTA was *always political and strategic.* This was especially true regarding Mexico, as several prominent economists frankly pointed out – though there is an irony in saying that. The irony is that it fell to economists, rather than specialists in foreign policy or national security, to make this most fundamental political point. In an article aptly subtitled "It's Foreign Policy, Stupid," Paul Krugman reminded Americans of Mexico's national security relationship to the United States:

Not that long ago U.S. intelligence analysts worried that a Mexico hammered by the debt crisis and plunging oil prices might become a radicalized national security nightmare. The friendly neighbor it has instead become is like a State Department dream come true.[51]

In the NAFTA debate in 1993 that drew so much American attention, economics should have been a minor issue, and never the main point. The reason was that for generations before NAFTA was even dreamed of, the US already dominated the foreign trade and investment profiles of both Canada and Mexico. Again, economist Krugman put it well: "The United States and Mexico have already moved most of the way to free trade in advance of NAFTA." The same was true in Canada, as I have already pointed out. In 1985, for example, four years *before* the US–Canada free trade agreement, 86 percent of Canada's imports, and 75 percent of its exports, were with the United States.

The Clinton Administration's misleading claim – that NAFTA would produce significant US gains in employment – was largely in response to Ross Perot's famous and false warning that American jobs would experience a "giant sucking sound." That led to much overselling and hyperbole about prospective US economic gains, and just three years later the Clinton administration essentially conceded as much.[52] The central truth about NAFTA, however, was well put by another economist, who was also a prominent NAFTA advocate: "*The primary objective of US policy toward Mexico has always been to assure maximum social stability. ... Greater prosperity also reinforces stability, hence NAFTA.*"[53]

That, after all, is the main point about NAFTA's relationship to American national security. It has helped to reinforce the enviable strategic position of the United States: a great power whose extensive land borders, with Canada and Mexico, are now more secure than ever before. The Canadian border has long symbolized near-total security and predictability,[54] but the same could not be said for Mexico. NAFTA's essentially *political* contribution is its impact on Mexico's capacity to resolve its long-term internal problems – principally of an economic and social nature – in ways that can ultimately affect American security.

That substantial political accomplishment brings us back to the question raised at the outset of this chapter: "Why did the United States launch its 'Free Trade for the Americas' initiative in the first place"? Any national security gains that realistically could be attributed to the FTAA would not be of the same order of magnitude as those brought about by NAFTA. Quite the opposite: if the US were to pursue energetically its FTAA goal, it would also intensify two foreign policy headaches: one centered on Brazil, stemming from its commitment to MERCOSUR, and the other in Asia, which will be dealt with in the next chapter.

Brazil's commitment to MERCOSUR, as I pointed out earlier, is strongly tied to its political and economic self-image, and has been tested repeatedly by recurring economic tensions with Argentina, Brazil's main MERCOSUR partner. Those tensions flared up very seriously in 1999, in the wake of Brazil's currency devaluation (which made Brazil's exports to Argentina "cheaper," and Argentina's exports to Brazil more expensive), and similar problems are predictable in the future.[55] Nevertheless, in spite of those past and altogether likely future problems, it is extremely unlikely that Brazil – in order to smooth the way for a US-inspired Free Trade Area for the Americas – will give up on its MERCOSUR commitment.[56]

The principal reason, even aside from Brazil's perception of the US as its "competitor" for hemispheric influence, is that it has little economic incentive to look favorably on the FTAA. For many other developing and newly-industrializing nations (Chile and Singapore come quickly to mind), the prospect of improved access to the American market draws them to seek "free trade" agreements with the US. For two main reasons, however, that lure does not apply to Brazil. The first is that aside from possibly-larger exports of citrus products to a US market that presumably would be more open in an FTAA (Brazil is the world's largest producer of frozen orange juice), there is not much else Brazil might supply. After all, in 1999 Brazil ranked only 15th among exporters to the already quite open and competitive US market – well below *all* the Asian NICs, and even below the Philippines.[57] Consequently, while it would be nice to sell more orange juice to the Americans, there are few other opportunities, either in new products, or in greater quantities of traditional ones. Coffee consumption, after all, can only be expanded so far, even in the US.

The second factor is Brazil's well-grounded worry that under an FTAA, *imports from the US* would represent a formidable challenge to Brazil's highly-protected economy. "Our industry may be wiped out by US industry," cautioned a Brazilian manufacturers' association in 1999: "the Americans are much more competitive, not only in industry but also in agriculture."[58] Those sentiments precisely echo President Cardoso's warning in 1997 that the US has "the potential to destroy Brazil's industrial base." Views like that are hardly consistent with the model the United States expects will characterize a Western hemisphere "Free Trade" agreement (and which have made Chile's low-tariff and export-promotion policies such a favorite in Washington). Nor are they consistent with the low-tariff goals proclaimed by the Treaty of Asuncion, when it established MERCOSUR in 1991.

Those attitudes recall instead Brazilian views during the 1960s and 1970s, a period when Brazil's intense political nationalism reinforced its high tariff, import-substitution economic policies. A similar approach was followed by South Korea and some others in Asia in those years, but with an important difference: the Asians simultaneously undertook very strong export promotion measures. Brazil, however, did not, and even in much more recent times, the import-substitution model still resonates strongly among its leaders. At the end of 1999, for example, when MERCOSUR was severely strained by its intra-regional economic tensions, there was much talk of a need to start over, to "re-launch" MERCOSUR. At that point, Foreign Minister Lampreia offered the following prescription, which fairly reeked of the old "make it here" syndrome:

> I believe that what we also have to aim for is a greater integration in the productive process. Thought is being given, for example, to refrain from making a shoe in one [MERCOSUR] country or in the other, but rather to integrate, and make one part of the shoe in one [MERCOSUR] country and another part in the other [MERCOSUR] country. *Industrial complementation.* This would assist us in gaining a stronger international position.[59]

That pattern of thinking, along with the results of Brazil's earlier experiments with buy-local, import-substitution policies, led to the sad conclusion expressed in 1999 by Senator Roberto Campos, a former Brazilian Cabinet Minister and Ambassador: "My generation failed to launch Brazil on the path to sustainable development."[60]

The full weight and intensity of Brazil's commitment to MERCOSUR became very public in late 1996. Prominent newspapers in London and New York revealed that the first empirical analysis of MERCOSUR had been completed, under the auspices of the World Bank, but it had been suppressed, and its author silenced, both at Brazil's insistence.[61] The Bank's senior trade economist (Alexander Yeats) had prepared the study, but Brazil attacked it as his "personal opinion"; labeled its substance "totally flawed"; and insisted it "not be published under the auspices of the bank." What led to this remarkable, and as it turned out, revealing, turn of events? The answer was in the study's main query, which since Viner's time has been the central and time-honored question about every effort in economic cooperation: is it trade-creating or trade diverting?

Although the full text of the study (provocatively titled "Does Mercosur's

Trade Performance Raise Concerns about the Effects of Regional Trade Arrangements?") was suppressed for many months, its central finding was clear. MERCOSUR had indeed expanded Brazilian–Argentine trade, but because *MERCOSUR had diverted trade from lower-cost producers*, those "gains" had come at the expense of both nations' economic efficiency and welfare.

After some internal turmoil at the Bank over the censorship issue, the report was ultimately released several months later. The published version included findings and qualifications that may or may not have been in the original, but which made it clear that, at least for Brazil, MERCOSUR was to be understood in *political* as well as economic terms. For example, the study included a statement – without explanation – that economic gains *alone* might not be the whole purpose of a regional *economic* effort. Likewise, the study's "Summary" stressed that it "does not comment on the many other possible effects . . . such as *benefits from political cooperation [or] enhancing the credibility of reform strategies.*" Finally, it added that MERCOSUR'S legitimate "other benefits" could include "*enhanced negotiating power and better credibility for the members' general economic reform programs* [and] the possibility of achieving otherwise unattainable economies of scale."

All of the above represent transparently obvious *political* wrappings, related only distantly to the customs union model on which MERCOSUR is allegedly based. Nevertheless, even in its published form, the World Bank study contained so many other phrases about MERCOSUR in practice ("clearly discomforting," "another disturbing pattern," "the evidence . . . is both compelling and disturbing") that the author's overall and ultimately negative evaluation could not be missed. Its central conclusion is to the point, and worth repeating here:

> The changing trade patterns analyzed in this study suggest that Mercosur was not internationally competitive . . . domestic producers were re-orienting exports to local markets in order to charge the higher prices associated with the most restrictive trade barriers . . . *consumers in Mercosur's internal markets are being denied access to higher quality and lower priced goods due to discriminatory trade barriers* . . . the quality produced (within Mercosur) . . . continues to be much lower and prices much higher than in other producing countries.[62]

The story of this World Bank study, including Brazil's efforts to suppress it or to strongly attenuate its findings, has two meanings for us. The most obvious is that the study of MERCOSUR found that indeed it reflected important trade-diverting problems, of the sort that may be expected in any effort in regional economic cooperation.[63] That conclusion was echoed by another prominent trade specialist at the World Bank. Commenting about the internal World Bank uproar surrounding the Yeats study, he conceded that "it's easy to get overly enthusiastic" about regional free trade agreements, because "they might confer significant benefits, *but there are also very significant dangers.*"[64] That was precisely the conclusion of the previous chapter, when Europe's regionalism was discussed. Chapter 3 stressed two points worth recalling: the extent to which Europe increasingly trades with itself, and that its economies and products are less internationally "competitive" than they might otherwise be.

The second meaning of the World Bank story is the warning it provides to the US of Brazil's very clear and very firm commitment to MERCOSUR. Since Brazil is extremely unlikely to give up on its commitment, that means that in connection with the FTAA–MERCOSUR issue, the US and Brazil are on a collision course. American policy needs therefore to ask whether the potential gains from the FTAA are worth the near-certainty that South America's largest nation will become even more distrustful of United States foreign policy aims than it already is. Since there is no overriding US national security goal involved, as there was in connection with NAFTA, the question then turns on the extent of American economic interests in South America. But as this chapter has already shown, while those interests are substantial, they do not rise to the first rank, and in relative terms they are declining. The 30-year record of US trade with South America's two largest economies revealed that the US is not their principal trade partner, nor is it their principal investor. Moreover, in terms of America's total trade, even the broader region of South America as a whole represents just *eight percent* of America's total trade, and an even smaller proportion of its investments.

If, however, the United States continues to press ahead with its FTAA goal, in the face of such a relatively small economic stake, that action will certainly send a signal to nations in other world regions. Intentionally or not, it will signal that America's long post-war commitment to a global trade regime – as now reflected in the WTO – has moved to a lower place than before on the US agenda. Asia in particular will be affected, because to date that is the one major global region which so far has not yet become involved with the "appeals" of regionalism. Yet there is evidence, to which we will now turn, that Asia's exclusion from those developments is now ending. In May, 2000, Japan, which had for the entire post-war period remained committed to a global trade regime, made the first public and direct policy shift in that direction. Japan's steps were accompanied by similar signs from both Korea and Singapore, and there is a strong likelihood that others may soon follow. In the following chapter we will deal with those developments, which are liable to have a profound impact on the post-war international order.

Notes

1 Cardoso interview with Argentine newspaper *La Nacion*, 12 December, 1999, in FBIS (Foreign Broadcast Information Service) 12 December, 1999.
2 "A Momentous Debate," *Jornal do Brasil*, 11 May, 1997, in FBIS, 12 May. Similar views were expressed by Industry and Finance Minister Dornelles on *Rede Globo Television*, in FBIS, 13 May, and Foreign Minister Lampreia, in the *Financial Times*, 14 May, 1997.
3 Foreign Minister Lampreia in *Gazeta Mercantil* (São Paulo), 23 December, 1999, in FBIS, 23 December, 1999.
4 *São Paulo Agencia Estado*, 13 January, 2000, in FBIS, 13 January, 2000.
5 Kenneth MacKay in Brasilia, quoted by *Correio Brazilense*, 26 August, 1999, in FBIS, 26 August, 1999. At an FTAA conference in Toronto, MacKay again said Congress would not vote fast track before the next Presidential election, but insisted it was not essential (*O Estado de São Paulo*, 2 November, 1999, in FBIS, 2 November, 1999).
6 *Jornal do Brasil*, 27 October, 1999 in FBIS, 27 October, 1999.
7 Brazil has a population of 172 million (the world's 5th largest); a land area almost equal to the US; and a $1 trillion GDP economy (slightly less than Italy) that represents 70 percent of MERCOSUR's GDP and 80 percent of its manufacturing output.
8 A good statement of the US–Brazil situation, by an empathetic close observer of Brazil, is in R. Roett (ed.), *MERCOSUR: Regional Integration, World Markets*, Boulder and London, Lynne Rienner, 1999, especially Chapter 8.
9 See "Brazil Upset by Overtures to Neighbour," *Financial Times*, 22 August, 1997.
10 Jose Sarney, "Menem's Ill-Advised Moves within Mercosur," *La Nacion* (Buenos Aires), 12 November, 1999, in FBIS, 12 November, my emphasis. At the time, Sarney was Chairman of the (Brazilian) Senate's Committee on Foreign Relations and Defense.
11 Throughout 1999, the media in both nations was filled with inflammatory accounts of their roiled relations. As an Argentine newspaper remarked in early 2000, "the fact is that the devaluation ... brought the [MERCOSUR] integration process to a grinding halt. ... Tension has eased of late, but relations with Brazil are still far from optimal" (*El Cronista* [Buenos Aires], 17 January, 2000, in FBIS, 17 January).
12 Roett, *ibid.*, p. 111.
13 This is clearly the view, based on his long and close experience, of L. E. Harrison in *The Pan-American Dream*, New York, Basic Books, 1997, p. 141. He was for 13 years the director of US AID missions in several Latin American nations, and has written several excellent books on the region's economies. Roett, *ibid.*, p. 114, acknowledges that *Itamarati* is "inbred," and that others find it pompous.
14 R. E. Feinberg (a former White House official who attended the meeting), in *Summitry of the Americas*, Washington, Institute for International Economics, 1997, p. 141, cited by Roett, p. 114.
15 From Barshefsky's Senate testimony, 29 January, 1997, in Roett, p. 116 (my emphasis).
16 In the President's words, "With 160 million consumers, Brazil is one of today's biggest emerging markets" (*The New York Times*, 21 April, 1995).
17 For more on the Kissinger view, see Chapter 1, this volume.
18 Daley's prediction was reported by the Brazilian economic newspaper *Gazeta Mercantil* on 27 February, 2000 (in FBIS, 28 February). In July, 2000, his

prediction ironically was confirmed when the election-year platform of the *Republican* Party pledged to extend NAFTA to all of South America.

19 Good discussions are in Harrison, *op. cit.*, pp. 14–16, and A. Fishlow, "The Mature Neighbor Policy," in Joseph Grunwald (ed.), *Latin America and the World Economy*, London, Sage Publications, 1978, pp. 30–7.

20 All trade data in this paragraph is from IMF, *Direction of Trade Statistics Yearbook*, 1999. Population data from Central Intelligence Agency (CIA), *World Factbook*, 1999. Available at http://www.odci.gov/cia/publications/factbook/

21 Fishlow, *ibid.*, p. 44.

22 Mark Falcoff, in the *Financial Times*, 7 May, 1997. Falcoff is the author of four books and many articles on the region, and was the Latin America specialist for the US Senate Foreign Relations Committee.

23 Edward Schumacher, *The Wall Street Journal*, 7 May, 1997, and Ambassador Charlene Barshefsky, before the House Ways and Means Committee, 18 March, 1997. My emphasis.

24 What *is* attributable to NAFTA is the continuing high rate of growth of Mexican imports from the US, so much so that in 1997 Mexico surpassed Japan to become America's second largest market. Only Canada buys more from the US.

25 Claude Barfield, "Regionalism and U.S. Trade Policy", p. 148, in Bhagwati and Panagariya, *The Economics of Preferential Trade Agreements*, Washington, AEI Press, 1996. Barfield adds that because "The United States is the destination for only 20 percent of Brazil's exports and 9 percent of Argentina's exports," both countries have reason to favor MERCOSUR over the hemispheric FTA.

26 Fishlow, *ibid.*, p. 30. My emphasis.

27 H. Bailey and A. Nasatir, *Latin America: The Development of its Civilization*, Englewood Cliffs, Prentice-Hall, 1968, pp. 755–7. Emphasis added to each reference to "Latin America" in this and the other excerpts in this paragraph.

28 M. Kryzanek, *U.S.–Latin American Relations*, New York, Praeger, 1990, pp. 8, 12.

29 W. Keylor, *The Twentieth Century World, An International History*, New York, Oxford University Press, 1992, p. 216.

30 Robert J. Alexander, *Today's Latin America*, New York and Washington, Praeger, 2nd Edition, revised, 1968, p. 240.

31 In the remainder of this paragraph, mid-1970s data for investment in Argentina, Brazil and Mexico, are drawn from United Nations, Economic and Social Council, *Transnational Corporations in World Development*, 1978, Table III-49. The same table was reproduced, with no change, in Isaiah Frank, *Foreign Enterprise in Developing Countries*, Johns Hopkins University Press, 1980, Table 4, p. 14.

32 United Nations, *External Financing in Latin America* (E/CN.12/649/Rev.1), p. 14. My emphasis.

33 Fishlow, p. 31. See also R. Grosse, *Multinationals in Latin America*, London, Routledge, 1989, p. 16.

34 Grosse, p. 12.

35 UN, *External Financing in Latin America, ibid.*, p. 19

36 L. Whitehead, "Britain's Economic Relations with Latin America," in J. Grunwald (ed.), *Latin America and World Economy, op. cit.*, p. 91.

37 *ibid.* My emphasis.

38 The same pattern applies when Venezuela is seen as a portion of US investments in *South America*: it represented just 7 percent of US FDI (United States' Foreign Direct Investment) in South America in 1998, down from a high of almost 50 percent in the 1950s.

39 The few exceptions, both in trade and investment, were in parts of Central Europe, where Germany was Britain's main rival, and in US-dominated Mexico

and Cuba (D. Platt, *Latin America and British Trade, 1806–1914*, London, A. and C. Block, 1972, Chapter VI).

40   *External Financing in Latin America, op. cit.*, p. 23.

41   The percentage-shares for Western Europe–US investment in Argentina in 1980, 1985, and 1989 were, respectively, 53–42; 49–46; and 48–45 (UN, UNCTAD, World Investment Directory, Vol. IV, *Latin America and the Caribbean*, 1994, Table 10, p. 36).

42   United Nations Conference on Trade and Development (UNCTAD), *World Investment Report 1991, The Triad in Foreign Direct Investment*, United Nations, New York, 1991.

43   *ibid.*, Table II, p. 54.

44   UN, *World Investment Directory, 1994, op. cit.*, p. 162.

45   Inter-American Development Bank and Instituto de Relaciones Europeo-latinoamericanas (IRELA), *Foreign Direct Investment in Latin America and the Caribbean*, 1999, Madrid, January 2000, citing Section 4.3, "European Investment in Latin America and the Caribbean" (available at http://www.lanic.utexas.edu/~sela/eng_docs/spdi1-2000-2.htm).

46   The US decision in May 2000 to formalize permanent trade ties with China is also expected to facilitate new investment there, and will accordingly much increase the portion of US FDI in the Pacific region.

47   *Financial Times*, 6 June, 1994.

48   The phrase, to "lock in" Mexico's reforms, was widely used in discussions of NAFTA. An early example was *Financial Times*, 9 June, 1992; another was in W. Orme, "Myths Versus Facts," *Foreign Affairs*, November–December, 1993, p. 11, who argued that NAFTA would provide "an intangible comfort" to outside investors, "knowing that Mexico was somehow legally linked to the United States" (p. 5).

49   Mexico began exploring a free trade agreement with the US in early 1990, and formally proposed it to President Bush in September. For a well-informed account of Mexico's trade-strategy history from the 1980s on, see N. Lustig, "Mexico's Integration Strategy with North America," in C. F. Bradford, Jr, *Strategic Options for Latin America in the 1990s*, Inter-American Development Bank, Washington, 1992. For good discussions of the background of political attitudes and economic conditions in Mexico that brought about the radical decision to seek tighter ties with the US, see Harrison, *The Pan American Dream, op. cit.*, and J. Heath, "Economic Sovereignty in Mexico," in Hoebing, Weintraub, and Baer, (eds), Washington, DC, The Center for Strategic and International Studies, 1996. Heath's chapter, while sympathetic to Mexico, does not ignore its history of political corruption and grossly unequal income distribution; it is an excellent treatment of the wrenching changes already taken and still needed.

50   Jorge G. Castaneda, "Can NAFTA Change Mexico?" *Foreign Affairs*, September–October, 1993, p. 73.

51   "The Uncomfortable Truth About NAFTA," *Foreign Affairs*, November–December, 1993, p. 18.

52   It was required to report to Congress on the extent to which NAFTA had brought the US economic gains, which were now seen as "modest." This was also the conclusion of several independent studies, which concluded that on balance, NAFTA was neither a big job-loser nor a significant job-gainer (see "Experts' View of Nafta's Economic Impact: It's a Wash," in *The Wall Street Journal*, 17 June, 1997). On the other hand, the political benefits I have stressed here were precisely those emphasized by Treasury Secretary Rubin: "A healthy growing economy in Mexico is . . . very much in the national economic

and security interests of the US" (quoted in "Modest US Gains Seen From NAFTA," *Financial Times*, 13 July, 1997).

53 S. Weintraub, "NAFTA and U.S. Economic Sovereignty," in *NAFTA and Sovereignty, op. cit.*, p. 150. He preceded that conclusion with this remark: "The United States discovered long ago that having a poor, low-wage country next door limited its control over who enters the country. There is much rhetoric about regaining control over the U.S. border, but the truth is that this control never really existed. This became evident in 1995 as Mexican incomes declined and incentives to emigrate to the United States rose" (p. 148).

54 It is worth recalling that in 1968, when the USSR was at the height of its relative power and influence, Charles de Gaulle of France briefly encouraged Quebec's independence. That raised the possibility of a divided Canada, at least one of whose parts would have represented an appealing target of opportunity to a then-adventurous Moscow.

55 "Brazil continues to devalue, and nobody can compete with the *real* at two to the dollar," was a typical Argentine complaint in early 1999 ("Brazilian Turmoil Threatens Argentine Car Exports," *The Wall Street Journal*, 1 February, 1999). Tensions reached a crescendo the following year as dozens of Argentine manufacturers and branches of major international firms moved to Brazil ("Argentina Cries Foul as Choice Employers Beat a Path Next Door," *ibid.*, 2 May, 2000). See also "Brazil Tie to Argentina at Breaking Point," *The Wall Street Journal*, 28 July, 1999.

56 This point was made early in MERCOSUR's history by Winston Fritsch, "Brazil's Trade Strategy for the 1990s," p. 148, in Bradford, *op. cit.*

57 US Commerce Department, *Foreign Trade Highlights*, 1999, Table 11.

58 Roberto Macedo, former President of Brazil's National Association of Electro-Electronic Manufacturers, quoted in Estado Sao Paulo, 1 July, 1999, in FBIS, 4 July, 1999. He added that European industrial products cause less concern to Brazil, because "some of our products are cheaper than European ones."

59 Interview with Brazil's Foreign Minister in *El Cronista* (Buenos Aires), 10 December, 1999, in FBIS, 13 December, 1999. Emphasis added. An economic approach called "Industrial complementation" is precisely what the ASEAN states in Southeast Asia tried as a policy in the 1970s and 1980s, and is discussed in two articles by R. B. Suhartono, "Basic Framework for ASEAN Industrial Co-Operation," and "ASEAN Approach to Industrial Co-Operation," in *Indonesia Quarterly*, Vol. XIV, Nos. 1, 4, 1986. The plan called for each ASEAN member to have its particular "national" industrial mission. Singapore, for example, was to produce diesel engines for the group; Thailand would produce soda ash for the group; while Indonesia was to be responsible for large-scale fertilizer production. Not surprisingly, this approach came to nothing.

60 See his lengthy interview in the *Financial Times*, 18 March, 1999.

61 The first pubic references to the leaked report were in *The Wall Street Journal*, 23 October, and the *Financial Times*, 24 October, 1996; for Brazil's campaign to suppress its findings, see M. O'Grady, "Brazil Wants a World Bank Critic of Mercosur Silenced," in *The Wall Street Journal*, 22 November, 1996.

62 A. Yeats, "Does Mercosur's Trade Performance Raise Concerns About the Effects of Regional Trade Arrangements?" Washington, The World Bank, February, 1997, Policy Research Working Paper 1729, p. 30.

63 One very brief and unpersuasive commentary *was* critical of the Yeats study. In addition to arguing that "statistics" should not be so heavily relied on (but what other measure *should* be used to gauge economic performance?), it concluded that the trade diversion found in the World Bank study was *not*

important; that its focus on the auto industry was misplaced; and that ultimately MERCOSUR's protectionist barriers would go away. See E. Hudgins, "Mercosur Gets a 'Not Guilty' on Trade Diversion," *The Wall Street Journal*, 21 March, 1997.

64 L. Winters, chief of the bank's international trade division, in *The Wall Street Journal*, "South American Trade Pact is Under Fire," 23 October, 1996.

5   Will the geese fly?

In the summer of 1962, when I first visited Tokyo, there were three Japanese economists I was anxious to meet, since each was involved with issues of Asian economic cooperation. The first was Kyoshi Kojima, one of a handful who even then were working on Pacific-area free trade issues. Another was Dr Saburo Okita, then Director of Japan's Economic Planning Bureau, and one of the intellectual godfathers of Japan's post-war economic recovery. Years later, as Foreign Minister, he was instrumental in the steps that led to APEC. Finally, in Bangkok, I met with Professor Hiroshi Kitamura, who as research chief at "ECAFE" (the United Nations Asian economic headquarters),[1] was doing some of the spade work on Asian regionalism. They were the originators of the concept with which this chapter is concerned, and a few words about each are warranted.

Kojima and Okita in particular were closely associated with the "flying geese" model, a term introduced in 1935 by Japanese economist Kaname Akamatsu. It deals mainly with developmental stages in newly-industrializing countries, but its closely-related second meaning, in the post-war period, suggests a V-shaped ("flying geese") regional pattern of Asian economies.[2] Japan is alone at its head; in the next rank are Korea and Taiwan (and probably Singapore and Hong Kong); they are followed next by the ASEAN countries and China; and bringing up the rear are Asia's least-developed economies. Because of its similarity with the "co-prosperity" label of pre-war days, "flying geese" has never of course been formally endorsed by Japan's leaders as a post-war model. Nevertheless, it retains its power in Japanese thought, and as we will see in this chapter, the image does seem related to some contemporary developments.

Professor Kojima, who was at Hitotsubashi University, and who was the first of the post-war economists to popularize the flying geese imagery, had concentrated on issues of Asian economics since at least the early 1960s. His studies on Japan's relationship to the concept of a Pacific-region free trade area grew from that work, and as early as 1968, he edited a joint volume called *Pacific Trade and Development*.[3] Even now, some of his writings are well recalled, and are summarized in his 1971 book, *Japan and a Pacific Free Trade Area*.[4]

Hiroshi Kitamura's work on Asian economic cooperation probably began even earlier. He had left a teaching post at a Japanese university for Bangkok in 1957, and in 1961 he had already been responsible for the publication of an ECAFE study called "The Scope for Regional Economic Cooperation in the Far East." In 1964, in another ECAFE study, he helped introduce the concept of "harmonized" regional economic development in East and Southeast Asia.[5]

Okita was the most senior of the three, and the one with the longest roots in the subject. The first of his post-war studies on Asian economic cooperation was undertaken for ECAFE, when he served as one of its three "wise men" on Asian regionalism. Their work – the "Report of the Consultative Group of Experts on Regional Economic Cooperation in Asia" – was completed in December, 1961.[6]

I say his "post-war studies," because Okita's interest in Asian regional economic cooperation began *before* the Pacific war. As a 1937 electrical engineering graduate of Tokyo University, he was selected in 1938 to join the private school ("Showa-juku") that Prince Konoe had established, in order to train promising young men. Konoe had been very prominent in Japan since World War I (he attended the Paris Peace Conference), and from 1937–41 he served three times as Japan's Prime Minister.

The school Okita attended was part of Konoe's elite policy-study group ("Showa Kenkyukai"), that focused on Japan's "peace" program for Asia, and it was there that Okita heard Konoe's statement on the "Creation of a New Order in Eastern Asia."[7] It introduced the young engineering graduate, post-war economic planner, and eventual Foreign Minister to the world of international politics. Some have even identified Okita as the principle post-war popularizer of the "flying geese" model.[8] His own words are relevant: although he was at the school for only a few months before being transferred to China, Okita later said "his experience there had a lifelong impact on his later life."[9]

I recount this early background to emphasize two main points. The first is that Asian and Pacific regionalism has long and deep roots that are clearly traceable to Japanese thinking. As Russell Fifield wrote in 1981, "In the sum total of study and political activities [on regionalism] the Japanese are in the vanguard."[10] The second point is that regionalism's post-war resurfacing in the 1960s, as Chapter 1 has already pointed out, was part of a worldwide attraction to the concept that stemmed directly from the EC's evident success. In that era, regional "integration" was all the rage,[11] and the reason, as Kojima himself acknowledged in 1972, was Europe's experience:

> The establishment of the European Economic Community was a major event of the 1960s ... [it] represents a formidable agglomeration of economic wealth and power ... [it] will continue and strengthen its inward-looking policies, intensifying intra-regional development and raising the degree of its self-sufficiency which are

the purposes of the integration. *Now, which free world countries are left outside the Eurobloc? They are mostly Pacific basin countries. . . . Is it not logical that these Pacific basin countries should promote their economic integration, following the successful example of the European Community?. . .*[12]

These concerns, about Europe's tendencies to be "self-sufficient and inward-looking," inclined some Japanese to continue their interest in regionalism well into the 1990s, but that interest did not spill over to the government. As an official policy-related issue, the concept of regionalism was largely set aside by the mid-1960s. Without ever formally or completely rejecting the idea, Japan turned away from any temptation it might have had to follow a specifically Asian policy, and aimed instead to pursue what was called at the time its "all points" diplomacy: a policy in which no one region would be emphasized.

In Japan's post-war history, this shift is symbolized by Prime Minister Ikeda's time in office, a period when Japan's "income doubling" goal was put in place, and when Japan's "low posture" policy, associated with Prime Minister Sato, was adopted. Along with the effort to "separate politics from economics," these were all part of a deliberate Japanese stance to seek or accept no leadership position in Asia, and certainly nowhere else. In those years, critics regularly complained that the definition of Japan's foreign policy was that it *had* no foreign policy. It was a period when Japanese opinion polls, which regularly asked "Which nation do you most admire?" or "Which nation do you think Japan should emulate?" found that large percentages most often named Switzerland!

Of course there were good reasons for Japan's approach. As early as 1955, Japan had been enrolled in GATT, which committed it to the world of open, multilateral, and non-discriminatory trade (at least for most manufactured goods), and by 1964 Tokyo gained OECD membership, thereby signifying its status as a major industrial nation. In those same years, Tokyo hosted the Olympics; inaugurated the *Shinkansen* ("bullet train"); and entered the massive post-war economic boom symbolized by GATT's "Kennedy Round." The GATT "Round" ran from 1964–7, and achieved substantial tariff cuts (over half exceeded 50 percent, and the average was nearly 40 percent). The mid-1960s was also the period of America's increasing involvement in Vietnam, not an easy time for Japan in its role as America's principal Asian ally. Tokyo obligated itself to not openly differ from the US in its Asian policy, but instead to follow the path of high economic growth and prosperity – always under the protective wing of the United States.

In that environment, an era in which Japan (and many others in the industrialized and developing world) began the trajectory of high, and often export-led, economic growth, Japan's "no involvement" approach was in no way irrational. Any thoughts of an overtly "Asian" policy were put to the side, and in the view of Robert Scalapino (one of America's most prominent specialists on Japan), that was precisely where they should stay. Scalapino, writing a decade later, acknowledged that the continuing "Asian versus Western" identity-dilemma was powerful and real in Japan,[13] and that the appeals of an "Asian" policy had deep roots. But he concluded, nevertheless, that "Pan-Asianism, *still a dream for some Japanese*, is highly unrealistic":

> Japan would not be in a position to make regionalism the primary focus of its foreign policies, economic or political. The nature of its development has made *Japan one of the few societies of the contemporary world with truly global interests*. Its future hinges partly on the emergence of a new economic internationalism. ... Exclusively or primarily regional policies would not serve either of these requirements ...[14]

Those words, especially their emphasis on Japan as one of the few truly globally-involved economies, are as true and applicable today as they were in 1977. If anything, they have been reinforced by the secular changes that have transformed the global economy since the 1970s. Those changes have made an Asian "regional" policy even less *objectively* correct for Japan today than in the 1970s, and to list the reasons is also to identify the interrelated features of what has come to be called globalization:

- the explosion in foreign investment;
- the worldwide diffusion of technology;
- the generation-skipping, global spread of productive capacity;
- the decline of the costs of distance, as a result both of sea-borne containerization and the remarkable expansion of airfreight; and
- suffusing all of the above, the instant movement of money and information.

The results are visible to consumers all over the world. Computer parts may come from China, Malaysia, or Ireland; shoes and textiles may come as readily from South Asia as from South America; and major industrial firms – themselves often globally decentralized – are linked instantaneously with suppliers everywhere. Together, all these factors have enormously reduced the economic consequences of physical distance, and reduced even further the previously strong economic attractions of geographic and regional proximity. The policy-consequence is that Scalapino's 1977 prediction – that a "new economic internationalism" would make "regional policies" unsuitable for Japan – is objectively more true than ever before.

Japan changes course

Nevertheless, something *has* happened, and something *has* changed, especially in Japan, that runs counter to all those forces, and it promises to accelerate and reinforce the revival of global regionalism. The change became official in May, 2000, with the publication by MITI (the Ministry of Trade and International Industry) of Japan's yearly "White Paper" on trade. Its centerpiece was the announcement that Japan had reversed 50 years of policy, and had formally moved *away* from the single, multilateral, and global system of world trade and economic interaction to which Tokyo had adhered since the end of the American occupation. Yet the shift had been strongly hinted at since early 1999: first when the head of JETRO, the leading foreign trade association, announced "a change of the Japanese government's attitude towards regional agreements"; and then when the 1999 MITI White Paper put its imprimatur, for the first time, on regional trade arrangements.

In February 1999, for example, the JETRO Director acknowedged that while "Japan's fundamental position was that such agreements are against the spirit of the GATT . . . there is a change":

> Tokyo had suddenly begun to feel somewhat alone in its opposition to the regional deals. . . . We cannot prevail alone. We have to face reality . . . 26 of the world's 30 main economies were or would be partners in such accords – the European Union, the North American Free Trade Agreement and the Association of Southeast Asian Nations' planned Free Trade Agreement (AFTA).[15]

MITI's 1999 White Paper went further than that. It pointedly noted that "some 90 percent of the WTO's 134 members belong to regional trade integration systems, and those without membership of such regional systems, *such as Japan, South Korea and Hong Kong, are in a minority*."[16] Its conclusion? That "Japan should work for regional trade integration in Northeast Asia."

MITI's next White Paper, in May, 2000, pulled together these hints and thoughts by stating frankly that because of the "growing interdependence between the Asian economy and Japan," Tokyo would now seek "free trade" agreements with Asian nations. Those few words, the formal linkage that MITI drew between (1) Japan's asserted "growing interdependence" with the Asian economies, and (2) Japan's decision to seek free trade agreements in the region, contained two lessons.

The first lesson was that MITI's announcement represented a culmination of trends that have long been developing, and about which this book has repeatedly cautioned. To recall those cautions is *not* to predict an early or formal institutionalized political cooperation arrangement between Japan and nations in East Asia. It is, however, to say that it will no longer be possible completely to insulate Japan's projected economic interdependence with East Asia from some forms and degrees of political coordination between the two.

The second lesson of MITI's announcement was that it provided yet another example, if more were needed, of the iron law of unintended consequences. This becomes clear when we recall Japanese attitudes towards America's revived interest in Western hemisphere regionalism. Signs of that interest surfaced in the final years of the two Reagan administrations, and were unmistakable in the Bush administration.[17] In that period, Japanese officials were openly worried about these indications of new directions in American policy, and they increasingly expressed the view that it would be difficult to expect Japan to long continue as the only major industrialized economy *not* included in regionalism's revival.

The evident vitality of its revival was reflected both in the EU's plans to intensify European integration (the outlines of what would become Maastricht were already underway), and by Washington's newly-aroused interest in some new Western hemisphere trade arrangement. In response, a number of Japan's leaders, including specifically the Prime Minister, the MITI Minister, and the most senior Foreign Ministry official, all publicly expressed their worries about the "increasingly regional focus of US trade policy."

In October, 1992, for example, the Japanese Vice Minister for Foreign Affairs told a large business and official group in San Francisco that

> questions have begun to be asked whether the United States . . . has shifted its emphasis from a global to a regional approach. . . . Utmost care is necessary in order to prevent regional integration from leading to . . . trade blocs.

A few days later, Kiichi Miyazawa, then Japan's Prime Minister, underlined the same point when he met with Canadian leaders. He urged NAFTA to be careful, because, as he said, Asian nations feared the creation of a "fortress North America." Finally, Japan's Minister for International Trade and Industry used "even stronger terms" when he told Carla Hills, the US Trade Representative, of Japan's worries.[18]

These reactions should have surprised nobody. Two years earlier, in 1990, the Tokyo correspondent of the *Wall Street Journal* reported that both the EU and the NAFTA proposal were "viewed with alarm by some Japanese as the beginning of a regional, protectionist bloc." And an influential *Keidanren* voice, commenting precisely on that point, agreed: "There is a little bit of cohesion among the nations of the Pacific Rim. Largely, they are afraid of American protectionism or European protectionism."[19] That prescient answer was affirmed a decade later in the MITI 2000 White Paper. It concluded that free trade agreements "are in line with . . . economic analysis and economic realities . . . policy attention [should] be paid to *new moves . . . in EU, NAFTA, Mercosur, etc.*"[20]

The publication of the MITI 2000 White Paper prompted a number of reports and editorials in all of Japan's leading newspapers, and their comments show that both the substance and causes behind the policy change were well understood. *Mainichi* and *Tokyo Shimbun* pointed to the previous

December's disastrous WTO meeting in Seattle as a prime factor, but *Mainichi* put Japan's policy change into a broader perspective:

> In the 1990s, moves for regional integration were observed across the world, as seen from the currency integration in the EU, the conclusion of the NAFTA, and the formation of MERCOSUR. As a result, only Japan, China, and the ROK are not involved in any regional integration schemes.

The policy lesson of Seattle, it concluded, was that "as U.S. leadership declined," multilateralism was harder to achieve, and "under such circumstances it is natural for Japan ... to conclude free trade agreements, though [it is] too little too late."[21] Similarly, *Tokyo Shimbun* perfectly described Japan's sharp policy shift, but worried at the same time that it might be over-read: "[Japan] has advocated 'multi-lateralism' since it joined GATT ... in 1955," and "in order not to cause misunderstanding that 'Japan has changed its stance to regionalism,' " Tokyo should take the initiative for a new WTO trade round.[22]

The American press, true to its pattern of covering events in Japan only when they are on the scale of the Kobe earthquake, ignored all this. Neither the *New York Times*, the *Wall Street Journal*, or the *Washington Post* reported the MITI turnaround; only the London-edited *Financial Times* did, and its account accurately described Japan's new policy as a sign of a basic post-war change. It wrote correctly that the MITI paper "highlights an emerging philosophical shift," and MITI officials did not deny the point. Quite the opposite: they acknowledged "there is a change – we realise we have to refine our position," and they argued that it stemmed in essence from four factors:

- the growth everywhere else of regionalism ("we are just doing what everyone else does");[23]
- intra-Asian trade growth, which called for special arrangements;
- WTO weaknesses also called for exploring alternatives;
- trade pacts – for example with Singapore and Korea – might encourage de-regulation and liberalization in Japan.

Nevertheless, the steps that led to the change were *not* inevitable, nor have they moved single-mindedly toward a pre-determined goal. Instead, like the crab that walks sideways and forward at the same time, Japan's movement toward regionalism has headed towards two general goals: fuller economic involvement in East Asia, and wider latitude for Japan's political initiatives in the region.[24] In these respects, Japan's new approach for the new century reverses its "low posture" and "all points" diplomacies of the mid-1960s. It aims instead to stamp East Asia's future with Japan's imprint, though not, of course, along the lines of the pre-war "Greater East Asia Co-Prosperity Sphere." That approach is far too firmly associated with the disastrous experiences of military expansionism to have any hope of contemporary support.

The shift does, however, need to be placed in the context of Japan's continuing dilemma as either an "Asian" or a "Western" nation. Consequently, while four recent developments accelerated the shift, they did not account for it. Those four developments were:

- the 1997 Asian economic collapse;
- the different US and Japanese responses to the event;
- the December, 1999 WTO debacle in Seattle;
- and not least important, the continued rivalry between the Ministry of Foreign Affairs on the one hand, and the two money ministries (MITI and Finance) on the other.[25]

All these factors facilitated the change, but the signs pointing to it were older and did not come out of the blue.

Take as one example a 1994 study of "NAFTA's Impact on Japan," published by the Woodrow Wilson Center in Washington, and prepared by a Tokyo University scholar. It reported – again correctly – that NAFTA's short-term consequences for Japan were negligible, but "if the US moves to enlarge NAFTA into WHFTA [a Western Hemisphere Free Trade Area], it could pose serious problems for Japan":

> The enclosure of Mexico alone is manageable. *But what if all of the major Latin American economies are enclosed by the United States? . . .* What can be pointed out presently is the danger that Asian regionalism will be strengthened if large-scale trade and investment diversion occurs.[26]

His findings were similar to those I encountered in Tokyo in late 1996, in my discussions with Foreign Ministry and MITI officials, and with staff members at *Keidanren* and *Nihon Keizai* (Japan's leading business federation, and Tokyo's principal economics newspaper). In those meetings, one point was emphasized by all: an acute awareness that Japan was the *only* major industrialized state not a member of any regional trade group, and the unlikelihood that status could long endure. A similar conclusion is in a recently-published study of economic regionalism in Northeast Asia: its report of MITI and Foreign Ministry interviews, in 1994, found that "all stated that Japan had no intention of creating a concrete regional economic bloc. *On the other hand, however, these officials acknowledged that some . . . regionalism was already under way in East Asia . . .*"[27]

The Asian monetary fund and Asia's reaction

Probably the clearest sign of Japan's steady interest in, and support for regional initiatives, was the brouhaha caused by Tokyo's proposal for an

"Asian Monetary Fund (AMF)." This controversy, which continues today, erupted in September, 1997, at the annual meetings of the G–7 Finance Ministers, the IMF, and the World Bank. Japan's proposal surfaced just before that, when the Asian Finance Ministers met in the immediate wake of the collapse of the Thai *baht*,[28] but it came as a surprise to both the G–7 and IMF meetings. Especially at the IMF meeting, the Japanese proposal ran into stiff and open opposition from US Deputy Secretary of the Treasury Lawrence Summers and IMF leaders.[29] They argued that an Asian Monetary Fund would needlessly complicate (read 'compete with') the IMF's global role; that it could lead to looser "conditionality" requirements for funding than those levied by the IMF; and in a related vein, that it could create problems of "moral hazard": the prospect that borrowers would delay putting their fiscal houses in order, because (or if) they believed additional funds could come from non-IMF sources.

Finance Ministry spokesmen, however, argued that in a case like Thailand, where \$20–\$30 billion in emergency funds might be needed, IMF resources might be insufficient, and could also prove too cumbersome. The central idea in their AMF proposal was to have a regional facility, to which ample resources – Japan identified a total of perhaps \$100 billion – would already have been committed, and which could disburse them more quickly, and with fewer restrictions, than normal IMF procedures might allow.[30]

The Ministry's brief was presented by Deputy Minister Eisuke Sakakibara, widely regarded at home and abroad as "Mr Yen" (for his reputed ability to influence currency values). Indeed his standing in Japan led Tokyo to nominate him in 1999 – well after his retirement – for the post of IMF Director. As expected, that effort was unsuccessful, but it was nevertheless the first time Tokyo had backed one of its own for the job, and it reflected Mr Sakakibara's continued status. More importantly, it underscores the view that Japan's AMF defeat in 1997 was a watershed, both in its relations with the US and with other Asian nations.

The reason is that the United States, in the person of Treasury representative Summers, directly rebuffed Japan, which then stood down in the face of strong and public US opposition. Sakakibara and Summers were already well known to one another, both from their earlier US–Japan negotiations, and their common backgrounds as economists. Summers had been especially prominent as a prolific and impressive Harvard Professor, and was widely regarded as a *wunderkind*. Sakakibara (who earned his PhD at the University of Michigan and also briefly taught at Harvard), had similarly enjoyed unusual and positive prominence in Japan – in part because he deviated strikingly from the "normal" model of a self-effacing Japanese bureaucrat. Moreover, in an environment already known for quick minds, both men were considered especially sharp (in an article after the event, Sakakibara called Summers a true "genius"). Finally, like Secretary of State Dean Acheson in a different era, neither man was known, as the phrase goes, "to suffer fools kindly."

The substantive issue that pitted the two against one another was of course a microcosm of their two nations' respective stands. One was Japan's emerging region-centered view, in which Tokyo had the capacity, and hopefully the legitimacy, to be Asia's voice and representative. The other was America's long-standing support for a single, multilateral system, reflected in monetary terms by the IMF – whose roots, after all, are in Bretton Woods and the world environment that was forming in 1944. Furthermore, the issue was allowed to be framed in classic zero-sum terms, in which the US/IMF position was that any change from the status quo would represent not only a significant decline in the IMF's role, but a challenge to the US-framed broader system as well. The consequence was that the AMF confrontation and its outcome were not easily forgotten, partly because the two men most directly involved may have identified personally with it. Their somewhat competitive relationship was not helped when, at one point in the discussions, Summers – in an evident jibe aimed at Sakakibara's "Mr Yen" nickname – referred to himself as "Dr Dollar."[31]

Moreover, the issue that helped lead to Japan's proposal – the Thai case – was itself was very sensitive for the United States, and it soon became clear that America's defeat of Japan's AMF proposal also significantly soured US dealings with Thailand. When Thailand's financial collapse hit in midsummer 1997, the US Treasury Department did not make emergency funds available quickly, as had been done in the case of Mexico two years earlier. Although the reason was Treasury's problems with Congress – themselves rooted in the Mexican bailout[32] – Thailand's leaders concluded the US had essentially ignored their problems. In their view, the Americans had not taken the Asian crisis seriously until Korea, a very close US military ally, also got into financial trouble.

Whatever America's internal reasons and problems, many leading Thai, in government and out, were clearly furious at the US failure to help. Their reactions led American officials in Bangkok to warn that the resulting backlash would bring trouble for the US not only in Thailand, but generally in Southeast Asia. Indeed Secretary of Defense Cohen himself later complained that "The very notion that the United States was unwilling to participate in some form ... sent the signal that perhaps the United States was pulling away."[33] That was true as far as it went, but it did not go far enough. Thai and other reactions to the financial catastrophe extended beyond foreign policy, and caused new doubts among Asian leaders about the "Washington consensus": the US and Western developmental model. Among some in Southeast Asia, new attention was focused on China and India, whose far more closed economies had avoided the crisis. As a Thai banker and government advisor put it, "We will have to think about whether it is worth it to open ourselves up as demanded by the West."[34]

Other ideas were also bruited – for example pegging the Thai *baht* (and other local currencies) to a "basket" of currencies not so dominated by the dollar, and the related possibility – as we will see in a moment – of forming a "Yen bloc." There were also suggestions that Washington's slow response was deliberate; that it represented a "calculated policy" aimed at damaging the Thai economy. At least three variations on that theme were expressed, and the mildest was voiced by a top official in Thailand's Foreign Ministry: "the United States had been a major proponent of liberalization and globalization," and was now "reaping greater benefits from it." A second and more critical theme was expressed by that same Thai banker and government advisor who questioned whether the West's model was the right one. He argued that America's inaction stemmed from more selfish motives, and said many others shared his view that "the US cannot compete with Asian countries ... *they keep suffering from high trade deficits. So they pull out this monetary scheme of destabilizing [our] currency.*"

The most extreme of the explanations was that America was racist and anti-Asian, and in the summer of 1997, that approach fell on fertile ground in Southeast Asia. Its leading voice was Malaysian Prime Minister Mahathir, who himself rose to fame on the basis of a book – *The Malay Dilemma* – that was long banned in his own country because of its anti-Chinese sentiments. A hallmark of Mahathir's tenure (he came to power in 1981) has been his public disputes with the press and governments of Britain, Australia, and the United States, all of which, he claims, are "anti-Malaysian."[35] In one instance, in the mid-1980s, he banned the Asian edition of *The Wall Street Journal*, charging that its American parent aimed to weaken his country. In another, sounding somewhat like Louis Farrakhan, the Muslim black-separatist in the United States, Mahathir wrote that whereas "tolerance is a typically Asian quality [sic] *white people in contrast are racists.*" That charge had a special irony, since Mahathir's government had sought, several years earlier, to change the program of the New York Philharmonic – because its scheduled visit to Malaysia included music by a long-dead Swiss composer who was also Jewish.

Even against that background, in the immediate wake of the Asian crisis, the Malaysian leader's extreme, and frequently sinister, criticisms of the American financial community attracted worldwide attention. New York bankers were regularly pictured as profiting from Asians' distress, and at an unforgettable point in these events, Mahathir claimed that financier George Soros in particular was part of a "Jewish agenda" that aimed to destroy Malaysia's economy.[36] "Jews are not happy to see Muslims prosper," he charged, adding that, "The Jews robbed the Palestinians of everything, but in Malaysia they could not do so, hence they do this, depress the ringgit."[37] Remarks like that led one Malaysian official who did not share Mahathir's view to hope "he would just shut up," and others to conclude that "He's Malaysia's I.B.M. – International Big Mouth."[38]

In retrospect, and in addition to the misery the Asian crisis brought to Asia's poor and middle classes, its political legacy was a revival both of anti-American sentiment and renewed interest in closer intra-Asian relations. In that respect, the crisis was a boost for Asian regionalism, and the last time that had happened was in 1988–9, when the GATT multilateral system of world trade threatened to break down. But even then, a wide body of opinion concluded that, as long as GATT was effective, proposals for regional integration, and regional "free trade areas," especially with an outside partner, were undesirable on almost all other grounds.[39] Nevertheless, despite the fact that the next decade saw substantial accomplishments under GATT, the Asian crisis breathed new life into Asian regionalism.

The main reason was the lesson that Asians drew from the stark contrast between Japan's quick and generous AMF offer, and America's initially-slow response to the crisis. The enduring nature of the legacy became clear several years later, as the region's economies improved, but the anti-US resentment generated by the financial collapse did not disappear or much decline. In Thailand, for example, the same senior Foreign Ministry official who had complained in 1997 that the US benefited from globalization, while Thailand suffered, expressed new bitterness in 2000 about America's seemingly continued unconcern with Southeast Asia. The issue that brought this into focus was the level of American representation at a UN conference, planned for Bangkok. The event prompted Thailand's Foreign Ministry to draw a pointed contrast between the US approach, and that of Japan and several others:

> The leaders of eight ASEAN countries have confirmed participation. *The Japanese prime minister will attend.* ... EU leaders will ... attend [but] *I am a bit disappointed with the US participation* ... The US domestic economy is large and sound, which is probably why it does not attach much importance to participation in international forums.[40]

Thai opinion outside of government, likewise several years after the 1997 crisis, was even more cutting. Thailand's press is now quite genuinely open and free, and one reflection of its freedom is that newspapers in Bangkok readily excoriate the Thai government. As the following excerpt shows, the financial crisis provided an excellent occasion to condemn the US, and at the same time label Thailand's government as a US puppet, for having "surrendered to the IMF conditions":

> the IMF conditions were aimed at compounding the Thai economic plight ... so that the foreign capitals financing the IMF could come in to buy the assets they wanted and control the Thai people's life forever, in the same way they succeeded to do in several Latin American countries [this] ... will only turn Thai people into slave workers and economic slaves forever. These days the Thai people hope that a knight will appear to drive out foreigners and annul all the IMF conditions ...[41]

In contrast, Japan's readiness to materially help an Asian friend in need, and to propose the generous funding levels the AMF offer implied, was welcomed among the ASEAN states. It seemed a good case of Japan as the nearby Asian neighbor willing to "walk the walk," while the US just "talked the talk." For a short while after the AMF defeat in 1997, when Prime Minister Hashimoto briefly seemed again to support the IMF's central role, it appeared unlikely that Japan might fill those high expectations, but Tokyo's indecision did not last long. Within only months of the AMF setback, Japan returned to, and indeed enlarged, its efforts to materially assist the nations affected by the emergency. In early 1998, for example, Japan announced a $44 billion aid program for the depressed Asian economies, of which almost half was part of an IMF program. Then in October, Finance Minister Kiichi Miyazawa (the former Prime Minister) introduced a $30 billion aid program that quickly became known as the "Miyazawa Plan."[42] Not long afterwards, with the first $30 billion from that effort already drawn down, Japan announced a second stage; this was envisaged to bring as much as $80 billion in new aid and loan-guarantee funding.

A yen bloc?

All these efforts were related to earlier Japanese discussions of proposals to "internationalize" the yen as a widely used currency. In 1990, for example, the *Far Eastern Economic Review*, in an introduction to several articles on the subject, wrote that "the notion of a yen bloc emerging in the region is being taken more and more seriously." Among other points, it reported that a senior Bank of Tokyo official had said, "if Asia needs a reference currency, the yen is a good candidate."[43] The year before, the *Economist* carried an article also titled, "The Yen Bloc," which reported that Japan's planners "saw the rest of Asia as a means of expanding and diversifying markets for Japan's goods":

> ensuring access to needed material and labor inputs, and permitting Japanese manufacturers to move upmarket while retaining a role in the production of lower technology goods elsewhere in Asia.[44]

Despite these early signs of interest, for the next several years the idea did not draw any significant or broad support beyond Japan itself. Singapore's Lee Kwan Yew, for example, said in 1988 that "No leader in the East favours a yen bloc. It would be a retrograde step."[45] But in the wake both of the Asian crisis in 1997, and the introduction of the Euro in 1999, circumstances had much changed. The advent of the Euro prompted Robert Mundell, one of the world's leading authorities on currency issues, to quickly predict that its adoption would "provoke steps toward an *Asian monetary bloc*, spearheaded by Japan, China, or the members of ASEAN."[46]

He was, of course, not alone: as I pointed out in Chapter 3, Prime Minister Obuchi also reacted quickly when the Euro was introduced. He immediately called for the Yen's adoption as the third global currency; in his words, "Having three key currencies could serve to further reduce exchange rate risks."[47] In sum, the new European currency, along with the Asian crisis two years earlier, were among the *external* developments that revived yen internationalization.

Two other developments, more directly related to Japan, emerged in the early 1990s, and all brought new attention to the assets and liabilities of yen-internationalization, both for Japan and the other East Asian economies. One was Japan's emergence as the world's largest creditor country. That meant its economy was far more subject to potentially-damaging exchange-rate changes, but it also meant that Japan's risks could be reduced if more of its foreign assets were denominated in yen rather than in dollars (or other currency). Wider use of the yen would also bring other benefits: as in the cases of New York, London, and Singapore, it would add more business to Tokyo's banks and financial-security houses.[48]

The other factor that made wider use of the yen potentially more feasible was the phenomenal growth of several of the East Asian economies – often matched by Japan's increasing role in their trade, aid, and investment. From the mid-1960s on, as the Senior Economist and Director of Asia Research at the Nomura Research Institute pointed out,

> real GNP multiplied 12 times in the Asian NIEs (Hong Kong, Taiwan, Korea, and Singapore), 11 times in Japan and 6 times in ASEAN and China. *This compares with 2.5 times for the United States and 3 times for the world economy.*[49]

In the early 1990s, moreover, Asian and Pacific imports from Japan rose more sharply than from any other supplier, and also more sharply than their overall, or *world* imports.

The following three charts illustrate this heightened Japanese role in the early 1990s. The first (Figure 5.1) shows the pattern most starkly: it traces the growth-rates for imports from Japan in "Northeast Asia," a construct which includes South Korea, Taiwan, Hong Kong, China, and in some cases Japan itself.* Figure 5.1 shows that the highest rate of increase was for imports from Japan; it suggests why the nations included in "Northeast Asia" (some would add Singapore) are often regarded as the most likely candidates for early yen-use.

The next two illustrations, Figures 5.2 and 5.3, deal with the "Pacific Rim," and then with ASEAN. Included in the "Pacific Rim" shown in Figure 5.2 are all Asia–Pacific nations *except for Japan*. The chart shows that in the Pacific Rim, the growth rate for imports from Japan was higher than from any other source, including each nation's overall, or total world

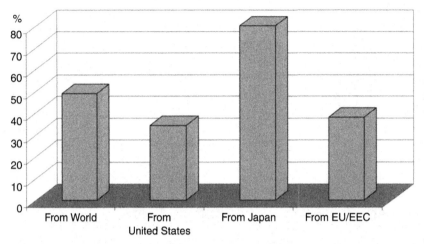

Source: Author's calculations from data in IMF, *Direction of Trade Statistics Yearbook*, annual issues.

* When "Northeast Asia's" imports are shown from the US, the EU and the world, the imports of Japan – as one of Northeast Asia's constituent parts – are included.

Figure 5.1 Growth of Northeast Asia's imports, 1990–4.

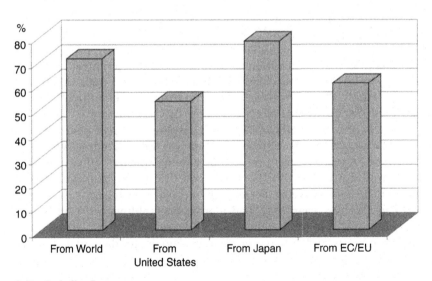

* Not including Japan.

Figure 5.2 Growth rate of Pacific Basin* imports, 1990–4.

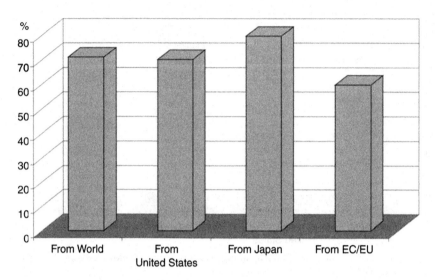

Figure 5.3 Growth rate of ASEAN's imports, 1990–4.

imports. Figure 5.3 shows that in ASEAN, the growth of imports from Japan was less than in the two previous illustrations, but higher than the ASEAN import record from any other supplier.

When the Asian crisis hit, therefore, there were already somewhat favorable conditions surrounding yen-internationalization, and those conditions were broadened and intensified by the 1997–8 collapse. In its wake, many in Asia began to examine the possible advantages of linking their currencies' values to a standard wider than the US dollar alone, and in that context, Tokyo's evident interest in a "Yen Currency Area," or even a so-called "Yen bloc," had more resonance than ever before.

This was true especially among those developing Asian countries that critics had regarded as "over-reliant" on the US dollar. Their view was reminiscent of French President de Gaulle's famous protest, 30 years earlier, that worldwide reliance on the dollar gave the US an "exorbitant privilege."[50] In 1997–8, however, the charge of dollar over-reliance as the principal cause of the Asian crisis had many takers, although it is at best an exaggeration that serves mainly political purposes. The fact is that, even now, economists and other specialists remain in fundamental disagreement about the causes of the Asian crisis.[51] The most sober-minded explanation – in important respects anticipated by some prominent economists – is that its causes were rooted in the *internal* political and economic circumstances of the East Asian nations.[52]

Although for very different reasons than in the 1960s, it is true nevertheless that in the wake of the crisis in Asia, many in the region became interested in loosening their own relationship to the dollar. Malaysia's Prime Minister Mahathir was in the vanguard of that group: in a 1997 speech, he referred to the "unstable American dollar," and called instead for a "common basket of currencies." Not long afterwards, the *New York Times* reported that leaders in Thailand, the Philippines, and Singapore, "after meeting Mr Mahathir . . . supported using regional currency for regional trade."[53] One possibility was the Singapore dollar, "Southeast Asia's sturdiest currency," but as a currency specialist in Hong Kong remarked about that suggestion, "It comes from a trading bloc mentality, that we should take care of ourselves. . . . I don't give it much credence."[54]

The obvious other and possibly-real choice is Japan's yen, and there is strong and growing evidence that Japan's most powerful voices are now increasingly committed to the goal. Achieving it, however, depends in large part on Japan itself because, to bring it about, Tokyo would need to take a number of basic domestic changes that would be politically and culturally difficult to manage.[55] Among them would be significant structural adjustments, including greater opportunities for foreign direct investment; more transparency in financial and business transactions; a reduced governmental willingness to "bail out" troubled companies; and probably most important, a fundamental restructuring of Japan's notoriously interconnected banking and business system.

Some steps in that direction have already begun, and Japan's effort to reform and open its banking structure – in a series of de-regulations often referred to as the "big bang" – is the best-known example. The effort has seen some back-sliding, but in early 1998 Japan nevertheless undertook full liberalization of foreign exchange transactions, and in mid-2000 there were other promising signs of change. The best known was the case of the famous and two-centuries-old Sogo department store group, which faced imminent bankruptcy and employee layoffs. Japan's familiar pattern of a government bailout seemed likely, but a public uproar surprisingly intervened, and the episode showed – just as many critics have hoped – that even such well-known enterprises (and their banks) will in fact be allowed to go bust without a publicly-funded rescue.

But equally-difficult problems remain, and prominent Japanese and Western economists have long pointed to a number of other quite concrete reasons why wider use of the yen should not be soon expected.[56] Among them is the slight use of the yen in international finance, compared with other currencies' usage. Regardless of the fact that Japan is the world's second-largest economic entity, its currency plays a far smaller role than that global economic standing would imply. One careful analysis, based on IMF data, pointed out that although the yen accounts for 14 percent of global financial activity, it "rarely is used outside [Japan's] domestic borders."[57] Similarly, an examination of the yen's role in other nations' foreign reserves showed that when compared to the dollar, yen-use actually *declined* in the late 1990s. Another measure is the currency-composition of international bond issues, and this too revealed that in 1998 the yen dropped to just 1 percent, while dollar use rose to 76 percent. These and other indicators suggest that, despite Japan's revived and growing interest in achieving wider use of its currency, the yen has become "increasingly irrelevant" in the world economy.

Some Japanese officials are said to agree; they regard yen-internationalization as a longer-term prospect, rather than "an emergency policy move."[58] Nevertheless, in mid-1999, the second stage of the Miyazawa Plan was introduced; this added at least $17 billion to the original $30 billion, and gave every indication it was designed to promote the yen's use in East Asia. The Finance Ministry then made that goal official, first by identifying the establishment of "*the international role of the yen . . . as a vital issue*," and second by establishing a Commission to lay out concrete recommendations on how to get there.[59] In an important follow-up step, MITI then added its powerful backing, and when the Foreign Ministry also came on board, all the essential bureaucratic points were covered.

Perhaps the clearest evidence of this growing institutional and political support for internationalizing the yen was that Mr Miyazawa himself formally lent his name to the effort. In 1999 he announced that he too regarded "over-reliance" on the dollar as a chief cause of the Asian financial crisis, and early 2000 brought new evidence that not only the defeated AMF proposal, but the earlier "Yen bloc" idea as well, had been fully resuscitated. Both steps were promoted as good medicine to protect against another Asian currency crisis, and a truly ground-breaking development came at meetings of the Asian Development Bank (ADB) in April and May, 2000.

At those sessions, Japan proposed an all-Asian, "funds-swapping" agreement, that would include *China, South Korea, and the ASEAN countries.* Its aim, which seemed transparently designed to neutralize America's opposition to any weakening of the IMF's central role, would be to "allow [Asia's] central banks ... *to trade their national currencies for dollars, yen or other in-demand currencies held by the Bank of Japan.*"[60] Japan has the resources to make this happen: it has the world's largest gold and foreign-currency reserves (about $340 billion), and if the proposal develops as Tokyo hopes and intends, the Asian "funds-swapping" scheme promises to be a decisive step on the path towards regionalism and a regional currency.

These efforts were accompanied, in the same month, by a proposal of the now-retired Mr Sakakibara. In a speech to the World Bank in Washington in April, 2000, he called on East Asian nations to take three interrelated actions that would not only put Asia more roughly on a par with America and Europe, but also implicitly lead to a new role for the yen.[61] Mr Sakakibara proposed (1) quick development of a liquid and efficient bond market; (2) a regional currency; and (3) – no surprise here – an "Asian Monetary Fund." Published comments in Japan made it clear that the far-reaching and essentially political purpose of these steps was quite well understood.

For example, the prominent journal *Foresight* described their aim as the Finance Ministry's "*overwhelming desire to internationalize the yen,*" and added that an innocent-sounding, but politically-motivated, bureaucratic step was also involved. It combines Japan's Export–Import Bank with its foreign aid agency, and *Foresight*, in a comment that accurately reflected the warrior-like style of Japan's bureaucratic politics, described the merger as the "Ministry's new fortress":

> Since the top posts are usually reserved for retired Finance Ministry officials ... *the New Miyazawa Plan [will] protect the Ministry's new fortress* ... the new scheme allows the Ministry to increase its clout on the diplomatic stage, not to mention its already strong voice in the government."[62]

Even more revealing was an April, 2000 report on Japan's new "fund-swapping" proposal, which appeared in *Sankei*, the prominent Tokyo newspaper that is closely associated with the governing Liberal-Democratic Party. *Sankei* is widely read in most offices in *Kasumigaseki*, the downtown Tokyo district where Japan's powerful Ministries are located, and is reliably thought to reflect important and often-authoritative LDP and government thinking. For that reason, two elements in its explanation of Japan's new funds-swapping scheme are worth special mention.

The first and relatively technical point was that the scale of the "currency-swapping fund" scheme would be "in the tens of billions of dollars." Other accounts indicate a likely total of $100 billion, with Japan expected to provide half that amount. The second, and more broadly political perspective, came as part of *Sankei's* commentary that the fund-swapping scheme "*derives from [Japan's] desire to realize an Asia Monetary Fund (AMF).*" It warrants a full quote:

> Japan's strategy this time is to conclude a multilateral agreement voluntarily among Asian countries, [and] develop it gradually to the AMF *without causing America's resentment. China's participation is vital* for launching the AMF. Talking China into accepting the plan seems easier with a multilateral agreement on swapping funds. There is [also] a zealous call for the AMF in ASEAN ... [and] *skepticism about the United States' active assistance should another crisis occur.* Japan's strategy, to realize internationalization of the yen [and] to break away from excessive dependence on the dollar ... as well as to adopt the AMF swiftly, is likely to be tested once again.[63]

Japan and the EAEC: an idea whose time has come?

The statement above, so thoroughly infused with political and strategic content, highlights several points which, if considered separately, are neither exceptionable nor even surprising, given what has so far been said in this chapter. But taken together, and seen as a whole, the *Sankei* commentary reflects a coherent Japanese foreign policy view on relations with the US, ASEAN, China, and finally on the funds-swapping and yen-internationalization issues.

Regarding the US, it speaks to Japan's deep and continuing economic and strategic dependence on the United States, the sleeping giant who may be irritated if it fully recognizes Japan's aims – but whose "resentment" – in *Sankei's* words, can be lulled by developing those aims "gradually." On ASEAN, Japan's task, as the emerging voice of Asia,[64] is both to respond to ASEAN's "zealous calls" for Japan to take on more responsibility, and to be sensitive to ASEAN's "skepticism" about the US. On China, which is, of course, the most difficult relationship of all, the *Sankei* commentary reflects the central reality that for Japan's funds-swapping scheme (and much else) to work, "China's participation is vital" – but it can be achieved by "talking China into accepting the plan."

On the issues of the Asian Fund, yen-internationalization, and the "funds-swapping" plan, the *Sankei* editorial accurately reflected not only the substantive purpose of those proposals, but the durability and persistence of Japan's efforts to see them realized. The editorial could be said merely to confirm and corroborate much evidence already brought to this discussion, but it does something more important as well. It underlines this book's finding that Japan *has* embarked on a process, notably including the revival of the Asian Monetary Fund, that will strongly encourage regionalism in Asia, and thereby contribute to the regionalization of the globe. That is clearly what a Yen bloc would mean today. The Asian Monetary Fund, now in its up-dated and expanded version, and calling itself an Asian "funds swapping" regime that formally includes *all* East Asian nations in a format heavily backed by the yen, will be a major step to a 'Yen bloc' in all but name.

With regard to the long-term durability of the issue, recall that at the end of the 1980s (when the possibility of internationalizing the yen first came to public attention), several issues had just emerged that were considered favorable to the yen's wider role in Asia. One, as we have already pointed out, was the set of difficulties the GATT negotiations were then experiencing: "if GATT's current Uruguay round ... ends later this year in failure, the result will accelerate the drift towards trade blocs."[65] Moreover, if GATT did indeed falter, the newly-established APEC was thought to be its main beneficiary in Pacific Asia. In other words, the indirect effect of a weak or much-wounded GATT would be to promote, as an acceptable alternative, intensified cooperation in APEC. And to add substance to APEC, it was thought likely that Japan would take two long-overdue steps: open its markets wider to imported goods from Asia, and liberalize its financial markets, in part to encourage yen regionalization. A third factor, the clincher so to speak, was the widespread expectation in the 1980s, especially among many Japanese, that the United States was of "waning importance in the world economy." In that event, as the then-Vice President of Nomura Research in Tokyo predicted:

> Asian nations are likely to be less willing to hold and settle transactions in dollars, while the likelihood of a larger regional and international role for the yen would grow ... [and] Japan would create the kind of domestic financial markets which would allow for regionalisation and internationalisation of the yen.[66]

Most of this has *not* come to pass. Certainly GATT did not collapse; indeed the years immediately following those early thoughts of yen-internationalization saw instead the major trade-expanding successes of GATT's Uruguay Round, and flowing from those successes, the establishment on a more permanent footing of the WTO. APEC, moreover, confounding predictions, clearly has fallen on hard times. It was launched amidst high hopes, and President Clinton put it on the world's agenda when he hosted its meeting in Seattle in 1993, and gave it an added boost with his support for the Jakarta meeting in 1994. But even then, there were doubts about what APEC might accomplish. When the European Commission was denied its request to send observers to the Jakarta session, an Asian diplomat explained, "The reason was simple. We didn't want them to discover there was nothing to discover."[67]

APEC, of course, has had some successes, most notably in helping to achieve some single-sector trade agreements, but its ambitious plans for trade liberalization have been severely criticized for doing far too little. Late in 1997, for example, a report to the APEC summit by business leaders concluded that "APEC has yet to reach a consensus on how free trade should be defined."[68] And the most recent and thorough analyses about it are replete with references to APEC's lack of focus; its weak or non-existent organization; its meager tangible accomplishments; and much else that has saddened many observers.[69]

The same has happened to ASEAN, that other much-touted effort in Asian regional cooperation. It established its reputation in political and security cooperation, essentially as a "Foreign Ministers' Club," and then, probably unwisely, ASEAN expanded its membership and simultaneously attempted to take on issues of trade and economic collaboration. Its most notable advertised accomplishment in that guise was AFTA, the "ASEAN Free Trade Area," but here too the product never met marketers' expectations. In 1999 and 2000, it suffered grievous body-blows when Prime Minister Mahathir first signaled, and then announced, that unless ASEAN agreed to delay for several years certain already-scheduled tariff cuts, Malaysia would leave ASEAN altogether.[70] No other ASEAN Prime Minister or President was willing to call his bluff, and amidst much grumbling, finger-pointing, and – most important – likely responses in kind by other members, ASEAN blinked and gave in.[71]

The result is that contemporary sentiment in and about ASEAN is dour at best, and was reflected in an article aptly titled "ASEAN in Danger of Plunging Into Dustbin of History." It covered the annual ASEAN meeting in July, 2000, and was prepared by a long-time Philippines observer, who wrote that ASEAN today "is in danger of joining such august predecessors as Maphilindo (Malaysia–Philippines–Indonesia) and the Southeast Asia Treaty Organization (Seato)":

> The speeches at the opening of the organization's 33rd annual meeting in Bangkok on July 24 had a distinct "I-have-come-to-bury-ASEAN, not-to-praise-it" note to them. Thai Prime Minister Chuan Leek-Pai warned of the association's rapidly falling behind other regional economic blocs in global trade. *But it was Singapore Foreign Minister S. Jayakumar who best captured ASEAN's near-terminal state when he described it as being stuck with the image of a "sunset organization" in international circles.*[72]

Yet despite what contemporary jargon calls these "counterfactuals" – events that *did not occur* but which were expected to promote wider use of the yen – internationalization of the yen has not evaporated. It has instead very much persisted, and as we have repeatedly shown, in contemporary Japanese thinking it is a front-burner and Finance Ministry-designated "vital issue." Nor is it, by any means, restricted to the nation's economic and financial leadership; the "Prime Minister's Commission on Japan's Goals in the 21st Century" gave it the same emphasis:

> In order to promote the use of the yen internationally, we must make it a more smooth process for foreign nationals to manage and procure funds in yen . . . it will be in the basic interests of emerging-market countries, *including Asian countries, to strive for the inter-nationalization of the yen.*[73]

Much of the reason for the issue's durability is that it represents a long-term national interest among Japan's leadership. As the *Sankei* commentary also reflected, yen-internationalization has been revived, both in Japan and among the crisis-hit Asian economies, by the bitter legacy of the AMF defeat. In that respect it is reminiscent of the sour taste left a decade earlier by the "FSX affair": a US–Japan program to jointly develop an advanced fighter-support aircraft – despite the initial and strong objections of Japanese industrialists and others, who preferred to go it alone. Larger financial and strategic considerations in both nations dictated the co-development agreement, but a multitude of problems led to openly-expressed US doubts that Japan would fully share its innovations, and President Bush ultimately insisted that the agreement be re-negotiated.[74] The resulting mistrust added to the slights – real and imagined – that are themselves one factor in Japan's reviving Asian identity, and in that regard was similar to the consequences of the AMF defeat.

In that case too, Japan's long-standing goal – to internationalize the yen – was thwarted, but Tokyo neither fully accepted nor became reconciled to the 1997 defeat. Both because and in spite of that reversal, Japan returned to the goal, now in the guise of the "funds-swapping" scheme. Indeed Mr Sakakibara explained the initial loss of the AMF only as a matter of his weak tactics, rather than the idea's substance:

> It was somewhat premature on our part, but we were consulting with some of the Asian countries about this [AMF] idea, and they reacted very favorably. . . .We wanted to consult the U.S. after that, but Larry Summers somehow got information about it and he didn't like it at all . . . I regret that I didn't nurture it a bit longer.[75]

New and added confirmation of the 1997 defeat's bitter legacy beyond Japan came at the July, 2000 meetings of ASEAN. The New Zealand Prime Minister (Helen Clark) described Asia's perspective on what had happened: "A slow and inadequate response by the US and other industrial countries to the crisis." She then added that in her own view too, the crisis left "terribly bitter feelings."[76] We have already mentioned similar evidence from Southeast Asia, and argued that it produced two results: a rise in Asian "regional" sentiment, and a revival of attitudes critical of the Western developmental model in general, and the role of the United States in particular. In the worst-hit of the Asian economies, the American response was seen as at best insensitive, and at worst malevolent – for reasons that were thought to include private profit, state policy, and ethnic Western racism – and possibly a combination of all three.

The sad consequence is that in contrast to what was conceived of in 1989–90 as an Asia–Pacific region, represented organizationally by APEC, has now begun instead to degenerate into a racially-configured East Asian preference for an "Asians only" arrangement. The best evidence for this is the growing reality of the "ASEAN-plus three" format, in which the "three" are Japan, China, and Korea, while the United States, Australia, and Canada – all with major stakes in the Pacific region's strategic, political, and economic fortunes – are formally and explicitly excluded. This "ASEAN plus three" label is, of course, simply another term for Malaysia's decade-long goal of an "East Asia Economic Group." Known later as the East Asian Economic *Caucus* (in a moment we'll explain why "Caucus" was substituted for "Group"), the Mahathir proposal had long been thought to be in decline, but it is clear now not only that it is still alive, but is rapidly gaining strength and prominence.

Before more is said about this "ASEAN-plus-three" format, three points about the early ASEAN-APEC-EAEC relationship need to be briefly explained. First, ASEAN was initially wrong-footed by what it feared were APEC's likely directions and outcomes, largely because of its American membership. The US was not dismissive of ASEAN, but it nevertheless strongly supported APEC's creation. Indeed Secretary of State Baker and other very senior members of the Bush Cabinet represented the President at APEC'S first formal meeting in Australia, and the first Clinton administration, in particular, maintained that level of interest and support.

ASEAN members, however, had two worries: that the US, and possibly some others, saw APEC as a more institutionalized group than they were comfortable with, and that the new organization might soon endorse very liberalized trade and other formal economic agreements. ASEAN members also feared that APEC would overshadow their much smaller effort. It was not so much that ASEAN could point to concrete material benefits, but it *could* point to important intangibles. Its "post-Ministerial" meetings (attended by Foreign Ministers from the major industrialized nations) were one example. Those meetings enhanced ASEAN's voice in Asian and even global affairs, and no ASEAN leader was willing to lessen that status.

The second point concerns Indonesia, whose size and population gave it "key state" status in ASEAN. In 1989–90, when these events were taking shape, President Suharto's external reputation was still largely unblemished, and both he and Foreign Minister Ali Aletas shared these concerns about the direction in which APEC might be moving. They were nevertheless upstaged by the EAEG proposal of the much smaller Malaysia, as represented by its outspoken Prime Minister. As a result, neither Indonesia nor Singapore fully endorsed the Mahathir proposal.[77] In an effort, however, to accommodate the Malaysian proposal, and at the same time to dilute it, Singapore and Indonesia won ASEAN support to change its name from "group" to "Caucus," as in East Asia Economic *Caucus.* One wag quickly remarked that this would nevertheless leave it a "Caucus without the Caucasians."

The third point relates more directly to Japan, and its place in the newly-energized East Asian format. When Malaysia first called for an "East Asia Economic Group," there were early alarms, especially in the US, because the EAEG included only those who were ethnically and racially "East Asian." There was some speculation that Japan, too, toyed with the idea of an "Asians-only" grouping, and there were even suggestions that Tokyo, and not Kuala Lumpur, inspired the original EAEG proposal.[78] We will not have an answer to that question any time soon, but it is no secret that US Secretary of State James Baker took famously strong exception to the proposed group's racial and especially *economic* exclusion of the United States. The consequence was that at the 1991 APEC meetings in Seoul, Japan and Korea were confronted by Malaysia's insistence to support the EAEG, and simultaneously by America's very strong opposition.[79] In the end, both Korea and Japan supported APEC, but Japan's choice was reliably reported to be dictated, not by a principled disagreement with the East Asian format, but instead by Japan's dependent relationship on the United States: Tokyo concluded that to give any encouragement to the EAEG was likely to be taken "as an expression of *kenbei* (dislike of America)."[80]

In the wake of the 1997 financial crisis, those initial fears of America's opposition to the EAEC format, now in its new clothing as "ASEAN-plus-three," have lost much of their force. In November, 1999, the ASEAN summit meetings were joined by the leaders of Japan, China, and Korea, and together they agreed to a new format, initially to be known as "EAC," or East Asia Cooperation. Not surprisingly, the Malaysian Foreign Minister and others waxed lyrical over the transformation:

> Malaysia's dream to see the establishment of a special forum for East Asian countries has come true. ... Whatever name is used ... is not important. Whether the name is ASEAN Plus Three or EAC, Malaysia's wish to see the establishment of a special forum for East Asia has been successfully realized.[81]

As Thailand's Foreign Minister correctly observed, the change was a clear result both of the 1997 crisis, and other nations' responses to it. In his words, both developments "highlighted the need to strengthen the interdependence between countries of the region."[82] There were similar reactions in the Philippines: in the *Manila Business World* a columnist wrote that "Mahathir ... can rejoice that the East Asian Economic Caucus is actually coming to pass, although in another name."[83] Likewise, former Philippines President Ramos, who for years was friendly to the US (he is a graduate of the US Military Academy at West Point), was obliged to tell a Washington audience in July, 2000, that an EAEC-style group was on the way to becoming a reality.[84]

Along with these developments has come a rapidly-accelerating schedule to develop several unprecedented, and Japan-based, "free trade areas" within Asia. Immediately after the failed WTO meetings in Seattle, Singapore's Prime Minister Goh Chok Tong spent a week in Tokyo in December, 1999, and met with all the relevant Ministers, including then-Prime Minister Obuchi. He successfully urged that negotiations begin for a Singapore–Japan FTA,[85] and the two governments expect a formal agreement, covering trade both in goods and services, to be completed during 2001. Similar discussions were begun between Japan and Korea even earlier, and in mid-2000, both nations requested detailed free-trade studies by non-government research bodies.[86] They too expect a bilateral accord within a year.

Certainly, while none of these Asian developments will by themselves alter Asia's international structure, they are a reminder nevertheless of two points. The first is the cumulative effect of individually-small steps; in US Senator Everett Dirksen's famous phrase about American budget expenditures, "a billion here, a billion there, and soon you're talking real money." Secondly, they reflect a widespread East Asian perception that the United States is both less engaged in East Asia than it was in recent years, and that the US is itself less committed to the global trading environment than it was. As usual, Jagdish Bhagwati, writing in *The Economist* in 1997, put the issue perfectly into context:

> Proliferating 'free-trade areas' have become a pox on the world trading system. It is a mark of Washington's blurred vision that, departing from a half-century of steadfast adherence to non-discriminatory multilateralism in trade, the administration has sought to build discriminatory free-trade areas instead.[87]

To the extent, moreover, that Washington's behavior signals a lesser degree of interest and involvement in East Asian developments, it presages a regional structure – including a political and economic arrangement that formally links China and Japan to all the other East Asian nations – that will inevitably affect the national interests of the US and several others. In January, 2000, former Singapore Prime Minister Lee Kwan Yew, who for years welcomed the American military presence in Asia, spoke precisely to this point. He was asked whether he saw any prospect that the US was "withdrawing from Asia," and responded "probably not, for the next 30 or 40 years," but then added that

> The United States confines itself to stopgap measures, giving almost no thought at all to how one goes about rebuilding an international system of cooperation. It probably thinks that kind of behavior is in its national interest, but the other countries aren't going to follow along.[88]

The stakes are not small

I pointed out earlier that only the United States, among the world's major industrialized nations, is a truly *global* exporter. In 1999, just over half its exports were divided almost equally between Europe and Asia, and more than a third went to Canada and Mexico. In other words, almost 90 percent of America's exports are sold in roughly equal proportions to the globe's three main economic regions: North America, East Asia, and the EU.

The contrast between that US export pattern and Europe's experience is very great. The European Union is the world's single largest economic powerhouse, and as a unit, the EU is the world's largest exporter. But as

Chapter 3 pointed out, almost *two-thirds of EU exports* are concentrated in just one market: the EU itself. The next illustration (Figure 5.4) is based on 1998 trade figures, and makes this point. It shows that 9 percent of EU exports were directed to the three NAFTA economies (US, Canada, and Mexico), while the entire East Asia and Pacific region received less than 7 percent. As the illustration shows very clearly, more than 60 percent was represented by intra-EU exports.

Japan's exports are more widely dispersed than that. Figure 5.5 shows that roughly equal portions of Japan's exports (35 percent each) were sent to the Asia–Pacific markets and to NAFTA, but the EU took a much smaller portion: just 18 percent. To complete these comparisons, Figure 5.6 illustrates the more equal distribution of US exports: 22 percent in Europe, 26 percent in Asia, and 35 percent in North America.

That well-diversified US export performance, along with America's substantial investments in East Asia (to which we will turn in a moment), adds to the problematic and worrisome nature expressed by former Prime Minister Lee, that after "the next 30 or 40 years" the US might be "withdrawing from Asia." By "withdrawing," he no doubt meant mainly a much-reduced US military presence, and possibly – though this is more difficult

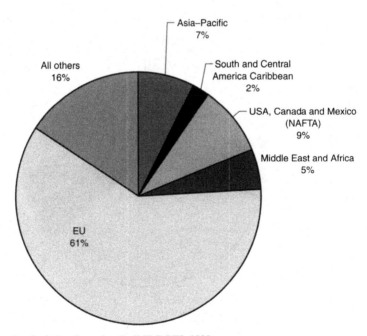

Source: Author's calculation from data in IMF, DOTS, 1999.

Figure 5.4 EU export markets, 1998 (total = $2,219 billion).

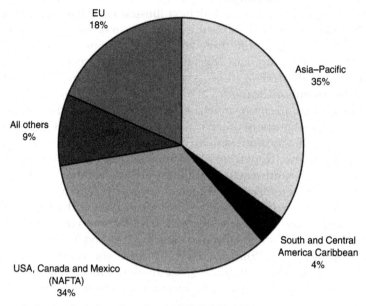

Source: Author's calculations from data in IMF, DOTS, 1999.

Figure 5.5 Japan's export markets, 1998 (total = $388 billion).

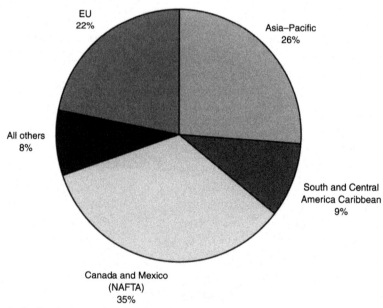

Source: Author's calculations from data in IMF, DOTS, 1999.

Figure 5.6 US export markets, 1998 (total = $680 billion).

to measure – a reduced political presence as well. Both notions, however, are very difficult to square with two fundamental realities.

The first is the permanent reality that the United States is geographically a very large and major Asia–Pacific nation. Its 1500-mile-long west coast is home to Oregon, Washington, and California (the last is America's most populous state). Its two non-contiguous states, Alaska and Hawaii, give the US a further physical presence in the Pacific that is no less real and enduring than that of China and Japan. Add to that the increasingly Asian ethnicity of America's western states, and that in the United States, ethnic composition has a legitimate role in shaping national attitudes and policies. In that respect, America's Asian and Pacific populations are directly analogous to the roles historically played in US foreign policy by the European origins of America's East Coast and Midwest populations.

The second point to emphasize is the already high value, and *increasing global share*, of US exports to the Asia–Pacific region. Of the nearly $700 billion in US global merchandise exports in 1999, a quarter – $180 billion – was sent to Asia alone. (That was more, incidentally, than the entire European Union exported to the US the year before.) Just before the Asian financial crisis, moreover, both the percentage and value of US exports to Asia were even higher. Figure 5.7 strikingly illustrates this. It shows that in 1995, US sales to Asia represented almost 33 percent of America's worldwide exports, and in 1997 (the year of the crisis), US exports to Asia reached $202 billion. That performance is all the more impressive when we focus on the first-year trade numbers in Figure 5.7. In

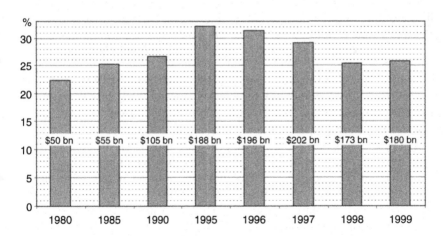

Source: from data in *Foreign Trade Highlights*.

* China, Japan, Korea, Taiwan, Hong Kong, ASEAN, Australia and New Zealand.

Figure 5.7 US exports to Asia–Pacific as percentage of US total exports, 1980–99 (export values in billions).

1980, the share of US exports sent to Asia was fully ten percentage points lower than in the 1990s, and the value was just $50 billion.

These considerations are a reminder of two points: the sheer size of America's Asia–Pacific exports, and that as the devastation of the 1997 financial collapse recedes, those exports have again begun to rise. Add to that the issue of jobs, and the related employment impact of changes in the *composition* of US exports: 85 percent are now manufactured goods, and a substantial and growing proportion of those are high-technology products. Using any of the measures mentioned earlier to calculate jobs derived from exports, the $200 billion in exports to Asia translates to *10 million jobs*. Even if that number were halved, it would represent a politico-economic factor of critical consequence to the democratically-elected leadership of any nation.

The political relevance is clear: in the context of the nearly 20 percent of America's GDP now represented by trade, the size of America's exports to Asia means that the US has a higher-than-ever stake in the nature of Asia's future. For policy makers in a democratic society, where a government's performance-rating is closely tied to the number of jobs in its economy, the fact that a *single* region's export share is in the $200 billion range – and regularly accounts for 25–30 percent of its total exports – is a prize not to be regarded lightly.

Finally, when we consider again the prospect that the US may be seen to be "withdrawing from Asia," it is essential also to recall that in *investments* as in trade, the United States is one of the two major industrialized actors involved in the region. The *accumulated* value of those US investments – which is, after all, what FDI "stock" reflects – makes it all the more difficult to contemplate a reduction of US interests in the region. Japan's role is similarly large and extensive, but Japan is not, as we will see now, already the region's "dominant" actor. That is decidedly not the case, as Figure 5.8 shows.

As this illustration makes clear, the US is the principal FDI source in four of Asia's economies, as Japan is in six. Tokyo's larger total accumulation ($145 billion versus $115 billion), stems mainly from its investments in Indonesia, a principal source of Japan's raw materials imports, and in China, where a sizeable Japanese presence has long been dictated by proximity and history, as well as by present-day politics and good financial opportunities. The point of this comparison, however, is not to minimize or explain away Japan's role. It is instead to show that the US investment presence is also very large, quite comparable to Japan's, and in terms of geography, widely-dispersed as well.

Asia's *imports* from Japan and the US reveal a roughly similar pattern. In 1998, the most recent year for which these data are available, the region as a whole imported more from Japan than from the US ($143 billion versus $121 billion), but as Figure 5.9 shows, two economies (China and Hong Kong) again accounted for much of that $20 billion difference. In five of

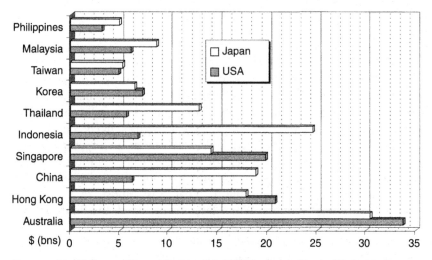

Sources: for *US, Survey of Current Business,* July 1999; for Japan, *Finance Ministry,* in Japan
Economic Report #35A, 17 September, 1999.

Figure 5.8 Total investment stock of Japan and US in Asia (through 1998).

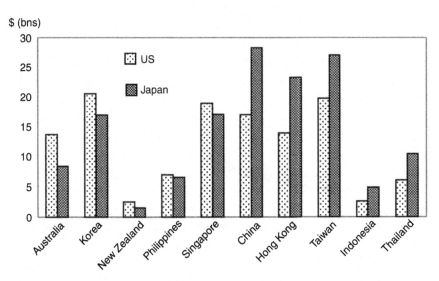

Source: Based on data in IMF, DOTS, 1999.

Figure 5.9 Comparing Asia's imports from USA and Japan, 1998.

the other eight economies, imports from the US were greater (Malaysia is not shown because it imported an identical $11 billion from each). As in the case of investment, this illustration also shows that when Asia's US and Japanese imports are put side by side, the American role is both quite comparable and geographically well-dispersed.

The high value and global dispersion of American exports has been a main theme of this book. Exports have been emphasized because of the role that foreign markets increasingly play in US attitudes and policy. When we turn the coin over, and consider Asia's likely perspectives towards the US, we find that the American role as an *importer* of Asia's goods is no less important. In 1998, for example, and even without including America's large imports from Japan, US imports from the Asia–Pacific nations accounted for $230 billion. That was almost 25 percent of America's worldwide imports. When Japan is included, the figure rises to more than 37 percent. Figure 5.10, the final illustration in this chapter, shows that *over the 30-year period from 1968-98*, the Asia–Pacific imports of the United States have consistently been larger than Japan's.

The lesson of all these comparisons is that, both for the US and the Asian nations, the stakes in today's Asian economic structure, which have brought such enormous gains to the peoples of the region, are not small. Yet this chapter has presented much evidence that in Japan and elsewhere in the region, significant alternatives to the present structure are under serious consideration. Among the signs are Tokyo's long-standing, and recently-heightened commitment to much greater Asian use of the yen; its insistence

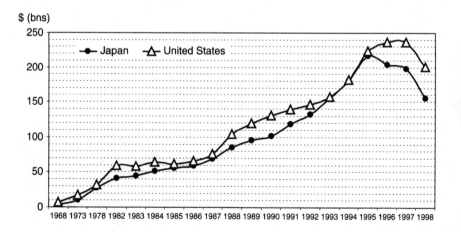

Source: IMF DOTS, annual issues.

* Asia–Pacific nations = China, Japan, Hong Kong, Taiwan, Korea, ASEAN, Australia and New Zealand (Japan imports necessarily exclude Japan itself).

Figure 5.10 US and Japanese imports from Asia–Pacific nations* 1968–98.

on an Asian Monetary Fund in one or another form; and its altogether new participation in an East Asian economic structure that includes Japan, while formally excluding the United States and several others.

Although these developments do not predict with certainty the formation of an Asian regional economic bloc in the form of the "flying geese" model, that is their tendency. Yet American policy appears increasingly diffident to such patterns; indeed the Presidential election campaign of 2000 made it powerfully clear that American leaders, of both parties, are increasingly committed to a Western hemisphere economic system along the lines of the "Free Trade Area for the Americas." To that extent, the United States may well appear either to be resigned to a world of regional blocs, and to some Asians, even to be "withdrawing from Asia." Those are signals no responsible US leadership should give, first because they run counter to the facts and continued significance of America's engagement in the Asia–Pacific region, and second because a world of regional blocs will not be compatible either with American interests, or with conditions likely to be supportive of an international environment of lessened tensions and widening prosperity.

Notes

1 ECAFE was the acronym for the "Economic Commission for Asia and the Far East." It is known today as "ESCAP" (Economic and Social Commission for Asia and the Pacific).
2 For discussions of the "flying geese" label and its uses, see the chapters by T. Pempel, J. Koschmann, B. Cumings, and T. Shiraishi, in P. Katzenstein and T, Shiraishi, *Network Power: Japan and Asia*, Ithaca, Cornell University Press, 1997.
3 Japan Economic Research Center, Tokyo, February, 1968.
4 University of California Press, 1971. Among several related publications was his "A Pacific Free Trade Area Proposed," *Pacific Community*, April, 1972, pp. 585–96.
5 UN, ECAFE, "Approaches to Regional Harmonization of National Development Plans in Asia and the Far East," E/CN.11/CAEP.2/1.45 (26 September, 1964), mimeo.
6 In mimeo, marked "strictly confidential," 17 December, 1961.
7 Konoe's thinking is well-captured in an essay he wrote just before leaving for Paris, at the end of World War I. It is reprinted as "Against a Pacificism Centered on England and America," in *Japan Echo*, Special Issue, 1995.
8 K. Pyle, *The Japanese Question: Power and Purpose in a New Era*, Washington, DC, AEI Press, 1992, p. 70.
9 I reported on Okita's earlier background in "Japan and the Pacific Basin Proposal," *Korea and World Affairs*, Summer, 1981, pp. 268, 270. My article drew on the lengthy Editorial, "Pacific Rim," in *Japan Quarterly*, April–June, 1980, pp. 147–52, which also points out that several of Japan's post-war leaders came from the *juku* Okita briefly attended. In yet another connection from pre-war days to the post-war world, Konoe's pre-war "Showa Kenkyukai" was regarded in Japanese commentary at the time of APEC's founding as the "forerunner of Prime Minister Ohira's [1979–80] private advisory group" – both of which, of course, included Okita.

10 R. Fifield, "ASEAN and the Pacific Community," *Asia–Pacific Community*, Winter, 1981, p. 15.

11 My own work in that period was no exception; examples are my "Economic Impediments to Regionalism in Southeast Asia," in *Asian Survey*, May, 1963; Chapters 5 and 6 in *Dimensions of Conflict in Southeast Asia*, Englewood Cliffs, Prentice-Hall, 1966; and "Rhetoric and Reality in Regional Cooperation," *Solidarity* (Manila), July, 1971.

12 "A Pacific Free Trade Area Proposed," *Pacific Community*, April, 1972, pp. 585–6. My emphasis.

13 For a good statement of this more than century-long issue, see Koro Bessho, "Identities and Security in East Asia," *ADELPHI* paper No. 325, London, International Institute for Strategic Studies, 1999, p. 13–25.

14 "Perspectives on Modern Japanese Foreign Policy," in R. Scalapino (ed.), *The Foreign Policy of Modern Japan*, Berkeley, The University of California Press, 1971, p. 399. My emphasis.

15 Noboru Hatakeyama, head of the Japan External Trade Organization (JETRO), 10 February, 1999, in FBIS, 10 February, 1999.

16 MITI White Paper on Trade, 1999, "For Stable Growth in the World Economy in a Global Era," Kyodo Press, 21 May, 1999, reported in FBIS, 21 May, 1999. My emphasis.

17 President Bush's interest in the "Enterprise for the Americas" proposal dates from the same period, and was a conceptual precursor to the geographically more limited NAFTA.

18 Remarks of Koji Watanabe, MITI Minister; Koji Kakizawa, Parliamentary Vice Minister for Foreign Affairs; and Prime Minister Kiichi Miyazawa, in Japan Economic Institute, JEI Report No. 41B, 30 October, 1992.

19 *Keidanren* is Japan's Federation of Business Organizations. The quotation is from Kazuo Nukazawa (then its managing director, later Japan's Ambassador to Hungary, and a very highly regarded voice on Japanese industry and trade), in *The Wall Street Journal*, special section on World Business, 21 September, 1990, p. R31.

20 From the Executive Summary, [Japan] Ministry of International Trade and Industry, "White Paper on International Trade 2000," available at www.miti.go.jp/report. My emphasis.

21 *Mainichi Shimbun*, 17 May, 2000, in US Embassy (Tokyo) Office of Translation Services, 17 May, 2000. My emphasis.

22 *Tokyo Shimbun*, 19 May, 2000, in US Embassy (Tokyo), Office of Translation Services, 19 May, 2000.

23 Comments of Japanese officials, reported in the *Financial Times*, 12 May and 17 May, 2000.

24 A good example of Japan's views of its Asian role came in early 2000, in the planning for the G–8 summit in Okinawa later that year. As part of that process, Prime Minister Obuchi toured widely in Southeast Asia, in an effort, as the Foreign Ministry said, "to put out an upbeat and forceful message that fully reflects Asian interests and aspirations" (*Financial Times*, 14 January, 2000).

25 Tales of MITI/MOFA rivalry are legion; at the APEC meeting in Manila in November, 1996, reporters encountered separate briefers from each Ministry, who then openly disagreed on what had just happened. See *The Wall Street Journal* (Interactive), 26 November, 1996, at wsj.com. Also see E. Krauss, "Japan, the U.S. and the Emergence of Multilateralism in Asia," prepared for the "After the Global Crises: What Need for Regionalism" 3rd Annual Conference, Centre for the Study of Globalisation and Regionalisation, The University of Warwick, Coventry, England, 16–18th September, 1999.

26 Keiichi Tsunekawa, "NAFTA's Impact on Japan," Washington, DC, The Woodrow Wilson Center, Occasional Paper No. 58, March 9, 1994. My emphasis.

27 K. Cai, "The Political Economy of Economic Regionalism in Northeast Asia: a Unique and Dynamic Pattern," *East Asia: an International Quarterly*, New Brunswick, Transaction Press, Summer, 1999. My emphasis.

28 *Financial Times*, "Idea Whose Time Has Come Closer," 7 October, 1997.

29 This discussion draws on the extensive report by A. Rowley, "Asian Fund Special: The Battle of Hong Kong," *Capital Trends*, November, 1997, Vol. 2, No. 13.

30 Good reporting on the AMF proposal and Japanese views are in Japan Economic Institute (JEI), *Japan Economic Report*, 26 September, 24 October, and 14 November, 1997.

31 Almost two years later, Mr. Sakakibara continued to ruminate over the AMF defeat, and in a 1999 speech in Australia, he referred to it as one of the two causes of the 1997 Asian Financial Crisis. See the report of his speech on 26 May, 1999, as reported by *Kyodo* [Japan's newspaper–NHK cooperative press agency] in FBIS, 26 May, 1999.

32 Opponents of the Mexican "bailout" were angry that the Treasury Department had acted without Congressional approval, and had used funds Congress may have intended for different, and probably largely domestic US purposes. In that environment, the Treasury was loath to repeat the action in the Thai case.

33 An extensive discussion was published a year later in *The Wall Street Journal*, 24 September, 1998.

34 Sura Sannittanont, advisor to Deputy Prime Minister Supachai, quoted in *The Wall Street Journal*, 20 January, 1998. The Foreign Ministry official quoted next is Kobsak Chutikul, *ibid.*

35 For a recounting of some of the public confrontations in which he has been involved, including his row with Australia's press and its Prime Minister, see *The Asian Wall Street Journal Weekly*, 6 December, 1993.

36 Prime Minister Mahathir's critique of Mr Soros was detailed in the *Financial Times*, 23 July, 1997. Among Southeast Asian governments, Mahathir's has been the most prominent for its anti-Jewish statements and policies, but it has had quiet company in the leaderships of Indonesia, Thailand, even Singapore at one point, and certainly – as testified by the sales figures of anti-Jewish screeds in Tokyo bookstores – in Japan.

37 Quoted in *The New York Times*, 21 December, 1997. There are dozens of similar quotes from Dr Mahathir along the same lines, for example his speech in Santiago, Chile, in September, 1997, where he commented that Malaysia and others in the region were "damaged unfortunately by some of the people we had been friendly with" (Mahathir's speech published in *The Star* [Kuala Lumpur], 2 October, 1997 in FBIS [Western Hemisphere], 3 October, 1997.

38 *New York Times*, 18 December, 1997.

39 See, for example, the conclusions in the Report to the [US] Senate Committee on Finance, "The Pros and Cons of Entering Into Negotiations on Free Trade Area Agreements with Taiwan, the Republic of Korea, and ASEAN, or the Pacific Rim Region in General," United States International Trade Commission Publication 2166, March, 1989, as well as the earlier study of Proposals for a US–Japan Free Trade Area Agreement (USITC Publication No. 210, September, 1988).

40 Director-General of the Foreign Ministry's Economics Department (Kopsak Chutikul), speaking to the Thai reporters association, in *Siam Rat*, 6 February, 2000, in FBIS, 6 February. My emphasis.

41 Commentary by Kamon Kramontrakun, "Thailand in Name Only," in *Bangkok Than Setthakit* (in Thai), 6–8 January, 2000, in FBIS, 6 January, 2000.

42 Details of this and related Japanese efforts are in M. Castellano, "Two Years On: Evaluating Tokyo's Response to the East Asian Financial Crisis," JEI Report No. 30A, August 6, 1999.

43 "Japan in Asia: Building a Yen Bloc," *Far Eastern Economic Review*, 11 October, 1990, p. 74. More recently, the concept has been carefully discussed by W. Grimes, "Internationalization of the Yen," Paper prepared for the conference on "Power, Ideology and Conflict," Ithaca, Cornell University, 31 March, 2000. There are in addition a number of references to the "yen bloc" idea in Jeffrey A. Frankel, *Regional Trading Blocs in the World Economic System*, Washington, Institute for International Economics, 1997.

44 P. Maidment, "The Yen Block," *Economist*, 15 July, 1989, quoted by M. Pierson, "Report on the International Trade Commission Study of 'East Asian Regional Economic Integration and Implications for the United States,'" in *Law and Society in International Business*, 1994, No. 3, pp. 1161–85.

45 Quoted in the *Far Eastern Economic Review*, 11 October, 1990.

46 "The Case for the Euro-II," in *The Wall Street Journal*, 25 March, 1998. My emphasis.

47 *Financial Times*, 6 January,1999.

48 See C. H. Kwan, *Economic Interdependence in the Asia–Pacific Region: Towards a Yen Bloc*, London and New York, Routledge, 1994, p. 163.

49 *ibid.*, p. 11. My emphasis.

50 His main argument was that, because the US could uniquely fund its debts by printing more money, America's behavior damaged nations whose policies were presumably more restrained. A secondary complaint was that the dollar's international currency role allowed the US to exercise "seignorage," i.e., to profit from what was in effect a "money tax."

51 See Chapter 5, "Global Financial Vulnerability," in R. Gilpin, *The Challenge of Global Capitalism*, Princeton, Princeton University Press, 2000, especially p. 136.

52 For two good statements about the *Asian* causes of the crisis, see G. Segal and D. Goodman, *Towards Recovery in Pacific Asia*, London and New York, Routledge, 2000, especially pp. 1–5, and Lee Kam Hing and Tan Chee-Beng, *The Chinese in Malaysia*, Oxford and New York, Oxford University Press, 2000, p. 156. Lee and Tan point to seven prime *internal* causes: "overvalued currencies; worsening current account deficits; excessive foreign and domestic borrowings; overinvestment in prestigious but unproductive projects; failure to exercise fiscal discipline or to impose strict controls over banks and financial institutions; lack of transparency; and corrupt business practices." The most prominent early caution about Asia's high-growth economies came from P. Krugman, "The Myth of Asia's Miracle," *Foreign Affairs*, November/December, 1994, pp. 62–78, but there were also early warnings (though in retrospect in too-general terms) from the IMF and World Bank.

53 *The New York Times*, 9 February, 1998. Mahathir's Santiago speech, as already noted, was reported in *The Star* (Kuala Lumpur, 2 October, 1997).

54 *The New York Times*, 9 February, 1998, quoting Eric Nickerson of the Bank of America office in Hong Kong.

55 See Bronwyn Curtis, "What Asia Could Learn from Europe," *The New York Times*, 25 January, 1998.

56 See, for example, R. McKinnon and K. Ohno, *Dollar and Yen, Resolving Economic Conflict Between the United States and Japan*, Cambridge, The MIT Press, 1997, where they argue (p. 107) that "If foreigners are not eager to borrow at long term in yen securities, nor willing to hold deposits in Japanese banks in yen … the model of Japan as an international financial intermediary is not robust."

57 Data from the IMF, in M. Castellano, "Internationalization of the Yen: A Ministry of Finance Pipe Dream?", JEI Report No. 23A, 18 June, 1999.

58 A senior Finance Ministry official, quoted in *Financial Times*, 22 February, 1998.
59 M. Castellano, in JEI Report No. 23A, *ibid.*, which cited two MITI Reports: "Internationalization of the Yen for the 21st Century," and "Resource Mobilization Plan for Asia," May, 1999.
60 Japan Economic Institute, JEI Reports No. 20B and 24A, 19 May, 2000 and 23 June, 2000. Emphasis added. The funds-swap arrangement became known as the "Chiang Mai Initiative," for the town in Northern Thailand where some of the ADB meetings were held.
61 *Wall Street Journal*, 19 April, 2000.
62 Hiroki Chino, "Unspoken Risks of the 'New Miyazawa Plan,'" in *Foresight* (Tokyo), November, 1999, in US Embassy (Tokyo), Office of Translation Services, *Review of the Monthly Magazines*, December, 1999. My emphasis.
63 *Sankei*, April 21, 2000, in US Embassy (Tokyo), Office of Translations Services, 21 April, 2000. Emphasis added.
64 Japan as Asia's "voice" is literally and precisely the role for which the late Prime Minister Obuchi often volunteered, both when he traveled in the region in early 2000, and in the planning for the G–8 Summit in Okinawa, which was his legacy. See for example his rhetorical question to reporters, reported in *Sankei*, 15 January 15, 2000, "I wonder if it would be acceptable to give the impression that Japan, as a Summit member country, is the representative of Asian countries." The Foreign Ministry added that since the "G8 comes to Asia only once every seven years, Mr Obuchi wants it to put out [a message] that fully reflects Asian interests and aspirations" (*Financial Times*, 14 January, 2000).
65 N. Holloway, "Japan in Asia: Building a Yen Bloc," *Far Eastern Economic Review*, *ibid.*, p. 73.
66 Yoshio Suzuki, quoted in *Far Eastern Economic Review*, *ibid.*
67 *Financial Times*, 10 November, 1994.
68 *ibid.*, 7 November, 1997.
69 There have been many commentaries on why and how APEC lost its way, but few doubt that it has. A recent and good summary discussion is J. Ravenhill, "APEC adrift: implications for economic regionalism in Asia and the Pacific," *The Pacific Review*, Vol. 13, No. 2, 2000, pp. 319–33.
70 *Financial Times*, 27 July, 2000. The proximate cause was Malaysia's long-standing (and essentially non-commercially-competitive) "national car" project known as "Proton." Thailand in particular would be damaged were Malaysia to forfeit its tariff-reduction agreements, since a number of automotive producers, as we saw in Chapter 3, have established production facilities in the Bangkok region.
71 For an account of the items on which Thailand might delay tariff-cuts if others followed that tactic, see the *Bangkok Post*, "Tariff Cut Delays Likely if AFTA Members Cannot Agree," 19 May, 1999, in FBIS, 19 May, 1999. For a broader discussion of AFTA's origins, processes, and prospects, see R. Stubbs, "Signing on to Liberalization: AFTA and the Politics of Regional Economic Cooperation," *The Pacific Review*, Vol. 13, No. 2, 2000, pp. 297–318.
72 W. Bello, in *Manila Business World*, 28 July, 2000, in FBIS, 28 July, 2000. Emphasis added.
73 From Chapter 6 of the Report, prepared by the "Subcommittee on Japan's Place in the World," in FBIS, 4 February, 2000. This 10-member subcommittee was chaired by Professor Mokoto Iokibe of Kobe University; its members included Keiko Chino of *Sankei Shimbun* (author of the *Sankei* commentary from which we have quoted here), and Yoichi Funabashi, chief diplomatic correspondent for *Asahi Shimbun*. It represents important contemporary mainstream Japanese thinking on foreign affairs.

74 The FSX project dates from 1987, and since going into limited production the aircraft has been designated the "F2." Recent discussions are in Japan Economic Institute, Reports No. 32B, 23 August, 1996 and No. 32A, 22 August, 1997.

75 Sakakibara interview with an Australian business newspaper, reported in *Kyodo* [Tokyo], 26 May, 1999, in FBIS, 26 May, 1999.

76 Quoted in the *Financial Times*, 21 July, 2000.

77 Singapore's reason was rooted both in its commitment to a trade regime as open as possible, and in its strong aversion to anything directly opposed by the United States. Suharto shared that view of the US, and resented Mahathir's proposal on personal grounds as well, largely because the sharp-tongued and confrontational Mahathir had never deferred to the courtly Javanese. Mahathir's call for an EAEG was not the first time he acted without clearing his initiative with Jakarta. For a discussion of the "seemingly frosty personal relations" between the two see M. G. G. Pillai, "Mahathir–Suharto talks augur well for ASEAN," in the *Bangkok Post*, 5 August, 1993, FBIS, 6 August, 1993. Pillai argues correctly that "The presumption in Kuala Lumpur is that Indonesia behaves like an elder brother, and in Jakarta that Malaysia was getting too big for her boots."

78 Further support for that view was in the report that "some of Tokyo's trade and foreign affairs bureaucrats favor a Mahathir-style Asian trade bloc if the GATT breaks down" (R. Fisher, Heritage Foundation Asian Studies Center *Backgrounder*, 9 November, 1993).

79 For a useful discussion of the conflicting pressures on Japan see the two articles in *Nihon Keizai*, 20 November and 25 November, 1991, in US Embassy (Tokyo) *Daily Summary of the Japanese Press*.

80 This point was made by the well-informed writer Yoichi Funabashi, in the *Asahi Evening News*, 31 January, 1992.

81 Foreign Minister Syed Hamir, in *Utusan Malaysia* (Internet version), in FBIS, 1 December, 1999.

82 *Financial Times*, 21 July, 2000.

83 Solita Collas-Monsod, "ASEAN+3 Informal Summit: Mahathir Vindicated," 30 November, 1999, in FBIS, 30 November, 1999.

84 *Financial Times*, 21 July, 2000.

85 *Kyodo* (Tokyo) 7 December, 1999, in FBIS, 7 December, 1999. In mid-2000, moreover, Singapore was also negotiating an FTA with New Zealand.

86 A Singapore–Japan study was readied by August, 2000, and the Free Trade Agreement was expected to be completed by early 2001. Japanese sources reported it would be a "new age" pact covering services and the information technology sectors.

87 "Fast Track to Nowhere," 18 October, 1997.

88 Interview with *Asahi Shimbun* (Internet version), 8 January, 2000, in FBIS, 16 January, 2000.

6 The high price of folly

In 1999, the Asian Development Bank published its annual *Asian Development Outlook*. An early chapter dealt with the "The Financial Crisis in Asia," and that very readable discussion can be commended to anyone interested in both the causes of the crisis and the major ways to avoid a new one. More to the point of this book, the 1999 *Outlook* also included, as part of its special chapter on Asia's "growth and recovery," an important and provocative section on "Regionalism." The chapter's overall tone and message were reflected in its brief first sentence, "Openness matters," by which it meant that the principles of liberal trade regimes, with their key features of export promotion and outward orientation, were largely responsible for the welfare gains in East and Southeast Asia.

In the same vein, the chapter's verdict on regionalism, both generally and in Asia, strongly confirms the approach this book has taken on the question of why regionalism has become so much the vogue today:

> In the early 1980s, in the face of EU reluctance to engage in a new round of multilateral trade negotiations, *the United States turned to regionalism* as a vehicle for trade liberalization. This switch in US policy has launched a *new wave of regional agreements around the world.*[1]

The *Outlook* then launched into a formidable, and highly critical, discussion of regionalism in Asia. It took head-on APEC's notion of "open regionalism," which it gently labeled as the subject of "considerable confusion." Less gently, it added that the confusion extends to "whether it is a useful concept at all ... *If arrangements are open, they cannot be regional.*" Then, in ways that will also be familiar to this book's readers, the ADB *Outlook* reviewed the main criticisms that have been directed at regional trade arrangements.

The downsides of economic regionalism

Its first point was to remind its readers of the prime question regarding any effort in economic regionalism: does it create or divert trade? Our discussion of MERCOSUR, in Chapter 4, reported clear evidence of trade diversion in South America. Chapter 3, which showed that two-thirds of Europe's trade is intra-regional, falls into the same category. It was no surprise, therefore, that the authors of the ADB *Outlook* correctly reported that "empirical studies confirm that regional trade arrangements [the EU, NAFTA, and MERCOSUR were specifically named] *have substantial trade diversion effects.*" They concluded, moreover, that those effects were "at the expense of the Asian Developing Economies," and they singled-out the trade diversion consequences already experienced by the Asian economies. Losses to important industrial and trade sectors were cited, as in Korea and Taiwan, as well as anticipated investment losses in ASEAN, specifically in Singapore and Malaysia.

The second negative feature the ADB identified was what Bhagwati has often called the "spaghetti bowl" effect: the proliferation, and inevitable administrative complexity, of overlapping tariff regimes.[2] This is a large and important issue, especially in practical and governmental terms, but it is too-little discussed in most writings about the workings of regionalism in practice. The three books by Jeffrey Frankel (two are a collection of several authors' essays) are roughly in this category. Although several separate chapters are valuable, none contains any reference to the practical realities that will bedevil governments if regional arrangements spread.[3] The reason for the omission may be that the great bulk of the writing on regionalism comes from economists, for whom governmental resources are not a research question, and who prefer, in any case, to remain relatively agnostic in the overall debate about regionalism.[4] Their work is reminiscent of President Truman's vain hope for a "one-armed economist," one who would not so consistently point both to the assets and the liabilities of every course of action under consideration.

The third criticism of regionalism in the ADB volume, and ultimately the most important, was its assessment of regional integration as a *concept* in the world economy. The ADB argued that at base, regional trade arrangements are *not* compatible with multilateral liberalization, which they frankly called a "superior route to international liberalization." In contrast, regional trade arrangements "reduce a country's incentive to liberalize trade on a nondiscriminatory basis," and each of the following were cited as current examples:

- "NAFTA undermined the momentum built up for unilateral liberalization in Latin America ... [where] tariff protection ... dropped from 40 percent in 1986 to below 20 percent in 1991, but since that time virtually no progress has been made ...
- "In the wake of Brazil's recent fiscal crisis, MERCOSUR *raised* its common external tariff by 3 percent."
- "Internal trade liberalization in the EU has been accompanied by more vigorous antidumping against outside countries."

- "Now that Eastern and Central European countries are implementing tariff preferences under association agreements with the EU, *they too are raising tariffs*.[5]

Those are sobering words for East Asian nations, especially since the Asian Bank, whose high quality staff has given it the region's respect, is the one international institution with which Asia's governments and specialists are most familiar. For that reason, it is important to recognize that the ADB's specific and operational recommendations about regionalism reflected not only an uncompromisingly negative view of the general concept, but also represented a stern warning of how Asia's economies would be affected if it flourished:

> If the trend toward regionalism continues, with the EU and NAFTA expanding to include more countries, the [Asian Developing Economies] *stand to suffer a considerable loss of market access and export demand*. Therefore, it is in Asia's interest to push for a *sunset clause on regional arrangements* . . . Such a clause would require that preferences . . . be extended to all WTO members within . . . less than ten years . . . [and] discourage . . . trade blocs that intend to stay closed.[6]

However sound that advice may be, we need to ask the question: is that advice destined to illustrate yet another case of "folly," as the word was famously employed by Barbara Tuchman? On present evidence, including much from all three regions this book's earlier chapters have recounted, the answer is a probable yes: the advice and warnings likely will be to no avail.

Tuchman, after all, wrote that a governmental "folly" is *not* simply an error or misjudgment made by a state or its leaders, not even an error of very large proportions. Instead, she wrote, we are in the presence of a true folly when a nation's leaders, ignoring or rejecting the warnings by *contemporary* advisors of disaster ahead, follow nevertheless a wrongheaded course. It is in that sense that in Asia today, developments that pertain to regionalism suggest a new folly in the making, and as Tuchman showed, such a course has proven uniformly disastrous for the nations and leaders involved.

The Western hemisphere, particularly as reflected in America's trade-driven campaign for a "Free Trade Area for the Americas," presents another example of a folly, this one in its late formative stage. Its roots, as Chapter 4 pointed out, are in America's romantic-historical view of "Latin America," although the US trade and investment record provides little evidence of those roots in *South* America, where the proposed FTAA would principally apply. This absence of a tight economic relationship between the US and South America is better understood now than in earlier years. Since the early 1990s, several prominent specialists have warned that implementing the FTAA would be harmful to the United States and its foreign policy goals.

A good example is the writing of C. Michael Aho, who in 1990 was Director of Economic Studies at the Council on Foreign Relations in New York. In arguments that directly parallel this book's concerns, he strongly urged *against* expanding NAFTA throughout the hemisphere: "For the United States to look beyond Canada, Israel, and perhaps Mexico in terms of regional agreements *would be a big mistake.*" Aho was equally clear and negative on the issue of compatibility between regionalism and multilateralism. Bilateral (or regional) agreements, he wrote, "are not building blocks [for] a stable multinational trading system," and only in very special cases, such as the European Community, are they justified. As we pointed out, it was Europe's long history of wars that made the EC one such special case. That history of conflict, especially between France and Germany, led to their historic post-war *rapprochement*, and then to the Treaty of Rome in 1957 that established the Community. Aho added that another special case was the US–Canada FTA, and he concluded that a similar agreement with Mexico "may also be a special case. *But beyond these, it would not be healthy . . . if the United States were to take the bilateral path.*"[7]

A similar argument was pressed in 1993, by Lawrence B. Krause, for many years a leading American specialist on the Asian economies (he has focused on APEC and Korea in particular). Krause wrote at a time when the possibility of a three-bloc division of the globe had first come under serious attention, and in terms even stronger than Aho had used, he criticized any thought of expanding NAFTA. Krause argued, as did this book at its outset, that it was *the United States* whose policies had brought about the danger of a three-bloc world:

> What gives the three-bloc concept some saliency is the formalization of . . . North America into NAFTA, and the *ill-considered trade elements* in President Bush's Enterprise of the Americas Initiative (EAI), which could extend NAFTA to the whole of the Western Hemisphere.

No less importantly, Krause also took issue with Henry Kissinger's strange argument, mentioned in Chapter 1, that a "Western Hemisphere-wide free trade system" would allow the United States to retain a *"commanding role no matter what happens."* In Krause's view, that was both factually wrong and dangerous, because of what it implied about the future directions of American policy:

> While analysis can clearly show that even an expanded NAFTA *cannot replace global economic linkages for the United States,* fear has been created that the United States may be turning inward within the confines of a protected subregion. This has led to suggestions for an East Asian economic group or caucus.[8]

His insightful work will be touched on again here, but it should be said now that Krause's essay, ironically in a book about regionalism, was replete with warnings about its *predictably negative consequences*, both world-wide and particularly in East Asia. Asian regionalism, he concluded, would be especially dangerous because it "would raise concerns elsewhere as to what its real intentions were. Hence the onus for undermining the world economy *would fall on East Asia*, not on the EC or NAFTA (*although NAFTA should not be enlarged*)."

Yet both Clinton administrations, and the Bush administration before it – in a perfect example of what Tuchman would call a wooden-headed way – proceeded precisely down the path of widening and extending NAFTA. Mr Clinton's plan to expand it to Central and South America, with Chile expected as the first new member, was frustrated only by Congressional refusal to grant him "fast track" negotiating authority. Even so, Congress was widely expected to renew fast track once Clinton left the scene, and it was predictable to a certainty that American policy would then again embark on its same wrongheaded course. After all, both the Republican and Democratic party candidates, in their campaigns to succeed Mr Clinton, clearly confirmed their intention to restart the FTAA initiative. As candidate George W. Bush put it in August 2000, "our goal will be free-trade agreements with all the nations of Latin America. ... We should do so with Chile, and Brazil and Argentina, the anchor states of Mercosur."[9]

This, despite all the evidence brought forward here that Brazil – South America's largest and most populous nation – is dead-set against that American design, and has its own quite different plan in mind. If that were ever in any doubt, it was resolved in September 2000, when Brazil convened a first-ever summit meeting of *all* the South American nations. It was held in Brasilia, the nation's capital, and as the *Financial Times* reported, the meeting was a "sort of coming-out party for ... Brazil [to] forge a new diplomatic role."[10] Local assessments were even more clear: one of Brazil's most prominent and influential newspapers wrote that "the Brazilian Government's main objective is 'the creation of a South American free trade zone.'"[11] A few days later, a columnist for the same newspaper summed up the meaning of the summit:

> Although the government denies it and Itamaraty [the Foreign Ministry] avoids it, there is no doubt that Brazil last week began a diplomatic offensive to become "a regional leader" or – as some neighbor countries are interpreting it – "the regional leader."[12]

Of course what prompted all this activity was Brazil's awareness that, in the United States, there is bipartisan support to press ahead with the FTAA, and that its momentum would accelerate after the Presidential elections in November, 2000. The Brazilian press put it this way: "Democrat Al Gore and Republican George W. Bush are promising to move forward quickly in negotiating the Free Trade Area of the Americas (FTAA)." With that in mind, there was a need to move quickly to stop or slow the American momentum, and Brazil's anxiety was heightened by its growing suspicions that Argentina's developing ties with the US would weaken its support for MERCOSUR. In that case, as a widely-felt caution had it, "the US Government would find it much easier to order the hemisphere's integration along the lines of a project 'made in USA.'"[13]

At the core of Brazil's concerns, however, are its fears of American economic competition. Recall the Brazilian manufacturer, whose words we quoted earlier: "Our industry may be wiped out by US industry ... the Americans are much more competitive, not only in industry but also in agriculture." A similar warning came on the eve of the September, 2000 summit, this time from the chief economist of Brazil's Industrial Federation (CNI). With MERCOSUR in mind, she cautioned that "the FTAA accord will take precedence over all regional trade pacts, unless the provisions of the latter are stricter."

One consequence of these worries was that, in the lead-up to the South American summit, Brazil and its partners – in order to better fend off the US and its FTAA attractions – were regularly urged to end their intra-MERCOSUR squabbling. A good example was an editorial titled "Mercosur Must Be Stronger to Stand Up to FTAA." It is also worth mentioning because it reflected Brazil's penchant to regard the US (and its free trade proposals) as Brazil's rival for leadership in South America. For example, while the editorial conceded that Argentina's "protectionism" – on cars, sugar, intellectual property, and much else – caused many irritants, Brazil nevertheless had to bear those burdens, because the FTAA alternative was worse. In sum, MERCOSUR members needed to get their house in order because:

> Acting together, they carry enough weight to force consideration of interests differing from those supported by Washington. ... The FTAA would be merely an extension of the North American Free Trade Area (NAFTA) under conditions perhaps even more favorable to the strongest partner. That risk remains, and will be all the greater to the extent that the Mercosur project is delayed.[14]

The downsides of political regionalism

This book has regularly cautioned that mistaken American trade views, especially on US export performance, have often driven foreign policy in ways that are harmful to overall American interests. The FTAA--MERCOSUR issue, however, *may* present an instance of the happy opposite: a case where broader political and security goals have begun to take precedence over a misguided trade policy. At least in this instance, as I will explain now, the hopeful outcome could be an improved US approach towards the nations involved.

In September, 2000, in their preparations for the upcoming South American summit, Brazilian officials were relieved, and probably surprised, by US government statements that were described as "in support of Brazil's decision to assume its natural position of leadership in South America." Admittedly those remarks, as a leading newspaper put it, "could sound like mere diplomatic rhetoric in the face of events over which Washington has no control":

> But statements of support for the Brasilia Summit made by US Ambassador to Brazil Anthony Harrington and echoed by US Secretary of State Madeleine Albright, in a recent visit to Paris, represent *much more than that*.[15]

By "much more than that," the report meant the US had shown greater sensitivity than before to Brazil's interests, and that Washington may have taken to heart the old adage to "not let the perfect become the enemy of the good." The background came in 1997, in the planning for President Clinton's scheduled visit to Brazil. The office of the US Trade Representative and other officials were said to have "argued that the president should use the trip to clear up Washington's doubts about the usefulness and viability of Mercosur." A possible confrontation with Brazil might have resulted if that advice were followed. What reportedly prevailed instead was a more sophisticated vision, "defended by US Undersecretary of State ... Pickering and the [National] Security Council staff":

> Their view was that, *even though Mercosur might hamper the realization of US trade policy objectives*, it is a factor of stability in a region notorious for its instability, and represents a step in the right direction for integration.[16]

Hopefully this is true, and credit should go to Professor Arturo Valenzuela, an American scholar of Chile and South America. At the time of these events, he was a senior US official, serving with the Clinton administration while on leave from his post at Georgetown University. His contribution dealt with Brazil's inclination to see the US as its hemispheric "rival," especially in South America. In Chapter 4, I argued that when the US deals with Brazil about MERCOSUR, it needs to avoid being cast in that competitive role, and that it must especially avoid being seen as Brazil's rival for hemispheric leadership. Professor Valenzuela reportedly made a similar argument in the 1997 discussions. In ways that appear to have been vindicated by the summit, he stressed that it "would be a mistake" to side with those US officials who regarded Brazil's MERCOSUR policy as the "start of a hemispheric rivalry between Brazil and the US." In his words, "As the Brasilia meeting proved, we are talking here of shared values. The US can only gain from Brazil's taking a leadership role."[17]

That is the mark of a sophisticated American policy; one that recognizes what the nature of US interests *are* in the Western hemisphere, and also knows what they *are not*. Valenzuela's contribution was to stress the essential *political* point that the United States interest, both in South America and the hemisphere, is in the widening of democratically-based political stability: what he referred to as "shared values." The expansion of South America's political stability, as a result of those shared values, is of far greater importance to the US than any tangible benefit that Americans might derive from the FTAA commitment.

Of course America's trade and investments in the region are important and valuable, and obviously they should always be encouraged. But the United States *does not*, after all, have a very large trade presence in the region, and its investments have sharply declined. In 1999, US exports to *all* of South America were *less than 5 percent* of the US global total, and its imports from South America were well *below 4 percent*. The steep drop in America's investments in the region were shown in Chapter 4. As Figure 4.14 demonstrated, they fell from 25 percent of US global investments in 1950, to *only 7 percent* in 1998.

Certainly these and related considerations were familiar to Professor Valenzuela, in his role both as scholar and official. They are also a sharp reminder of a main *economic* point highlighted by our discussion of US trade in the Western hemisphere: that outside of Mexico and Canada, the hemisphere is no "natural market" for the United States. As Krause put it, "The United States requires access to *global* markets and particularly to the growing markets of the Pacific Basin. The United States could not confine its economic activity to North America without severe economic hardship."[18] To that we would add a point now familiar to this book's readers: even if the United States included South America in an expanded NAFTA, that would do nothing to change the equation.

Similarly, in shaping the *political* aspects of US policy, especially toward Brazil, the United States needs to recall a central diplomatic point long emphasized by Hans J. Morgenthau. In his rightly-famous book *Politics Among Nations*, Morgenthau reminded his readers that every nation must always "Look at the Political Scene from the Point of View of Other Nations." He called this "diplomacy's fourth rule," and in support of the principle, Morgenthau quoted Edmund Burke, who in 1793 wrote that "Nothing is so fatal to a nation as an extreme of self-partiality, and the total want of consideration of what others will naturally hope or fear."[19]

America's relations with Brazil are a perfect illustration of that Burke–Morgenthau teaching. We have seen here that Brazil, whose size, population, and economy are the region's largest, views in existential terms its role as South America's regional leader ("or as some neighbor countries are interpreting it, 'the regional leader'"). In contrast, the United States, as the pre-eminent global power, needs for its part to gauge *its* national interest against that Brazilian interest – now further symbolized by the MERCOSUR commitment. With that dual measurement in hand, the US must certainly conclude that, however large is the American ideological commitment to the FTAA concept, it has no transcendent stake in the proposal. Morgenthau's words apply very well here: "For minds not beclouded by the crusading zeal of a political religion and capable of viewing the national interests of both sides with objectivity, the delimitation of these vital interests should not prove too difficult."

The values of multilateralism

The broader task for US foreign policy is always to recall how successful the United States has been as an actor in the global economy. That success is especially well reflected in America's continuing role as the world's leading exporter, as Chapter 2 demonstrated. Figure 2.4 showed that over the *100-year period from 1896-1996*, the United States retained a level of roughly 12 percent of world exports. American exports reached a significantly higher percentage than that in two war-related periods (especially the first 15–20 years after World War II), *but over the century-long period they have never been much lower than that 12 percent level*. The illustration also showed that, in the most recent years, from 1980–96, the US share of the global market was at the same constant level: not quite 12 percent. Its performance in the few years since then has become even slightly better. US exports rose to 12.2 percent of the world total in 1997, and in 1998 they rose again, to 12.4 percent.[20]

That 100+-year-record is an astoundingly successful accomplishment, and it stands in stark contrast to the often ill-informed dialogue on trade that continues to shape so much American thinking about the issue. That everyday dialogue, so resistant to readily-available evidence, regularly laments America's alleged difficulties in "penetrating" various world markets. Of course there remain problems of market access – and they are found *in all parts of the world*. In Western Europe, for example, the US Trade Representative complained that laws covering US biotechnology exports are "cumbersome and non-transparent, and the EU's approval system has ceased to function." Similarly in Poland, where US exports are blocked by agricultural quarantines that "do not meet the international definition," and in Brazil, the USTR office reported that "the lack of effective copyright and trademark enforcement is a serious concern."[21] Yet despite these obstacles, and the far better-known cases in Japan, China, and most other East Asian economies, the evidence remains that the US is the world export leader; indeed it has increased its global market-share in recent years. Those undeniable facts, which underline the ability of all types of US exports to compete successfully in all markets, make it all the more puzzling that Washington continues to support the rise of new "free trade areas."

The implications of that concept, especially to the extent that they lead to regional trade blocs, are decidedly unfavorable, both for the United States and more widely. In 1993, Krause warned that a "three-bloc world" already had become a "commonplace," and while the label was not objectionable as "literary shorthand," there were great dangers if it became more than that. If "three blocs were to become a reality, it could mean a disaster for the world economy":

> Analysis of a three-bloc configuration [centered on] Germany, the United States, and Japan ... suggest[s] that they would be internally contentious and externally aggressive. Game theory suggests that such a trading system would be very unstable ... there would be frequent changes in alliances, regions would follow tit-for-tat strategies, and short-term considerations would overwhelm long-term interests. The most serious problems would arise if Japan and the United States were ... in different and rival regions ... *It is unlikely that the global system as it exists today could be sustained in such an atmosphere.*[22]

That is not an extreme projection, either in its assessment of the probabilities, or in their likely consequences. Those who doubt the danger will argue that no modern statesman, given the course of recent history and its bleak lessons over the past century, is likely to knowingly take his nation down the path of aggressive "rival regions." The doubters would add that the realities of globalization would themselves act as a final impediment, and make such a course impossible to implement even if it were sought or attempted.[23] Indeed it does seem self-evident that today's globally decentralized supply and production networks (to name just one feature of economic globalization), would render "tit-for-tat strategies" and "externally aggressive" blocs so unlikely as not to warrant serious consideration.

Yet modern history has been there before. After all, the years of the late nineteenth and early twentieth centuries, from roughly 1850–1914, were characterized by an unprecedently open international economic system – so much so that the analogy is sometimes made between today's globalization and that era. That first period came to an end in 1914, and it has long been an easy debater's tactic to point to the demonstrated political-irrelevance of that early open economy. Although many of its cross-national economic factors objectively made war seemingly irrational, extreme nationalism in parts of Europe triumphed instead. Major portions of the world imploded with the outbreak of World War I, but there was no evidence of any mitigating impact of that first "globalization."

Without harking back too much to that period, it is undeniable that however defined, one feature of today's globalization is that its support-base is increasingly precarious. It has its enlightened advocates, of course, but some of them – President Clinton's performance at the WTO Seattle meeting comes to mind[24] – recall the old dictum that "with friends like that, who needs enemies?" The broader reality is that powerful forces in today's world economy oppose *what they regard as globalization*. Whether from the standpoint of farmers, organized labor, environmental and animal-rights advocates, or traditional protectionism in any of its other guises – from fair labor standards to "buy local" sentiments – the concept is now under sharp and growing attack. Its opponents are antithetical to the model in general, and they are especially hostile to the system of open and multilateral trade that has shaped the world economy since the 1950s.

Those forces were well-represented in Seattle in November–December, 1999, where they helped to scuttle the scheduled meetings of the World Trade Organization.[25] Alan Greenspan, the chairman of the Federal Reserve in the US, commented almost a year later that one result of that WTO failure was that the world's "ability to move forward on various trade initiatives has clearly come to a remarkable stall." From his vantage point of long experience and high responsibility, Greenspan warned that despite the welfare gains that have characterized so many economies in recent years, nothing could be taken for granted. "Should recent positive trends in economic growth falter," he said,

> it is quite imaginable that support for market-oriented resource allocation will wane, and the *latent forces of protectionism and state intervention* will begin to reassert themselves in many countries, *including the United States*.[26]

As every observer of the trade debate in the United States knows, Greenspan's assessment of the potential for a revival of protectionism is not only correct, but applies to the American economy and to all others, especially in the developing world. Much of the American debate about those economies has long rejected the "Washington consensus," despite its role in promoting so much of East Asia's growth. The American voices in that debate have expressed similar reservations about the dangers of globalization for the United States. They have warned in particular that much of America's burgeoning foreign trade is simply a cover-up for lost jobs and a "hollowing out" of the American economy. As applied to the developing world, they have argued especially against export-led growth, and urged instead a prescription comprised of local, demand-centered development. The implications of their ideas for world trade are as clear as they are depressing, as the following classic example of the anti-globalization perspective perfectly demonstrates:

What cannot be produced locally is produced nationally. What cannot be produced nationally is purchased from regional partners – which suggests the importance of *revitalizing regional integration institutions.* Only for those products for which regional producers cannot satisfy demand is trade necessary with countries on the other side of the globe.[27]

The legacy of the 1997 Asian crisis, and fears of a recurrence – despite much evidence of recovery[28] – has made those ideas again attractive. They add to Asia's receptivity for a revival of anti-globalization sentiment, and underscore Greenspan's warning that an economic slowdown also slows down economic openness. For the United States, the action-lesson is to once again take the lead in upholding the multilateral trade system that is now represented by the World Trade Organization. The WTO's importance is widely-recognized, but its challenges are less well understood. What should be clear to all, however, is the central relationship of the US to the question of whether the WTO can do its job. Early in the life of the WTO, an experienced observer described that critical connection, and made two inter-connected points: "The WTO can succeed only if the United States is perceived abroad to be playing by the rules, *and this will prove delicate because of its pursuit of regional trade arrangements . . .*"[29]

That challenge remains, and central to its accomplishment is the need for the United States to drop its truly dangerous flirtation with all "regional" efforts everywhere. In operational terms, that means that Washington has three tasks:

- bring an end to the FTAA chimera;
- resist any new or revived temptations to build a "transatlantic free trade area";
- oppose the further development of regionalism in East Asia, especially in ways that would sharpen lines in the Pacific between the United States and the vibrant economies on its other side.

In September, 2000, the editor of the "Americas" column in the *Wall Street Journal* broke new ground when, writing about Peru, she urged the US to "abandon the facile rhetoric of the Free Trade Area of the Americas."[30] That essay may come to be regarded as the opening first shot across the bow of a flawed enterprise, one that has been marked by much folly since its inception. Its errors have been further underlined by the damaging effects the FTAA proposal has already had on US–Brazil ties, and by its needlessly negative impact on political relations *within* South America, as in the case of Brazil–Argentina relations.

Even in Europe, there are dangers of new US involvement in regional developments. One example is a just-emerging proposal to create a "free trade arrangement" between the US and the United Kingdom. Its principal American advocate is Senator Philip Gramm, chairman of the Senate Banking Committee, which authorized a formal Congressional study. In Britain, the proposal has the support of some Conservative Party members who for years have had reservations about the EU, and now oppose London's announced intention to join its single currency.[31] Senator Gramm believes such a US–UK arrangement should also include Canada and Mexico, and while Britain's present leadership has made light of the whole idea (the Foreign Secretary referred to it as "pretty barmy"), it represents an incipient danger with the potential to attract wider support.

Worsening EU–US trade problems in 1999–2000 also led Stuart Eizenstat, the Deputy Secretary of the Treasury (and former US Ambassador to the EU), to warn of "raised tensions on both sides of the Atlantic."[32] Less cautious observers began to talk of "a new trade war," and to avoid that, Eizenstat urged the Europeans and Americans to negotiate their differences through existing bodies. He mentioned the regular EU–US Summit meetings, the OECD, and as part of the "Transatlantic Dialogues" we mentioned in Chapter 3, several Business, Labor, and Environment groups. All are good suggestions, but what must be resisted is any revival of the "Transatlantic Free Trade Area" (TAFTA).

The TAFTA proposal is superficially attractive, but has two fundamental flaws. First, as the German economists who were commissioned to study it wrote, TAFTA – when compared with the WTO – is, at best, only second best: "the WTO is an open club [but] regional liberalization discriminates ... the foremost risk of TAFTA is that bilateral agreements can hit third countries." Beyond that severe economic drawback, the second and even larger objection to TAFTA is political and strategic. Were Europe and the US to significantly institutionalize a transatlantic "free trade" arrangement, the certain result would be to encourage similar, and directly responsive measures in East Asia. As Chapter 5 demonstrated, the Asian financial crisis already has accelerated movements toward regionalism there, and Japan, to which we turn now, will be the critical factor determining how far those developments will go.

Avoid the self-fulfilling prophecy

We have seen that, in Japan, there is a long tradition, dating at least from the Meiji period, that questions whether it is truly "Western," or is it inevitably an "Asian nation." That debate is clearly continuing, but it has recently taken on an edge that affects nations throughout the Pacific region. In the interest of avoiding new and added tensions in the Pacific, especially between the US and Japan, it is essential that Japan resolve that identity question, without again seeking a role of leadership as an "Asian nation." There are, however, influential Japanese voices that *would* move in that direction, and while none are now dominant, and some are so frankly extreme as to have little prospect of drawing wider support, others are part of Japan's wide and respectable mainstream.

As an example, these last paragraphs will draw on the writing of Kazuo Ogura, a prominent and knowledgeable senior official in Japan's Foreign Ministry. He has been Director-General of the Ministry's Economic Affairs Bureau, and in mid-2000 was appointed Japan's Ambassador to France. His familiarity with Asia, and his knowledge of the region is reflected in his other two Ambassadorial assignments: first in Vietnam, and until mid-2000, as Ambassador to Korea. Ogura's public writing, which has concentrated on issues of Asia's identity, and the friction between Asia and the West, is worth special comment partly because it *is* public. His views provide an insight into the perspectives of Japan's foreign policy leadership for which there is simply no public parallel among the other major governments. By that I mean that in the US, as in Britain, Germany, and elsewhere, no *serving* senior official has the same latitude as in Japan to write *publicly* on foreign and national security affairs, in ways that do not conform closely to the government's policy of the day.

In 1999, in the prominent journal *Voice*, Ogura went further into a subject about which he had written before: Asia's identity. In the article, "Creating a New Asia," he signaled at the outset his overall approach:

> We have entered an age in which Asia must act in a unified way and in which Japan must shoulder a large part of the leadership needed to achieve that. One reason has to do with America's world dominance, *the concentration of power in the hands of the United States.*[33]

His reference to Japan's "leadership" in Asia underscores a theme already mentioned in Chapter 5: that in Japan, there is a continuing discussion among serious people about the nation's role as Asia's leader. It is sometimes thought that those discussions and views are restricted to Japan's so-called "right-wing nationalists," or to an older or "pre-war" generation. That is not the case. Ogura, for example, was born in 1938, received all of his training after 1945, and his education, at the University of Tokyo and at Cambridge (where he took an economics degree) has been top-flight by both Japanese and Western standards.

His emphasis, in the *Voice* article, on Japan's need to exercise Asian leadership reinforces another point raised in the previous chapter. I stressed there that the meaning of the Asian Monetary Fund's revival, both for Japan *and* Asia – as well as the significance of Tokyo's new "funds swapping" scheme – are closely inter-related, and that they are integral to broader Japanese goals. In Japan they are seen as part of the burden of leadership the nation must be expected to shoulder – a burden most recently reflected in the staggeringly-huge ($80 billion) "new Miyazawa plan" for East Asia.

The second part of Ogura's approach, its emphasis on America's "world dominance," and the "concentration of power in the hands of the US," clearly evokes the "hyperpower" view of the US associated with French Foreign Minister Vedrine. (For that reason alone, Japan's new Ambassador may be especially welcome in Paris.) More importantly, Ogura's perspectives on the US are tied tightly to his views on other key issues, and the following excerpts from his *Voice* article captures their overall flavor:

- "It is necessary for a united Asia, along with Western Europe, to be prepared to *check* America, so as to ensure that its leadership is free from self-righteousness and prejudice and that it does not lapse into protectionism and a narrow egoism";
- the "New Miyazawa Initiative" was launched to create "a new consultative mechanism in Asia";
- "The reason the Asian crisis [was] such a shock to many Asians was that Asians have not been given enough seats in international councils ... to have a significant voice in the international community";
- "Asian countries need to correctly perceive ... the great role postwar Japan's economic and technological assistance has played in their own countries' development ... they must show a positive attitude toward Japan's assumption of a greater international role ...";
- Asia's need to "heighten its sense of a distinct identity" has been catalyzed by "the advance of European integration," and by Europe's "strengthening political cooperation".

Each of these points could warrant a separate discussion, but suffice to say here that two fundamental propositions strongly characterize Ogura's argument. The first is the asserted need to "check" America; the second is a recognition of the supposed "limits" on America's capabilities, though that raises a logical question. Why, for example, is there a great need to "check" a power whose capacities are so "limited"? Nevertheless, these propositions led Ogura to the policy-conclusion he recommended: that Japan must do more as Asia's leader. The ostensible reason, he argued, is that:

Given America's military involvement in the Middle East and elsewhere ... it seems unlikely that the existing framework of bilateral ties between the United States and other countries will be sufficient to allow the U.S. military presence in Asia to continue to function effectively.

That statement is a near-perfect illustration of the "wish as father to the thought." To Americans, as to many others, it is *not* self-evident that there are such limitations on the ability of the US "military presence in Asia to continue to function effectively." As recently as late 1998, in a much-publicized formal report on strategy in East Asia, the US Secretary of

Defense affirmed, in unmistakable terms, America's "ability and intention to maintain a robust military presence of approximately 100,000 in the [East Asia] region."[34] In connection with Japan, moreover, the report added that "As our most important bilateral alliance in the region, the U.S.–Japan partnership in particular will remain critical ... The United States sees no substitute for this historic relationship." Those are powerful and serious words, and they depend ultimately on public understanding, a point the Defense Secretary acknowledged when he wrote, in his letter transmitting the report, that "The United States cannot long sustain its commitments without public support."

For that support to continue, however, it is essential for Americans and others to recognize that for the United States, in its role as the only truly *global* economic actor, the stakes are very high, and one of this book's aims has been to make the extent of that global involvement very clear. If that aim has been met, the prospect Ogura raises – of an America that needs to be "checked," but whose capacities at the same time are somehow "limited" – need not become a self-fulfilling prophecy. And if this book has been successful, we will not witness, as its subtitle warned, "How America is turning economic leadership into strategic weakness."

Notes

1 *Asian Development Outlook, 1999*, Oxford and New York, Oxford University Press, 1999, p. 224. Emphasis added.
2 He has used and explained this term in several writings, including (with A. Krueger), *The Dangerous Drift to Preferential Trade Agreements*, Washington, AEI Press, 1995, pp. 2–3.
3 In order of publication date, the three are: J. Frankel and M. Kahler, *Regionalism and Rivalry: Japan and the United States in Pacific Asia*, Chicago, The University of Chicago Press, 1993; J. Frankel, with E. Stein and Shang-Jin Wei, *Regional Trading Blocs in the World Economic System*, Washington, Institute for International Economics, 1997, and J. Frankel (ed.), *The Regionalization of the World Economy*, Chicago and London, The University of Chicago Press, 1998.
4 There are, of course, exceptions, led most notably by Bhagwati. Along with A. Panagariya, he has elaborated on the problem in, for example, *The Economics of Preferential Trade Agreements*, Washington, AEI Press, 1996, especially pp. 53–4. The issue of diversion of scarce governmental human resources has also been touched on by A. de la Torre and M. Kelly, *Regional Trade Arrangements*, International Monetary Fund Occasional Paper No. 93, Washington, IMF, 1992, pp. 44–5, and in J. Schott (ed.), *Free Trade Areas and U.S. Trade Policy*, Washington, Institute for International Economics, 1989, p. 35.
5 *ibid.*, p. 225. My emphasis.
6 *ibid.*, p. 227. My emphasis.
7 "A Recipe for RIBS – Resentment, Inefficiency, Bureaucracy, and Stupid Signals," in R. Belous and R. Hartley (eds), *The Growth of Regional Trading Blocs in the Global Economy*, Washington, The National Planning Association, 1990, p. 24. My emphasis.

8 L. Krause, "Comment," in Frankel and Kahler, *Regionalism and Rivalry*, *op. cit.*, p. 123. My emphasis.

9 From his speech at Florida International University in Miami, in *The New York Times*, 26 August, 2000.

10 *Financial Times*, 1 September, 2000.

11 *O. Estado de São Paulo*, Internet version, 2 September, 2000, in FBIS, 2 September, 2000.

12 Article by Vladimir Goitia, *O Estado de São Paulo* (São Paulo), Internet version, in Portuguese, 5 September, 2000, in FBIS, 5 September, 2000.

13 *ibid.*, 27 August, 2000.

14 *ibid.*

15 *ibid.*, 1 September, 2000. My emphasis.

16 *ibid.* My emphasis.

17 Quoted in *O Estado de São Paulo*, Internet version, 3 September, 2000, in FBIS, 3 September, 2000.

18 Krause, p. 123. Emphasis added.

19 H. Morgenthau, *Politics Among Nations*, New York, Alfred A. Knopf, 5th edn., revised, 1978, pp. 553–4, citing Edmund Burke, "Remarks on the Policy of the Allies with Respect to France" (1793), *Works*, Vol. IV, Boston, Little, Brown, and Company, 1889, p. 447.

20 Based on data in the IMF, *Direction of Trade Statistics Yearbook, 1999*.

21 *2000 Trade Policy Agenda and 1999 Annual Report*, Washington, United States Trade Representative, March, 2000.

22 Krause, *op. cit.*, pp. 122–3.

23 T. Pempel, "Gulliver in Lilliput: Japan and Asian Economic Regionalism," *World Policy Journal*, Winter, 1996/97, pp. 13–26, is a good statement of the doubts. He argued, though before the Asian economic crisis, that Asia needs the West too much to attempt to become "a closed loop," and everybody knows it; and that "Japan ceased to be exclusively Asian in anything other than geographic terms decades ago."

24 He angered and disappointed WTO participants when he said trade negotiations should include workers' rights issues: "[The WTO] should develop these core labor standards, and then they ought be a part of every trade agreement" (quoted in S. Mallaby, "The Irrelevant Election," Foreign Policy, September–October, 2000, p. 76).

25 For the views of one of the principal activists at Seattle, see "Lori's War," *Foreign Policy*, Spring, 2000, pp. 28–54. For a calmer view of the meanings of globalization, see R. Keohane and J. Nye, Jr, "Globalization: What's New? What's Not?, in *ibid.*, pp. 104–18.

26 As quoted in *The New York Times*, 26 August, 2000.

27 R. Broad and J. Cavanagh, "No More NICs," *Foreign Policy*, Fall, 1988, No. 72, p. 101. Emphasis added.

28 By 2000, growth rates again averaged almost 7 percent, with increases of economic growth of more than 8 percent expected in Hong Kong, Korea, and Singapore, and significantly lower rates projected only for Thailand and the Philippines. These data are from the Asian Development Bank's upward revisions of estimated growth-rates for 2000, as reported in the *Financial Times* and *The Wall Street Journal*, 19 September, 2000.

29 P. Morici, "Export our Way to Prosperity," *Foreign Policy*, Winter 1995–6, p. 12. Morici had been Director of Economics at the US International Trade Commission. Emphasis added.

30 M. O'Grady, *The Wall Street Journal*, 19 September, 2000. She wrote that the FTAA proposal ironically encourages Peru to "hold on to its remaining import tariffs until 2005 as bargaining chips."

31 See, for example, *Financial Times*, 29 August, 2000.
32 S. Eizenstadt, "The Cloud over Transatlantic Trade," *Financial Times*, 11 September, 2000.
33 Ogura Kazuo, "Creating a New Asia," in *Japan Echo*, Vol. 26, No. 3, June, 1999, p. 12. All of the excerpts quoted are from that *Japan Echo* translation, pp. 12–16. (Slightly abridged from "Atarashii Ajia no sozo," *Voice*, March, 1999, pp. 123–35). My emphasis.
34 US Secretary of Defense, *The United States Security Strategy for the East Asia–Pacific Region*, Washington, 1998, pp. 6, 61.

Bibliography

Aho, C., "'Fortress Europe': Will the EU Isolate Itself from North America and Asia?" *Columbia Journal of World Business*, 1994, Vol. 29, No. 3.

Alexander, R., *Today's Latin America*, 2nd edn, Revised, New York and Washington, Praeger, 1968.

Andersson, T., *Managing Trade Relations in the New World Economy*, London and New York, Routledge, 1993.

Asian Development Bank, *Asian Development Outlook, 1999*, Oxford and New York, Oxford University Press, 1999.

Averyt, W., Jr, *Agropolitics in the European Community*, Boulder, Praeger, 1977.

Baldwin, R., *Towards an Integrated Europe*, London, Centre for Economic Policy Research, 1994.

Barbezat, D. and Neal, L., *The Economics of the European Union and the Economies of Europe*, New York and Oxford, Oxford University Press, 1998.

Barfield, C. (ed.), *Expanding U.S.–Asian Trade and Investment*, Washington, American Enterprise Institute, 1997.

Barfield, C., "The Deceptive Allure of a Transatlantic Free Trade Agreement," *Intereconomics*, September–October, 1998.

Bergsten, C., "America and Europe: Clash of the Titans?" *Foreign Affairs*, March–April, 1999.

Bessho, K., "Identities and Security in East Asia," *ADELPHI* paper No. 325, London, International Institute for Strategic Studies, 1999.

Bhagwati, J., "Regionalism versus Multilateralism," *The World Economy*, September 1992, Vol. 15, No. 5.

Black, C., "Britain's Atlantic Option," *The National Interest*, Spring, 1999.

Blackhurst, R. and Anderson, K. (eds), *Regional Integration and the Global Trading System*, New York, St Martin's Press, 1993.

Bradford, C., Jr, *Strategic Options for Latin America in the 1990s*, Inter-American Development Bank, Washington, 1992.

Brinkley, D. and Hoopes, T., *FDR and the Creation of the U.N.*, New Haven, Yale University Press, 1997.

Cai, K., "The Political Economy of Economic Regionalism in Northeast Asia: a Unique and Dynamic Pattern," *East Asia: an International Quarterly*, New Brunswick, Transaction Press, Summer, 1999.

Carvounis, B. and Carvounis C., *United States Trade and Investment in Latin America*, Westport and London, Quorum, 1992.

Castaneda, J., "Can NAFTA Change Mexico?" *Foreign Affairs*, September–October, 1993.

Castellano, M., "Internationalization of the Yen: A Ministry of Finance Pipe Dream?", *Japan Economic Institute Report*, No. 23A, 18 June, 1999.

Castellano, M., "Two Years on: Evaluating Tokyo's Response to the East Asian Financial Crisis," *Japan Economic Institute Report*, No. 30A, August 6, 1999.

Cavanagh, J. and Broad, R., "No More NICs," *Foreign Policy*, No. 72, Fall, 1988.

Central Intelligence Agency (CIA), *World Factbook, 1999*. Available at http://www.odci.gov/cia/publications/factbook

Collins, S. (ed.), *Imports, Exports, and the American Worker*, Washington, Brookings, 1998.

Conquest, R., "Toward an English Speaking Union," *The National Interest*, Fall, 1999.

Corbet, H. (ed.), *Trade Strategy and the Asian–Pacific Region*, Toronto, University of Toronto Press, 1970.

Council on Foreign Relations, *Study Group Papers, U.S. Commercial Diplomacy*, New York, Council on Foreign Relations, 1998.

Dominguez, J., *The Future of Inter-American Relations*, London, Routledge, 2000.

Donges, J., *et al.*, "TAFTA: Assuring its Compatibility with Global Free Trade," *World Economy*, August, 1997, Vol. 20, No. 5.

Encarnacion, D. and Mason, M., *Does Ownership Matter?*, Oxford, Clarendon Press, 1994.

Feinberg, R., *Summitry of the Americas*, Washington, Institute for International Economics,1997.

Fenby, J., *France On the Brink*, New York, Arcade, 1999.

Feraru, A. and Simone, V., *The Asian Pacific: Political and Economic Development in a Global Context*, White Plains, Longman, 1995.

Fifield, R., "ASEAN and the Pacific Community," *Asia–Pacific Community*, Winter, 1981.

Frank, I., *Foreign Enterprise in Developing Countries*, Baltimore, Johns Hopkins University Press, 1980.

Frankel, J. *et al.*, *Regional Trading Blocs in the World Economic System*, Washington, Institute for International Economics, 1997.

Frankel, J. (ed.), *The Regionalization of the World Economy*, Chicago and London, University of Chicago Press, 1998.

Frost, E., *Transatlantic Trade, A Strategic Agenda*, Washington, Institute for International Economics, 1997.

Gaster, R. and Prestowitz, C., *Shrinking the Atlantic: Europe and the American Economy*, Washington, Economic Strategy Institute, 1994.

GATT, *Trends in International Trade*, Geneva, 1958 ("The Haberler Report").

Gilpin, R., *The Challenge of Global Capitalism*, Princeton, Princeton University Press, 2000.

Golich, V., "From Competition to Collaboration: the Challenge of Commercial-class Aircraft Manufacturing," *International Organization*, Autumn, 1992.

Goodman, D. and Segal, G., *Towards Recovery in Pacific Asia*, London and New York, Routledge, 2000.

Gordon, B., "Rhetoric and Reality in Regional Cooperation," *Solidarity* (Manila), July, 1971.

Gordon, B., "Japan and the Pacific Basin Proposal," *Korea and World Affairs*, Summer, 1981.

Gordon, B., "Regionalism in Southeast Asia," *Asian Survey*, May, 1963.

Gordon, B., *Dimensions of Conflict in Southeast Asia*, Englewood Cliffs, Prentice-Hall, 1966.

Griffiths, R. (ed.), *The Economic Development of the EEC*, Cheltenham, Elgar, 1997.

Grosse, R., *Multinationals in Latin America*, London, Routledge, 1989.

Grunwald, J. (ed.), *Latin America and the World Economy*, London, Sage Publications, 1978.

Hackmann, R., *U.S. Trade, Foreign Direct Investments, and Global Competitiveness*, New York and London, International Business Press, 1997.

Harrison, L., *The Pan-American Dream*, New York, Basic Books, 1997.

Hartley, R. and Belous, R. (eds), *The Growth of Regional Trading Blocs in the Global Economy*, Washington, National Planning Association, 1990.

Hashimoto, R., *Vision of Japan*, Tokyo, Bestsellers, 1994.

Henderson, D., *The MAI Affair: a Story and its Lessons*, London, The Royal Institute of International Affairs, 1999.

Hendriks, G., "Germany and the CAP: national interests and the European Community," *International Affairs*, Winter, 1988–9.

Hoebing, J. *et al., NAFTA and Sovereignty: Trade-offs for Canada, Mexico, and the United States*, Washington, The Center for Strategic and International Studies, 1996.

Inter-American Development Bank and Instituto de Relaciones Europeo–latinoamericanas (IRELA), *Foreign Direct Investment in Latin America and the Caribbean, 1999*, Madrid, 2000.

Inter-American Development Bank and Instituto de Relaciones Europeo–latinoamericanas (IRELA), "European Investment in Latin America and the Caribbean". Available at http://www.lanic.utexas.edu/~sela/eng_docs/spdi1-2000-2.htm (August, 2000).

International Monetary Fund, *Direction of Trade Statistics Yearbook*, Washington, annually.

Irwin, D. and Eichengreen, B., "Trade Blocs, Currency Blocs and the Reorientation of World Trade in the 1930s," *Journal of International Economics*, 1995, Vol. 38, No. 5.

Irwin, D., *Against the Tide: An Intellectual History of Free Trade*, Princeton, Princeton University Press, 1996.

Jackson, J., *The World Trading System*, Cambridge and London, The MIT Press, 1989.

Kahler, M. and Frankel, Jeffrey A. Jr, *Regionalism and Rivalry: Japan and the United States in Pacific Asia*, Chicago, University of Chicago Press, 1993.

Kelly, M. and de la Torre, A., International Monetary Fund, *Regional Trade Arrangements*, Occasional Paper No. 93, Washington, 1992.

Keylor, W., *The Twentieth Century World, An International History*, New York, Oxford University Press, 1992.

Kissinger, H. A., *Diplomacy*, New York, Simon and Shuster, 1994.

Kojima, K. (ed.), *Pacific Trade and Development*, Tokyo, Japan Economic Research Center, 1968.

Kojima, K., "A Pacific Free Trade Area Proposed," *Pacific Community*, April, 1972.

Kojima, K., *Japan and a Pacific Free Trade Area*, Berkeley, University of California Press, 1971.

Kolodziej, E., *French International Policy under De Gaulle and Pompidou*, Ithaca, Cornell University Press, 1974.

Konoe, F., "Against a Pacificism Centered on England and America," *Japan Echo*, Special Issue, 1995.

Kostecki, M. and Hoeckman, B., *The Political Economy of the World Trading System*, Oxford, Oxford University Press, 1995.

Krauss, E., "Japan, the U.S. and the Emergence of Multilateralism in Asia," prepared for the "After the Global Crises: What need for Regionalism?" 3rd Annual Conference, Centre for the Study of Globalisation and Regionalisation, The University of Warwick, Coventry, England, 16–18th September, 1999.

Krueger, A. and Bhagwati, J., *The Dangerous Drift to Preferential Trade Agreements*, Washington, AEI Press, 1995.

Krugman, P., "The Myth of Asia's Miracle," *Foreign Affairs*, November–December, 1994.

Kryzanek, M., *U.S.–Latin American Relations*, New York, Praeger, 1990.

Kwan, C., *Economic Interdependence in the Asia–Pacific Region: Towards a Yen Bloc*, London and New York, Routledge, 1994.

Lawrence, R., *et al.*, *A Vision for the World Economy*, Washington, Brookings, 1996.

Lawrence, R., *Regionalism, Multilateralism, and Deeper Integration*, Washington, Brookings, 1996.

League of Nations, *Industrialization and Foreign Trade*, Geneva, 1945.

Leipziger, D. *et al.*, "Mercosur: Integration and Industrial Policy," *The World Economy*, May, 1997, Vol. 20, No. 5.

"Lori's War," *Foreign Policy*, Spring, 2000.

Lougheed, A. and Kenwood, A., *The Growth of the International Economy, 1820–1990*, London, Routledge, 1992.

Mallaby, S., "The Irrelevant Election," *Foreign Policy*, September–October, 2000.

Mattli, W. *The Logic of Regional Integration: Europe and Beyond*, Cambridge and New York, Cambridge University Press, 1999.

Mayes, D. and Bollard, A., "Regionalism and the Pacific Rim," *Journal of Common Market Studies*, June, 1992.

Milner, H. and Mansfield, E. (eds), *The Political Economy of Regionalism*, New York, Columbia University Press, 1997.

Ministry of International Trade and Industry, *White Paper on Trade, 1999, "For Stable Growth in the World Economy in a Global Era,"* Tokyo, 1999.

Ministry of International Trade and Industry, *White Paper on International Trade 2000*, Available at www.miti.go.jp/report (August, 2000).

Morici, P., "Export Our Way to Prosperity," *Foreign Policy*, Winter, 1995–6.

Nasatir, A. and Bailey, H., *Latin America: The Development of its Civilization*, Englewood Cliffs, Prentice-Hall, 1968.

Newfarmer, R. (ed.), *Profits, Progress, and Poverty: Case Studies of International Industries in Latin America*, Notre Dame, University of Notre Dame Press, 1985.

Nye, J., Jr and Keohane, R., "Globalization: What's New? What's Not?" *Foreign Policy*, Spring, 2000.

Ogura, K. "Creating a New Asia," *Japan Echo*, Vol. 26, No. 3, June 1999.

Ohno, K. and MacKinnon, R., *Dollar and Yen, Resolving Economic Conflict Between the United States and Japan*, Cambridge, The MIT Press, 1997.

Organization for Economic Co-operation and Development (OECD), *International Direct Investment Statistics Yearbook, 1998*, Paris, OECD, 1999.

Panagariya, A. and Bhagwati, J., *The Economics of Preferential Trade Agreements*, Washington, American Enterprise Institute Press, 1996.

Panagariya, A. and deMelo, J., *The New Regionalism in Trade Policy*, Washington, The World Bank, 1992.

Pempel, T. (ed.), *The Politics of the Asian Economic Crisis*, Ithaca and London, Cornell University Press, 1999.

Pempel, T., "Gulliver in Lilliput: Japan and Asian Economic Regionalism," *World Policy Journal*, Winter, 1996–7.

Pierson, M., "Report on the International Trade Commission Study of 'East Asian Regional Economic Integration and Implications for the United States,'" *Law and Society in International Business*, 1994, No. 3.

Platt, D., *Latin America and British Trade, 1806–1914*, London, A. and C. Block, 1972.

Prestowitz, C., *Trading Places: How we Allowed Japan to Take the Lead*, New York, Basic Books, 1988.

Pyle, K., *The Japanese Question: Power and Purpose in a New Era*, Washington, AEI Press, 1992.

Ravenhill, J., "APEC Adrift: Implications for Economic Regionalism in Asia and the Pacific," *The Pacific Review*, Vol. 13, No. 2, 2000.

Robson, P., *The Economics of International Integration*, Fourth Edition, London and New York, Routledge, 1998.

Roett, R. (ed.), *MERCOSUR: Regional Integration, World Markets*, Boulder and London, Lynne Rienner, 1999.

Rowley, A., "Asian Fund Special: The Battle of Hong Kong," *Capital Trends*, November, 1997, Vol. 2, No. 13.

Scalapino, R. (ed.), *The Foreign Policy of Modern Japan*, Berkeley, University of California Press, 1971.

Schott, J. (ed.), *Free Trade Areas and U.S. Trade Policy*, Washington, Institute for International Econmics, 1989.

Schott, J. (ed.), *The World Trading System: Challenges Ahead*, Washington, Institute for International Economics, 1996.

Shiraishi, T. and Katzenstein, P., *Network Power: Japan and Asia*, Ithaca, Cornell University Press, 1997.

Stirk, P. and Weigall, D., *The Origins and Development of the European Community*, Leicester, Leicester University Press, 1992.

Stubbs, R., "Signing on to Liberalization: AFTA and the Politics of Regional Economic Cooperation," *The Pacific Review*, Vol. 13, No. 2, 2000.

Suhartono, R., "Basic Framework for ASEAN Industrial Co-Operation," and "ASEAN Approach to Industrial Co-Operation," *Indonesia Quarterly*, Vol. XIV, Nos. 1, 4, 1986.

Tan, C. and Lee, K. *The Chinese in Malaysia*, Oxford and New York, Oxford University Press, 2000.

Tsunekawa, K., "NAFTA's Impact on Japan," Washington, The Woodrow Wilson Center, Occasional Paper No. 58, March, 9, 1994.

Tuchman, B., *The March of Folly: From Troy to Vietnam*, New York, Ballantine Books, 1984.

UK Office for National Statistics, "Britain 2000: The Official Yearbook of the United Kingdom," London, 2000.

US Department of Commerce, *Foreign Trade Highlights*, Washington, annually.

US Department of Commerce, *Historical Statistics of the United States*, Washington, 1960.

US President, Council of Economic Advisors, *Economic Report of the President*, Washington, GPO, annually.

US Secretary of Defense, *The United States Security Strategy for the East Asia–Pacific Region*, Washington, 1998.

United Nations, *External Financing in Latin America* (E/CN.12/649/Rev.1), United Nations, 1965.

United Nations, Economic and Social Council, *Transnational Corporations in World Development,* United Nations, 1978.

United Nations, Economic Commission for Asia and the Far East (ECAFE), "Approaches to Regional Harmonization of National Development Plans in Asia and the Far East," E/CN.11/CAEP.2/1.45, Bangkok (mimeo), September, 1964.

United Nations, UN Conference on Trade and Development (UNCTAD), *World Investment Directory, Vol. IV, Latin America and the Caribbean,* New York, United Nations, 1994.

United Nations, UN Conference on Trade and Development (UNCTAD), *World Investment Report 1991, The Triad in Foreign Direct Investment,* New York, United Nations, 1991.

United States International Trade Commission, Publication 2166, "The Pros and Cons of Entering Into Negotiations on Free Trade Area Agreements with Taiwan, the Republic of Korea, and ASEAN, or the Pacific Rim Region in General," Washington, GPO, March, 1989.

United States International Trade Commission, Publication No. 210, "Proposals for a US–Japan Free Trade Area Agreement," Washington, GPO, September, 1988.

United States Trade Representative, *2000 Trade Policy Agenda and 1999 Annual Report,* Washington, 2000.

Viner, J., *The Customs Union Issue,* Washington, Carnegie Endowment for International Peace, 1950.

Whalley, J., "CUSTA and NAFTA: Can WHAFTA Be Far Behind?" *Journal of Common Market Studies,* June, 1992.

Wilkins, M., *The Emergence of Multinational Enterprise: American Business Abroad from the Colonial Era to 1914,* Cambridge, Harvard University Press, 1970.

Wilkins, M., *The Maturing of Multinational Enterprise: American Business Abroad from 1914 to 1970,* Cambridge, Harvard University Press, 1974.

Wilkins, M. (ed.), *The Growth of Multinationals,* London, Elgar, 1991.

World Economic Forum, *Report on Global Competitiveness,* 13 July, 1999, Available http: www.weforum.org (10 August 1999).

World Trade Organization, *Annual Report,* Geneva, 1999.

Woytinski, E. and Woytinski, F., *World Commerce and Governments: Trends and Outlook,* New York, The 20th Century Fund, 1955.

Yates, P., *Forty Years of Foreign Trade,* London, George Allen & Unwin, 1959.

Yeats, A., "Does Mercosur's Trade Performance Raise Concerns About the Effects of Regional Trade Arrangements?" Washington, The World Bank, 1997.

Yeung, M. *et al., Regional Trading blocs in the Global Economy,* Cheltenham, Elgar, 1999.

Zimmermann, R. and Freytag, A., "The Effects of a Transatlantic Free Trade Area on German Industry," Cologne, Institut Für Wirtschaftspolitik, University of Cologne, October, 1996.

Zimmermann, R. and Freytag, A., "What Role for TAFTA? Proposals for an Institutional Framework of a Transatlantic Free Trade Area" a paper presented to the 43rd International Atlantic Economic Conference, London, March, 1997.

Index

Philippines, 60, 122; exports, 44–5, 98; FDI stock of Japan and US, 137; and General Motors, 48; imports from US and Japan, 136–7
Platt, D., 104
Portugal, 36
Piller, Wolfgang, 67
preferential trade agreements, 52
preferential trade areas, 64
Prestowitz, Clyde, 46–7, 67, 69
protectionism, 5, 112, 155, 159; in Brazil and Argentina, 73, 150; in Europe, 40, 52; in US, 155
Puerto Rico, 76

Ramos, Fidel, 131
Real, 34, 73, 98
regional agreements, 146–8
regional blocs, 2, 3, 59, 139; in 1930s, 12; *see* trade blocs
regional councils, in postwar planning, 1
regional free trade agreements, 101, 146, 156
regional integration, 46, 156
regionalism, 118, 126, 161; in Asia, 139, 149, 156; consequences of, 5, 145; in Europe, 52, 101; in Japan, 109–10, 113, 157; practical realities of,146; revival of, 1, 9,11–15, 101, 108, 112–13, 147–9, 157; US role in, 2
regional trade arrangements, 146
Ricardo, David, 45
Ridley, Nicholas, 54
Rifkind, Malcolm, 51, 54, 66
ringgit, 117
Roett, R., 102
Rowley, A., 141

Salinas, Carlos de Gortari: proposes FTA with US, 96
Sakakibara, Eisuke, 141; and AMF defeat, 115–16; new proposals, 124, 129
Sankei, 126; on AMF, 125
Sannittanont, Sura, 141
Sarney, José, 102; on Argentina, 73
Sato, Eisaku, 109
Scalapino, Robert, 109–10, 140
Segal, G., 142
services: and GATT, 7; trade in, 7
Simone, V., 67
Singapore, 50, 122; exports, 20; FDI stock of Japan and US in, 137;

growth rates, 161; imports from Japan, 136–7; and trade diversion effects on, 146; imports from US, 75–6, 79, 136–7; regional FTA talks, 101, 113, 131, 144; US free trade talks with, 98
Skidmore, D., 32
Soros, George, 117, 141
Southeast Asian Treaty Organization (SEATO), 128
South America, 38, 72, 81, 149, 156; "dependence" on Europe, 83; comparisons, 44; European investment returns to, 91–3; foreign investment in, 90–1; and NAFTA, 14; summit, 151; trade diversion consequences of, 146; and US exports and imports, 152; and US market, 77, 152
Southeast Asia: intra-regional trade, 44–5
South Korea, *see* Korea
"spaghetti bowl effect," 146
Spain, 36: investments in Latin America, 92–3
Strauss-Kahn, Dominique, 65
Suharto, 130, 144
Summers, Lawrence, 64–5, 70; and AMF defeat, 115–16, 129
"Super 301": explained, 7
Sweden, 36
Switzerland, 44

TAFTA, 2, 11, 47–8, 50–1, 59, 64, 156–7; and free trade, 52, 60; and German–US ties, 54; and Klaus Kinkel, 50–53, 60; and NATO, 51; "Pacific tilt," 46
Taiwan, 1; and EC market, 40; exports, 20; FDI stock of Japan and US in, 137; "flying geese," 107; imports from Japan, 120, 136–7; imports from US, 136–7; imports from US, 79; trade diversion effects on, 146
tariffs: in MERCOSUR and NAFTA, 146
Thailand, 60, 118, 122; and GM; exports, 44–5; imports, 69; *Baht*, 115, 116; economy, 117; FDI stock of Japan and US in, 137; imports from US and Japan, 136–7
Thatcher, Margaret, 51, 68
The Malay Dilemma, 117
Thurow, Lester, 6

Printed in the United States
by Baker & Taylor Publisher Services